SERMON NOTES

OF

JOHN HENRY CARDINAL NEWMAN
1849–1878

THE WORKS OF
CARDINAL JOHN HENRY NEWMAN
BIRMINGHAM ORATORY
MILLENNIUM EDITION
VOLUME II

SERIES EDITOR

JAMES TOLHURST DD

SERMON NOTES

OF

JOHN HENRY
CARDINAL NEWMAN
1849-1878

EDITED BY

FATHERS OF THE BIRMINGHAM
ORATORY

with an Introduction and Notes by

JAMES TOLHURST DD

Gracewing.

NOTRE DAME

First published in 1913
Published in the Birmingham Millennium Oratory Edition in 2000
jointly by

Gracewing
2 Southern Avenue
Leominster
Herefordshire HR6 0QF

University of Notre Dame Press
310 Flanner Hall
Notre Dame
IN 46556 USA

Library of Congress Cataloging-in-Publication Data
Newman, John Henry, 1801–1890.

    Sermon notes of John Henry Cardinal Newman, 1849–1878/edited by fathers of the Birmingham Oratory; with an introduction and notes by James Tolhurst.

    p. cm. – (Birmingham Oratory millennium edition; vol. 2)
    Includes bibliographical references.
    ISBN 0-268-01771-9 (US: cloth) – ISBN 0-85244-444-3 (UK)
    1. Catholic Church–Sermons. 2. Sermons, English–19th century. I. Oratory of St. Philip Neri (Birmingham, England) II. Title. III. Series.

BX1756.N5 S47 2000
252'.02–dc21

00-064848

UK ISBN 0 85244 444 3
US ISBN 0-268-01771-9

Additional typesetting by Action Publishing Technology Ltd, Gloucester, GL1 1SP
Printed in England by Redwood Books, Trowbridge BA14 8RN

CONTENTS

Contents

CATECHETICAL INSTRUCTIONS—

NOTE ON THE TEXT

Sermon Notes was published posthumously in two identical editions (with a portrait of the Cardinal and twenty-three pages of introduction followed by the text of 344 pages) by Longmans, Green & Co., London, 1913 and 1914.

ACKNOWLEDGEMENTS

Those who know the work of Gerard Tracey, archivist of the Birmingham Oratory, can understand that without his help this edition would not have seen the light of day. His knowledge of the cultural background perfectly matches that of John Henry Newman. Every researcher owes him a great debt of gratitude.

I am also fortunate in having the guidance of Tom Longford of Gracewing who has had the courage to undertake this whole project, to which the Fathers of Newman's Oratory have kindly given their support. Jo Ashworth has been the model of a compassionate editor.

James Tolhurst DD.

WORKS INDEXED

Newman's works refer to the standard edition published by Longmans, Green & Co., London, 1868–1881. Other non-uniform titles mentioned are:

Autobiographical Writings, Edited by Henry Tristram, London, Sheed & Ward, 1956.

Catholic Sermons, Edited by C. Stephen Dessain, London, Burns & Oates, 1961.

Letters & Diaries of John Henry Newman, London, Nelson, 1961–72; Oxford University Press 1972–.

On Consulting the Faithful in Matters of Doctrine, Edited by John Coulson, London, Geoffrey Chapman, 1961.

Tracts for the Times, London, Rivington, 1839.

The Patrology Collection assembled by J. P. Migne from 1844 onwards, known as *Patrologia Graeca & Patrologia Latina* is referred to as *MG & ML*.

INTRODUCTION

On the inside of his notebook of sermon abstracts, John Henry Newman placed the quotation 'As we were allowed of God to be put in trust with the Gospel, even so we speak, not as pleasing men, but God, which trieth our hearts'.[1] This earnestness was remarked on by members of his congregation throughout his life. Gladstone, writing after Newman's death said

> Take the man as a whole, and there was a stamp and a seal upon him, there was a solemn sternness and music in the tone; there was a completeness in the figure taken together with the tone and with the manner which made even his delivery such as I have described it.[2]

The voice, which has been likened by Professor Shairp to that of a bell tolling, was of that distinctiveness that people would recall it after an absence of thirty years.[3]

[1] I Thess. 2:4 Ms. A.7.1.
[2] *Daily Chronicle* 12 August 1890.
[3] In Cambridge at the end of July 1861. q. Trevor, M., *Light in Winter* (London, Macmillan, 1962), p. 248.

Certainly there was a transparency that was evident when Newman spoke. It was not that he was revealing some strange truth or beguiling his hearers with tricks of oratory. He was speaking the truth which he had pondered on and totally believed – and that sincerity communicated itself so that it confronted the listener with the challenge. Professor Shairp says that 'He laid the finger how gently, yet how powerfully, on some inner place in the hearer's heart, and told him things about himself he had never known till then'.[4] Dean Church said that Newman's 'passionate and sustained earnestness' confronted the softness, restlessness and wordliness with the austerity of the New Testament with its real sternness.[5] There was a reverence for the word of God which never left Newman the preacher. William Lockhart said that Newman had the power of 'so impressing your soul as to efface himself, and you thought only of that majestic soul that saw God'.[6] This was confirmed by Fr Joseph Bacchus who wrote that

> it was only afterwards, if something had struck home and kept coming back to the mind, that one realised that it was not the words only, but something in the tone of the voice, in which they were said, that haunted the memory.[7]

But it is Newman's own admission that the impression

[4] Shairp, J. C., *Studies in Poetry and Philosophy* (St Andrews, 1866), p. 17.
[5] Church, R. W., *Oxford Movement 1833–1845* (London, 1891), pp. 21–2. Church, R. W., *Occasional Papers II* (London, 1897), p. 457.
[6] Lockhart, W., *Reminiscences of Fifty Years Since* (London, 1891), pp. 26–7.
[7] *Sermon Notes*, p. viii (original introduction to 1913 edition).

given by the preacher is always bound up with the personality behind the words. Preaching, like his university office, was seen as a pastoral charge and an expression of the ministry of shepherd which was conferred at ordination.

He knows his sheep, and they know him; and it is this direct bearing of the teacher on the taught, of his mind upon their minds, and the mutual sympathy which exists between them, which is his strength and influence when he addresses them. They hang upon his lips as they cannot hang upon the pages of his book. Definiteness is the life of preaching. A definite hearer, not the whole world; a definite topic, not the whole evangelical tradition; and, in like manner, a definite speaker. Nothing that is anonymous will preach; nothing that is dead and gone; nothing even which is of yesterday, however religious in itself and useful. Thought and word are one in the Eternal Logos, and must not be separate in those who are His shadows on earth. They must issue fresh and fresh, as from the preacher's mouth, so from his breast, if they are to be 'spirit and life' to the hearts of his hearers ... (he) comes to his audience with a name and a history, and excites a personal interest, and persuades by what he is, as well as by what he delivers.[8]

Fr Bacchus makes the point that those who knew Newman had the music of his voice in their memory as well as the printed words before their eyes, and

[8] *Idea of A University*, p. 426.

there was something in the voice which haunted the memory.[9] Others were to speak of the attraction of his words, not because of their poetic quality (although this was not lacking) but because of the personality behind the words:

> It seemed to me as if I could trace behind his will, and pushing so to speak against it, a rush of thoughts and feelings which he kept struggling to hold back but in the end were generally too strong for him and poured themselves out in a torrent of eloquence all the more impetuous for having been so long repressed.[10]

But again, there was no forced theatricality. Newman did not indulge in any particular skills and in fact there was a conscious effort to avoid any extravagance. Such antics could safely be left to Exeter Hall or the American revivalists that were pulling the crowds. If we look at his sermons they are always built around the power of the word of God and those who heard him did not consider that he preached at all but rather conversed very thoughtfully and *earnestly*.[11] The divine words were paramount and he was their instrument, which made Fr Bacchus comment that every sermon was a sermon on the objectivity of Revealed Truth.[12]

---

[9] *Sermon Notes* (SN), pp. viii, ix (original introduction to 1913 edition).
[10] Doyle, Sir F. q. *Oxford Movement*, p. 144.
[11] Bacchus, Fr Joseph SN, p. vii (original introduction to 1913 edition).
[12] Ibid., p. xii.

I. FROM *PAROCHIAL AND PLAIN* TO *SERMON NOTES*

Those who are familiar with the eight volumes of *Parochial and Plain Sermons* and the volume of *Sermons on Subjects of the Day* which comprise the printed output of his Anglican years will be aware of the fact that they were preached to a congregation. Most of the foregoing comments were made about such sermons which Gladstone called 'those indestructible classics of English theology'[13] recalling them from the time he had heard them as a student.

But when he became a Catholic, it was borne in upon him that its priests preach 'without book', that is not reading from a text. This does not signify a complete break from his earlier practice as it would at first seem. When Newman gave up reading his sermon, he did not preach extempore. He had always lambasted such eloquence. He was forthright in telling his congregation that he would not 'dishonour this service by any strangeness or extravagance of conduct or constraint of manner'.[14] He considered public extempore prayer 'plainly irreverent'.[15] Instead there should be 'sober words' and 'it will be a great thing if we enter into them'.[16] He argued therefore that 'for the sake of decency, and reverence, all public prayer, the whole of the priest's liturgy, should be settled beforehand and known'.[17] This principle was applied to his sermons as

---

[13] Gladstone, W. E., *Vaticanism* (London, 1875), p. 12.
[14] *Parochial and Plain Sermons VIII* 8, p. 164.
[15] MS, Sermon 225.
[16] *Parochial and Plain Sermons I*, p. 147.
[17] MS, Sermon 225.

a Catholic. He wrote to a seminarian from Maynooth, whose name has not come down to us, that much prior preparation was necessary before mounting the pulpit. He urged his enquirer 'to have your subject distinctly before you; to think it over till you have got it perfectly in your head'.[18] Nor was it to be a merely cerebral process; the thoughts should be put down on paper even in note form. He comments on this when he talks about university preaching:

> I think that writing is a stimulus to the mental faculties, to originality, to the power of illustration, to the arrangement of topics, second to none. Till a man begins to put down his thoughts about a subject on paper he will not ascertain what he knows and what he does not know, still less will he be able to express what he does know.

And he added, characteristically, with his mind on earlier days:

> To many preachers there will be another advantage besides; — such a practice will secure them against venturing upon really *extempore* matter.[19]

Newman adapted to the Catholic practice of taking short notes, although he did concede that one could take a text into the pulpit provided that it was carefully concealed. But he inclined to the opinion that the most effective method of all (which he termed the total concealment) was to get the sermon by heart

[18] *Letters and Diaries* XXIV, p. 44, 2 March 1868.
[19] *Idea of A University*, p. 422.

'whatever be its counterbalancing disadvantages'. One of these being that if you lost your concentration, as he did in later years, then there was no help but to resort to reading your old sermons, which he did.

But Newman did have on hand one obvious aid, since he was preaching divine truth – the Bible. Fr Bacchus says that Newman always had it in his hands, and after finding the particular spot, read from the *Douai* text. Fr Bellasis remembers that Newman held the Bible rather close to his face because he was short-sighted and the print was small and he constantly turned over its pages 'after the rather fumbling manner of an old man while he was speaking, presumably in order to find the next passage he intended to quote'.[20]

All noticed, as in his Anglican days that there was a great reverence for the words of Scripture, especially with regard to the words of Christ: 'Before and after these there was a kind of hush', relates Fr Bacchus,[21] but he remarks that Newman seems to have been listening to the words as much as reading. There was normally no change in the rather low and gentle voice, but this made any alteration even more memorable. Fr Bacchus describes how Newman, speaking of the crucifixion, came to the words 'as we fix a noxious bird up' and recalls the distress which came over his voice, which just as soon returned to calmness.

But the overall impression given was again of transparency as the preacher effaced himself behind the truth which he wished to convey. Newman argued

---

[20] *Sermon Notes*, p. vii (original preface to 1913 edition). Even the second sermon in *Catholic Sermons* has the note 'preached but not read' 20 February 1848 p. 32.

[21] *Sermon Notes*, p. xii (original introduction to 1913 edition).

that the personality needed to take second place, when he wrote to the anonymous enquirer from Maynooth:

> Humility, which is a great Christian virtue, has a place in literary composition – he who is ambitious will never write well. But he who tries to say simply and exactly what he feels and thinks, what religion demands, what Faith teaches, what the Gospel promises, will be eloquent without intending it, and will write better English than if he made a study of English literature.[22]

He returns to the theme in his lecture on university preaching when he says:

> Earnestness creates earnestness in others by sympathy; and the more a preacher loses and is lost to himself, the more does he gain his brethren ... Who could wish to be more eloquent, more powerful, more successful than the Teacher of the Nations [St Paul]? yet who more earnest, who more natural, who more unstudied; who more self-forgetting than he?[23]

As far as composition is concerned, Newman passes on to his seminary student in Ireland, and exemplifies in his own preaching, the need to concentrate on getting the point over, to the subordination of everything else. He tells him:

> to take care that it should be one subject, not several; to sacrifice every thought, however good

[22] *Letters and Diaries* XXIV, p. 45.
[23] *Idea of A University*, pp. 407, 8.

or clever, which does not tend to bring out your one point, and to aim earnestly and supremely to bring home that one point to the minds of your hearers.[24]

II. THE *SERMON NOTES*

We cannot disassociate the words of Newman from the man himself. We read them because of whom he was, and this is entirely consistent for he himself says 'People are drawn and moved, not simply by what is said, but by how it is said and who says it.'[25]

The *Sermon Notes* which date from 1849 to 1878 are in fact a collection of schemes of sermons preached within those years; and a series of catechetical instructions, starting on Tuesdays in 1849 and then given at varying intervals until 1850, resuming again on Sunday 3 January 1858 until 7 March and then on Sunday afternoon 8 May 1859 sporadically until the final lecture on Sunday 3 June 1860.

They are contained in two notebooks, averaging 24cms × 19cms[26] containing unlined cream paper. Into these have been pasted occasional scraps which Newman would have taken up into the pulpit. But apart from these *aides-memoires* Newman would have relied on his memory and the Bible, 'preaching is not reading, and reading is not preaching'.[27]

The notebooks have the words *Wm P. Neville, The*

[24] *Letters and Diaries* XXIV, p. 44.

[25] *Idea of A University*, p. 425.

[26] MS, A.16 4, I and II.

[27] *Idea of A University*, p. 424.

Oratory on the inside front page. Fr William Neville
was the Cardinal's secretary and literary executor and
he presented the books to Fr Henry Bellasis one
Christmas as a present.[28] Although it looks as if these
are notes to take up into the pulpit, it is clear that
Newman normally went to his room soon after
preaching and wrote out a summary of the sermon he
had just preached. We can see that he reflected on his
words because in the notes for 20 March 1870 he
provides three schemes for the same third Sunday of
Lent.[29] On another occasion he jots down:

> I was interrupted, or I meant to have written a sketch
> of a whole sermon. I have forgotten now my arrange-
> ment. I put down some isolated *topoi* (passages).[30]

Some five years after the last sermon scheme recorded
in this book, Cardinal Newman's memory began to
fail and instead of leaving things to chance, he took to
reading some of his old *Parochial and Plain Sermons*
which Fr Bacchus thinks were slightly 'touched up'
for their reprise.[31]

Readers of the footnotes which have been added
substantially for this new edition — there were two
previous editions, published by Longmans Green in
1913 and 1914 — will notice that similar embellish-
ments occur in quotations from the Scriptures, the
Fathers, classical authors and poetry. Newman freely
adapted what came to his prodigious memory, for the

---

[28] *Sermon Notes* (SN), p. vi (original introduction to 1913 edition).
[29] SN, pp. 198–200.
[30] SN, p. 181.
[31] SN, p. vi (original introduction to 1913 edition).

relevant passage in his sermon. He frequently had
recourse to the original meaning of the words. On
Palm Sunday 1850 he notes 'The wicked are like a
boiling sea'. The quotation is from Isaiah 57:20, but
the *Douai* version which Newman used says 'The
wicked are like the raging sea'. It is only when we go
to the *Vulgate* and see 'Impii autem quasi mare *fervens*'
that we understand where *boiling* comes from.[32]

The range of quotations will not surprise anyone
who has ever visited the Cardinal's room where poetry
jostles with geology and history with science, lives of
the Saints with plays of Calderón de la Barca, the latest
novels with volumes of Moral Theology. He was adept
at plucking out the illustrative quotation from history,
whether mythological or hagiographic. He presses into
service Catherine of Genoa, St Aloysius Gonzaga, St
Andrew Avellino, St Gregory Thaumaturgus, St Peter
Claver, St Rose of Lima, St Frances of Rome, St Philip
Neri and St Francis de Sales. But his selection from
other authors was also wide-ranging. He could make
use of Aristotle, Julian the Apostate, Horace, Virgil,
Cicero, Juvenal, Byron, Morier, Muratori, Malvenda,
Paley and Dollinger. We are reminded that those were
the years of not only a classical education but also of a
broader curriculum with no access to television. But
with all those points in mind, the preacher that was
Newman gave an interesting and constantly changing
picture to his congregation, which wove into the
theme of the sermon, contemporary events (Crimean
War, papal exile, railway journeys, astronomical observations and the Indian Mutiny) and large amounts of

[32] *Sermon Notes*, p. 39.

theology illustrated by commentators, ancient and modern, with effortless ease.

An illustration of his approach can be gathered if we take Newman's sermon for 14 July 1850. Fr Faber and his community are now in London but St Wilfrid's Cheadle needed supplying from both Birmingham and London. The Birmingham Oratory had not moved from Alcester Street. Newman preaches on the texts for the 8th Sunday after Pentecost[33] in particular, Luke 16:1–9 'The Unjust Steward'. He starts by setting the scene for his congregation. The situation is put in stark terms – here today – gone tomorrow: talking to each other, crossing the street 'so suddenly we may cross to the next world'. Then the corollary, that for his people just getting used to the idea of transport by rail, they could pass from this world in an instant, as soon as arrive in York. Today, we would say New York! Newman then brings in the note of apologetics, bearing in mind that some of his congregation may be Protestant or married to Protestants, or converted from Protestantism. Whereas, as an Anglican he would talk of the intermediate state which left matters tinged with vagueness, here he confronts Protestants with the fact that *they* are vague: 'They call it an unknown state ... After all, we know nothing'. Newman tosses the question around:

> Whether he will lose consciousness, or be asleep; whether in heaven, or what is heaven. In a word, he is all abroad; the question is new to him, and he has not one idea about it, no more than a pagan.

---

[33] List of Sundays and feastdays to be found in the appendix.

A pagan elegy in memory of Hadrian is thrown in for good measure!

At this point, Newman contrasts the Catholic position on life after death and the particular judgement each has to undergo. In terms which would be easily grasped, he reminds his people that judgement is immediate, like an inquest; and as necessary after death as an undertaker. Two illustrations are given, balancing each other. One urges that we must not deceive ourselves. Philip II rounded on his courtiers for telling him a lie. Mary Magdalen de Pazzi was afflicted with terror at the prospect of judgement when she fell sick.

Newman then returns to the theme of the Gospel and concentrates on stewardship and the account which we must all render at our judgement. Not only sins but idle and unthinking words, thoughts and the use of time and leisure as well as blessings and graces received and cooperated with. The question is asked 'Do we understand what is meant by stewardship?' His congregation are reminded to keep the thought of judgement before them.

We need to imagine the preacher himself talking to his motley crowd of immigrant labourers and middle class converts and friends, in a converted gin distillery near the present Birmingham coach station at Digbeth. What we lack is the tone of the voice which so haunted the memory but what we possess are the shafts of brilliance and the touches of genius which explain why they held his hearers as they had held undergraduates years earlier when he had spoken from the pulpit of St Mary's.

III. THEMES IN *SERMON NOTES*

The sermons follow the liturgical cycle of readings and can be seen as commentaries on them. But one can distinguish various themes throughout the volume which show us (like the *Philosophical Notebook*) the development of his ideas. This volume in a way exemplifies the principle of the development of doctrine for, as Newman says 'Every age is a semblance, a type in part of what then at last will be in fulness'.[34] We can see not only the working out of previous theological ideas that came to fruition in the 1830s, but also a growth in the mature thoughts themselves.

The Church

In his sermons of 1849, Newman fills out the thought that can be found in his *Essay on Development of Doctrine* where he states that the Catholic Church with its infallible authority fulfils the definition of Christianity as social and dogmatic.[35] In a sermon preached on 22 July he argues that it is because of their fear of the Church *as such a body* having a hold on them, that Protestants are deterred. He tells them that the reason for prejudice is that 'Catholicity, the Church, interposes between man and his God, teaching him, warning him, and judging for him'.[36] He would develop these themes in *Lecturers on the Present Position of Catholics* which he was to give in 1851. But here he deals with the *fact* of Catholicism as a challenge to the power of individual private judgement.

---

[34] *Sermon Notes* (SN), p. 225.
[35] *Essay on The Development of Christian Doctrine*, pp. 89–90.
[36] SN, pp. 4, 11.

For the average Englishman, it was one thing to be faced with the structure of a corporate body, but it was quite another for this body to incorporate *him*. Newman does not disguise the antipathy:

> Catholicity is a system which conspires against the peace and liberty of man; a tyrannical system which imposes a load of things upon the conscience, which terrifies the weak; anathemas; a grasping secret system.[37]

In the same year that he preaches his *Lectures on the Present Position of Catholics* he argues that the very existence of the Church as a growing and living reality engenders hatred, and is 'the mark of the true Church'.[38]

Newman had argued in his *Essay on Development* that Christianity proved itself by its ability to deal with and confront heresy. He quotes Bishop Horsley (in a sermon which he preaches in 1872) saying that the toleration of the most pestilent heresies would result in the toleration of atheism and in the persecution of Christianity.[39] Against this stood the bulkhead of the Catholic Church. She was a force to be reckoned with:

> a vast body with vast power all over the earth ... Such is the Catholic Roman Church, nay, far more fully, because it reigns more directly – not through other powers, as the British in India, etc.[40]

---

[37] *Sermon Notes* (SN), p. 10.
[38] SN, pp. 68, 84.
[39] *Discussions and Arguments*, pp. 107, 230.
[40] SN, p. 86.

Here was an image to be conjured with, the whole population was conscious of the jewel in the crown of Queen Victoria and the colonial administration as well as the network of military and legislative officers. The Catholic Church had that same visibility and also the power to exercise authority at the local level through the newly restored hierarchy, headed by Cardinal Wiseman in Westminster.

There was a vivid contrast between the British Empire and this spiritual empire which spread so widely and so diversely.[41] This was the fulfilment of the promise of Catholicity which the Anglican Church never achieved even though it established itself in all parts of the Empire. The difference between the two concepts of ecclesiology is that the Catholic Church had that capacity to root itself in all countries, not simply those which owed allegiance to the Crown: 'Its promise [was] that it was to be everywhere, and was *to be able* to be everywhere'.[42] This was bound up with the fact that it was everywhere united in one faith and under one Head. In his *Essay*, Newman spoke of the necessity that 'some authority there must be if there is a revelation given, and other authority there is none but she'.[43] He draws the conclusion that 'This awful unity of the Church is our consolation. While it proves the Church comes from God, it proves nothing comes strange and new to her'.[44] The very feature which repelled many people was in fact the

---

[41] *Sermon Notes* (SN), p. 33.

[42] SN, p. 32.

[43] *Essay on The Development of Christian Doctrine*, p. 88.

[44] SN, pp. 63–4.

reason for its ability to grow and preserve the truth of revelation.

Newman also looks back to his earlier evangelical sermons with their notion of the saved and the later development of the visible and invisible Church, and comes down firmly on the side of the existing body of the faithful. We judge the Church by her visible members, not by the saints in heaven and avoid making unjust comparisons: 'Those rich men who are in the Church may be holier than the poor'. Newman does not say that they *are* but that they may be for 'many of the saints [were both] rich and noble men'.[45] To redress the balance, he would also say that there was a continuity between the Church and the apostolic era and the present day which did not relate to finance but to intellectual ability. Newman noted that 'few were learned' but on the other hand 'just enough ... to keep it going'.[46] One could conjecture that this was uttered with a certain whimsical smile while the preacher reflected on the interplay between the unlearned, who needed instruction and the instructed who needed humility to teach them.

If the Church is not to be identified with any future invisible communion, it becomes obvious that Newman does not consider the Church as simply a teaching authority. His vantage point is that of the faith which is shared by prelates and faithful alike. He remarks (in 1851) that sinfulness does not destroy the Church because 'faith is independent of sin'.[47] In fact

---

[45] *Sermon Notes* (SN), pp. 101–2. Newman emphasises that 'best' clothes should be worn for Church (cf. SN, p. 6).

[46] SN, p. 101.

[47] SN, p. 77.

the prayer said by the priest before Communion at
Mass sums up the same thought: 'Look not on our sins
but upon the faith of your Church'. Newman points
out that faith is not only 'the beginning of all acceptable service, but is the binding principle of the
Church'.[48] It is for this reason that even though individual members of the Church may apostatise 'the
people are never wrong'.[49] This does not advocate
some brand of ecclesiological democracy, as Bishop
Brown of Newport would later conclude, but an
awareness of the encompassing nature of the Church
'as an Empire of faith' – it is the bond which unites all
and orders all things sweetly. The consensus of the
people does not make up for the silence of the Fathers,
nor is infallibility in that consensus, but the consensus
is an indication to us of the Church which is infallible.
That consensus in faith forms with the Magisterium a
totality, which Newman would call 'conspiratio
pastorum et fidelium' – a breathing together or a joint
sharing in,[50] which provided that harmony between
the teaching and listening Church. The *vox populi* is
that authentic response to the faith professed by the
bishops of the Church, but it is the response expressed
by the entire body of the faithful who cannot err.
Newman would have had no sympathy with those
who argue for some sort of receptionism based on the
acceptance of a section or an interested party of the
people of God. Such segments can, and often do err.

They would be the first, when they encounter
unpalatable pronouncements of the Magisterium on

[48] *Sermon Notes* (SN), p. 76.
[49] SN, p. 77.
[50] *On Consulting the Faithful in Matters of Doctrine*, p. 72.

matters of faith or morality conflicting with current mores, to reflect on the gloominess of Catholicity. For Newman, that gloominess was seen in terms of penance and mortification, confession and monasticism. It had all been said before about his 'monastery' at Littlemore when he became a Catholic. There continued to be those who hastened to interpret Newman's every move in the Catholic Church as an indication that he had regrets, and was in fact pining for the more congenial pastures of the Church of England. Newman pointed out to his congregation that there is an unfortunate tendency in mankind to dislike any bodily restriction. Nowadays we would invoke the spirit of Freud to justify our repudiation of mortification. Newman points out that in all this there is a complete disregard to the wounds being inflicted on the soul.[51] We might possibly add that this was the beginning of that materialism which would for the next century find the soul itself superfluous to any explanation of mankind's ultimate happiness. Those who imagined that he found that life was humdrum and disappointing in the Midlands were to learn that Newman saw things entirely differently. When he recorded his impressions eleven years later he remarked: 'Here has been the contrast – as a Protestant, I felt my religion dreary, but not my life – but, as a Catholic, my life dreary, not my religion'.[52] Those who read the *Sermon Notes* will discover that Newman had no doubts about his new allegiance. Indeed, he remarks without comment that Catholics

---

[51] *Sermon Notes*, p. 100.

[52] 21 January 1863. *Autobiographical Writings*; p. 254, see *Parochial and Plain Sermons* I, p. 317f.

are often surprised that every one does not share their religion.[53] He is quite adamant that if you are 'external' to the Church, you have no claim on divine grace.[54] The solution is simple: 'Seek Him where He can be found, i.e. in the Catholic Church'.[55] Yet this Empire of faith can be truthfully termed as much *Mother* as our own country; as a patriot, Newman would not allow the Church to be excluded from that classification which counted schools, and universities as *alma mater* and yet did not extend this to their Church. The implication in Newman's mind was clear – only Catholics could call Mary their mother, and therefore could also think of the Church in a maternal way.[56]

Mary

The *Sermon Notes* in their references to Mary provide an interesting 'section' (in the archaeological sense) of Newman's theology between 1851 and 1856. But they also present the culmination of his views in his Anglican days and look towards the *Letter to Pusey* which he would write in 1864.

As an Anglican he approaches the difficult subject of devotion to Mary in his sermon on the Annunciation in 1832. He is willing to accept that she is 'by nature a sinner', but in every other respect she is 'raised above the condition of sinful beings'.[57] God himself was bestowing his dignity upon her, He 'was

[53] *Sermon Notes* (SN), p. 4.
[54] SN, p. 46.
[55] SN, p. 51.
[56] SN, p. 81.
[57] *Parochial and Plain Sermons* II, p. 135.

taking upon Him her flesh, and humbling Himself to be called her offspring'.[58] Therefore we must conclude that the sanctified state of His mother 'of which God formed His sinless Son'[59] was marvellous indeed. He also compares her with Eve, as do the Fathers of the Church:

> In her the curse pronounced on Eve was changed to a blessing ... (God) sent Him forth as the Son of Mary, to show that all our sorrow and all our corruption can be blessed and changed by Him.[60]

The same point is made when he preaches two years later:

> He came by a new and living way; not, indeed, formed out of the ground as Adam was at the first, lest He should miss the participation of our nature, but selecting and purifying unto Himself a tabernacle out of that which existed. As in the beginning, woman was formed out of man by Almighty power, so now, by a like mystery, but a reverse order, the new Adam was fashioned from the woman.[61]

It is easy to see these words as a corollary of his study of the Incarnation in Athanasius and the early Fathers. He tells his congregation in 1849 that 'it was in order to *seal the doctrine* that He took a human mother'. On

---

[58] *Parochial and Plain Sermons* II, p. 128; see also *Parochial and Plain Sermons* VIII, p. 252.

[59] *Parochial and Plain Sermons* II, p. 132.

[60] cf. *Parochial and Plain Sermons* II, p. 31, also PPS II, pp. 129–30.

[61] *Parochial and Plain Sermons* II, p. 31.

the one hand it was necessary to assure mankind that
the Son of God had actually come in human flesh
since 'the human mind will evade it if it can'.[62] But at
the same time Mary had to be immaculate if she was
to be the Mother of the sinless Son. Newman has
resolved the difficulty of his Anglican days: 'one truth
follows from another'.[63] But we can notice a progress
in Newman's thought concerning the continuing
sinlessness of Mary. Since he believed that Mary cooperated with the grace she had been given, and
continued to merit, then, he argued 'she was peccable;
she *grew* in grace'.[64] But at the same time he concedes,
later on the same year that, as the new Eve, she is a
pattern of holiness for all mankind 'She holds up to us
what man is intended to be, as a type, the most perfect
submission of his powers to grace'.[65] Two years later
the process is complete: 'Go through her character –
so lovely, so perfect, so glorious; the ideal of painters
and poets; yet superhuman, the flower of human
nature. ... she is a better Eve ... She was the first fruits
of God's beautiful creation. She was the type of all
beauty ... Mary comes as a second and holier Eve,
having the grace of indefectibility and the gift of
perseverance from the first ...'[66]

This was manifested most obviously in the moment
of Christ's crucifixion, where with St John, Mary
stood beneath the Cross. Although Newman could
propose the opinion that she was protected from

[62] *Sermon Notes* (SN), p. 22 (Newman's emphasis)
[63] SN, p. 22.
[64] SN, p. 14.
[65] SN, p. 29.
[66] SN, pp. 74, 79.

diseases and wounds, and even the pain of childbirth[67] he was a firm believer in the fulfilment of Simeon's prophecy that a sword would pierce her very soul. He argued that her sinlessness brought her an over-whelming sorrow 'in this unholy world'[68] and that the vision of the suffering of her son overshadowed all the joys of being the Mother of God. In fact, because of that relationship and her unique holiness there was a sharing in her Son's passion.[69] Newman sees also a perfect reflection in Mary of the inward soul and the outward expression. Her perfection is such that the soul so beams through her 'that you could not tell her features'.[70] But he also says that artistic pictures of her draw people into the Church[71] which provides food for thought. In her suffering he is of the opinion that 'it quite changed her outward appearance to the end of her life'.[72] Artists have certainly subscribed to this — for Newman it is the theological expression of the perfect compatibility between soul and body that this should happen.

If Mary is the great work of God's love, then it is perfectly reasonable to accept that God took her to Himself at the end of her life, and that she died from love.[73] But although the Church in her definition of the Assumption in 1950 did not go into the question of actual death, merely saying that 'after her life on earth, she was assumed, body and soul into heaven',

[67] *Sermon Notes* (SN), pp. 104, 300.
[68] SN, p. 108.
[69] SN, pp. 135–6.
[70] SN, p. 74.
[71] SN, p. 112.
[72] SN, p. 92.
[73] SN, p. 105.

Newman did not hesitate to say that because her Son died, she died.[74]

Although he did not share in the widespread enthusiasm for Italian Marian devotions, thinking them not suitable for the English temperament,[75] he would not apologise for his belief in the power of her intercession. If we are to concede that Mary's dignity stems from her Son, then because of her closeness to Him, we can presume that her prayer has all the power that such a mother could possess. We believe in the power of prayer itself, but in Mary that power is magnified. He likens her to the importune widow in the Gospel 'who gains perseverance by prayer (and) overcomes God, as I may say'.[76]

To those who might say that this undermines the unique mediation of Christ, Newman tells his congregation that the Church does not give Mary this power but does give her the honour due to her maternity. If we so belittle her, then we end up by belittling her Son. For Newman there is a stark choice: 'Protestants say we make too much of her. Now which is best, to think too much of *her*, or of the *world*?'[77]

Grace

In his remarks on grace, Newman continues what he had earlier said in his *Lectures on Justification*. There he points out that God gives us the power to cooperate with Him, to accept the grace He bestows.[78]

---

[74] *Sermon Notes*, p. 104.
[75] *Apologia Pro Vita Sua*, p. 195.
[76] SN, pp. 44n, 47, see p. 116 (Luke 18:1–8).
[77] SN, p. 243.

Mary is the supreme example of perfect submission to grace.[79] Those who resist cannot blame it on any predetermined election but on their own free lack of response. God does give grace to people but it remains ineffectual in their case.[80] The possibility must be faced that it may be the last grace given, even if it is by nature stronger than any natural force, and capable of achieving superhuman results.[81] Newman argues that it is necessary to go beyond nature, to something higher if we are to understand the realm of grace, for it is the principle of immortality even in this life, joining us to the heavenly family.[82] It is, he argues, like a new nature, and its loss like a skin torn off leaving one raw.[83] He insists that all have grace even though they do not know it because it is the state in which God wills all mankind to be in, for Christ died for all.[84]

The Redemption

Fr Bacchus remarks that when the Cardinal spoke of the crucifixion some of his hearers were, without knowing why 'almost as shocked as if they had now heard of it for the first time'.[85] As suffering produced in Mary a physical result, so far more in Christ. For Newman the agony in the garden was no poetic

---

[78] *Lectures on Justification*, p. 94. 'He gives this grace in order that they may *come* into a state of grace'. *Sermon Notes* (SN), p. 111.

[79] SN, p. 29.

[80] SN, p. 88.

[81] SN, pp. 46, 67.

[82] SN, pp. 38, 144.

[83] SN, pp. 57, 144.

[84] SN, p. 111; cf. *Discourses to Mixed Congregations*, p. 188.

[85] SN, p. ix (original introduction to 1913 edition).

description but the recounting of the impact of the
whole horror of sin itself bearing down upon the
sinless frame of the Son of God. Just as extreme fear
can turn hair white, so the effect on Christ was the
sweat of blood.[86] Newman preached in 1849 on the
concept of mental suffering, pointing out that

> our Lord felt pain of the body, with an adver-
> tence and a consciousness, and therefore with a
> keenness and intensity, and with a unity of
> perception, which none of us can possibly fathom
> or compass, because His soul was so absolutely in
> his own power, so simply free from the influence
> of distractions, so fully directed *upon* the pain, so
> utterly surrendered, so simply subjected to the
> suffering. And thus He may truly be said to have
> suffered the whole of His passion in every
> moment of it.[87]

It is possible that we could imagine that Christ was
simply a paschal victim – the Lamb that was slain – but
Newman makes clear that there was always an active
will to accept the suffering and not simply to be the
object of it: 'Christ's mental pain would have swallowed up even His bodily, had He not willed to feel
it'.[88] In His passion, Newman sees Christ as the champion foreseen by Isaiah: 'In crimsoned garments from
Bozrah, he that is glorious in his apparel' (Isa 63:1).
This is the triumphant figure of the Fathers of the
Church who overcame sin and the devil by struggling

---

[86] *Sermon Notes* (SN), p. 40; see p. 149.

[87] *Discourses to Mixed Congregations*, p. 330.

[88] SN, p. 75.

with it in his own humanity and putting it to death on the Cross.

But Newman adds an interesting touch when he meditates on the cruelty of Christ's executioners and the words of forgiveness which He uttered. He sees this as an indication of that assumption of humanity without which it would not have been healed. The compassion which He expressed was because 'He felt a tenderness to that fallen nature which was showing itself so awfully devilish in His persecutors, for it was His own'.[89] This is all the more remarkable when we consider that this was preached during the horrors perpetrated in the Indian Mutiny where the son of Ambrose Lisle Phillipps, one of Newman's friends, would lose his life in gallant circumstances. There was no conflict in Newman's mind between such utter humanity, even to the extent of being considered by others, a sinner himself and the union with the Godhead which was his from eternity. Christ did not grow in grace, He 'had *all* grace from the first'[90] and that deepened His suffering as well as His compassion for sinners.

The First Death and the Second

As an Anglican, Newman possessed a strange ambivalence with regard to life after death. He would tell his congregation in 1836 that the soul

> has not passed away as a breeze or sunshine, but it lives; it lives at this moment in one of those many

[89] *Sermon Notes* (SN), p. 149.
[90] SN, p. 300.

places, whether of bliss or misery, in which all souls are reserved until the end.[91]

The reason is rooted in ignorance about the nature of the soul *and* the invisible world. It is like being cast out into the storm, and being left houseless and shelterless.[92] The same image returns thirty-five years later when he asks his congregation to consider 'being suddenly cut off from all intercourse except with ourselves – a truly solitary confinement; worse, for that there is only loss of hearing, i.e. conversation'.[93] It is this total isolation, far more than any pain of sense that Newman sees as constitutive of that second death which we call Hell. For there the soul is thrown on itself and cut off from God who is its reason for being and its source of love and life.[94] There is a horror about it, like the nightmare which turns into reality. A reality not so much of flames but of cold: 'Our soul can never die, but it can get older and older, ... colder and colder, so that the longer we lived the more miserable'.[95]

The punishment of living with oneself for ever[96] is merely consequent on what Newman sees as sin being selfishness in essence. The sin of Lucifer is 'a sort of *sensual* love of self' which combines presumption, ambition, hatred of God and jealousy roused by the creation of human beings who while sharing in the

[91] *Parochial and Plain Sermons* IV, p. 86, 27 March 1836.
[92] *Parochial and Plain Sermons* III, p. 370, 1 November 1835.
[93] *Sermon Notes* (SN), p. 251.
[94] SN, p. 28.
[95] SN, p. 160.
[96] 'Living with oneself for ever', *Parochial and Plain Sermons* IV, p. 82.

material creation will also participate in the spiritual order.[97] When he tempted our first parents, Satan knew full well that what he was offering was an impossibility – freedom from God ultimately means the eternal prison of Hell.[98]

Purgatory
But there was the dilemma concerning those

> against whom an unsettled reckoning lies, the issue of which is future, who have certain sins as yet unforgiven, and certain consequences of sins as yet unprovided for.[99]

The acceptance of the doctrine of Purgatory ('a fond thing vainly invented', according to Article 22 of the Anglican Articles) the question of admission of imperfect souls to heaven was solved. But the nature of their trial/punishment remained. Newman tells his people 'God might have saved us without pain, yet saves us with pain'.[100] If it is a pain/punishment, then he argues it must participate in some way in the aspect of that second death: '... it means something short of hell, though called hell.[101] Newman refers to the *Dies Irae* where hell is used both of purgatory and hell. In fact purgatory cannot in any way be hell because that is the rejection of God and Newman admits that those in purgatory are holy

---

[97] *Sermon Notes* (SN), p. 165.
[98] SN, pp. 234, 302.
[99] *Parochial and Plain Sermons* IV, p. 102, 6 August 1837.
[100] SN, p. 23.
[101] SN, p. 24.

souls – they know they have done with sin and are
assured of salvation and the eventual happiness of
heaven. But Newman persists that like Lazarus in the
bosom of Abraham they are 'in sight of hell' and
purgatory cannot be a happy place because it is not
heaven and 'the soul is downcast, miserable,
dreary'.[102] Although this seems contradictory – it all
occurs in the same sermon – we need to note that
the suffering of purgatory, although superficially like
hell ('at worst flame, at best and always, desolation'[103]) is the loving contact with the holiness of
God who 'is a consuming fire' (Deut. 4.24).

Those who are in purgatory are conscious of their
total unworthiness compared to the holiness of God
and willingly accept to be purified. In one of the few
written Catholic sermons, dating from 1848,
Newman says

> the sight of themselves will be intolerable, and it
> will be torment to them to see what they really
> are and the sins which lie against them. And
> hence some writers have said that their horror will
> be such that of their own free will, and from a
> holy indignation against themselves, they will be
> ready to plunge into purgatory in order to satisfy
> divine justice and to be clear of what is to their
> own clear sense and spiritual judgement so abom-
> inable.[104]

Although Newman does refer to the soul in purgatory

---

[102] *Sermon Notes*, p. 24.
[103] SN, p. 25.
[104] *Catholic Sermons*, p. 37, 20 February 1848.

as 'hungry', he says that this is like the feeling of sinking or fainting.[105] The image of being lowered into cleansing water borrows from the deep lake of the Requiem Mass liturgy[106] and will recur in *The Dream*:

> O'er the penal waters, as they roll,
> I poise thee, and I lower thee, and hold thee.
> And carefully I dip thee in the lake,
> And thou, without a sob or a resistance,
> Does through the flood thy rapid passage take,
> Sinking deep, deeper, into the dim distance.[107]

The willing plunge into the whirlpool which is purgatory, involves pain which may well be as acute as the pains of hell, but is borne with resignation because of the love which exists between the soul and God. In hell it is only darkness; there is no light of love.

Heaven

When Newman wrote to Pusey as his eldest daughter Lucy lay dying in 1844 he said

Do you not bear in mind the opinion of theologians that it is the grace which supplies all things, supersedes all things, and is all in all? I believe they hold, though a dying person were in a desert,

---

[105] *Verses on Various Occasions*, p. 365.

[106] Offertory prayer 'Deliver the souls of all the faithful departed from the pains of hell and from the deep lake.'

[107] *Verses on Various Occasions*, p. 365. *Discourses to Mixed Congugation*, p. 81.

without any one at hand, love would be to him everything.[108]

Our whole life must teach us how to love others not out of selfish reasons, but to the glory of God.[109] This theme will recur in a sermon preached in Dublin in 1857:

> There is no one who has loved the world so well, as He who made it. None has so understood the human heart, and human nature, and human society in its diversified forms, none has so tenderly entered into and measured the greatness and little-ness of man, his doings and sufferings, his circumstances and his fortunes, none has felt such profound compassion for his ignorance and guilt, his present rebelling and his prospects hereafter, as the Omniscient. What He has actually done is the proof of this 'God so loved the world, as to give His only-begotten Son'.[110]

The reality of our love can make familiar that place which we should call home. This was Newman's argument to those who thought that heaven was some sort of strange country, like going into space and seeing the wonders of the universe.[111] We need to be at home now with that other world which will one

---

[108] Tolhurst J. (ed.), *Comfort in Sorrow* (Leominster, Gracewing, 1996), p. 52.

[109] *Sermon Notes* (SN), pp. 161, 210. Hence purgatory 'burns away in every one of us that in which we differ from each other', SN, p. 284.

[110] *Sermons Preached on Various Occasions*, p. 106.

[111] SN, p. 207.

day be our happiness. Newman reminds his congregation that this world should be seen as a veil, hiding
that other world, not a mask shutting it out.[112]

There is also the phrase which harks back to his
Essay on Development, when he preaches on Christ's
second coming: 'Every age is a semblance, a type in
part of what then at last will be in fulness'.[113] As this
is one of two versions of the same sermon, one
wonders which was actually put into words.

Angels

It should not surprise anyone that the topic of angels
occurs to Newman as a fit subject for sermons. In
fact he preaches a series of four during September
1860. It will be recalled that in his childhood, he
thought life itself might be a dream and he an
angel.[114] When patristic studies began to monopolise
his time, he saw them as the real causes 'of motion,
light and life and of those elementary principles of
the universe ... the laws of nature'.[115] His remarks
on 30 September 1860 include the operation of
heavenly bodies, adding 'science need not [be
supposed to have] superseded this'.[116] We should not
infer by this that Newman embraced a fundamental-
ist approach to science. He objected to the
contemporary fashion of exalting scientific discovery
at the expense of God. In this sense we should understand his remark 'The tendency of this age to depress

---

[112] *Sermon Notes* (SN), p. 257; cf. *Essays Critical and Historical* II, p. 190.
[113] SN, p. 225.
[114] *Apologia Pro Vita Sua*, p. 6.
[115] *Apologia Pro Vita Sua*, p. 28.
[116] SN, p. 166.

man, fancying the stars inhabited'.[117] It also explains his reservations about certain currents in Natural Theology which concentrate on the wonders of creation but do not teach us our duty and tell us nothing about sin.[118]

From the perspective of the angels, the great mysteries of science are so much child's play[119] because such knowledge comes to them intuitively. But looked at from another angle, Newman repeats that the whole history of the world is wearying to them, and the guardian angels find their task odious.[120] Newman is possibly reacting to a saccharine interpretation of the heavenly powers, and injecting a note of asperity. He thoroughly espoused the Alexandrine concept of the angels as supremely strong executors of the divine will:

> For spirits and men by different standards mete
> The less and greater in the flow of time ...
> Not so with us in the immaterial world;
> But intervals in their succession
> Are measured by the living thought alone
> And grow or wane with its intensity.[121]

These are our guardian angels, who are also 'our constant friends ...'.[122] There are hints in fact that Newman would have liked to set this strong theology

117 *Sermon Notes* (SN), p. 23.
118 SN, p. 291 and *Parochial and Plain Sermons* I, p. 317.
119 SN, p. 162.
120 SN, pp. 9, 167.
121 *Verses on Various Occasions*, pp. 336-7.
122 SN, p. 138.

against a background of the immensity of the heavens, where light from distant stars had not yet arrived on this planet.[123] But he is not over-confident that mankind will make a success of his scientific riches as he adds 'the future quite dark',[124] and earlier on he had compared the course of events to a 'railway train, bowling away into the darkness'.[125] He falls back on his concept of Development to say that 'every age is a semblance, a type in part of what then at last will be in fulness'.[126]

The *Sermon Notes* are not the polished productions of the *Parochial and Plain Sermons* or the masterpieces of the *Sermons Preached on Various Occasions*. We can understand something of how they might have appeared by studying the first seven Catholic Sermons preached between January and the end of March 1848. But these are as much notes and observations as sermon schemes. Many contain alternatives and some were not preached at all. Others were outlines for later lectures. In this they resemble *The Philosophical Notebook* with entries from 1859 to 1880. As such the *Sermon Notes* provide a theological insight into Newman's thought over thirty years. If the *Theological Dictionary* had ever got off the ground, we may well have seen in Newman's contributions the developments of the chance phrases that can be found here. As it is, it repays patient study

[123] *Sermon Notes* (SN), p. 279.
[124] SN, p. 279.
[125] SN, p. 253.
[126] SN, p. 225.

and read alongside the *Letters*, where Newman enters into theological discussions, there emerges a coherent and surprisingly contemporary stance which vindicates his title as the Father of the Second Vatican Council.

SERMON NOTES

July 1, 1849

PURITY AND LOVE—LOVE IN THE INNOCENT AND THE PENITENT [1]

1. INTROD.—All the saints of God, all holy persons, all the faithful have, each in his measure, purity and love—the two graces go together. What is purity but the having the heart fixed [on], the loving (*al.* an affection for) things unseen? What turns away the soul from God so much as impurity? What is impurity but loving (*al.* having affection for) what is sinful? We have such an affection for money, etc.

2. Yet, though this be so, here as in other graces, some [saints] are instances of one grace, some of another; and therefore it may be said without exaggeration that there [are] two kinds of saints, the saints of purity, the saints of love—the lily and the rose.

3. St. John the Baptist, sanctified from his mother's womb, living in the desert. St. John the Evangelist, the virgin saint—perhaps he never voluntarily yielded to venial sin, and hence so much favoured—lying in our Lord's bosom. How different

[1] See Note 1, p. 334.

A

these two, yet agreeing in this that they lived *out
of* the world.   It is the characteristic of the virgin
saints that their love [is] contemplative, tranquil,
etc.—nay, can hardly be called love ; so intimately
one with the Supreme that it is with Him rather
than it loves Him.   It does not approach towards
Him so much as already have Him ; it *is* heaven
rather than loves heaven ; it is a partaker of the
divine Nature rather than a lover of it.   Therefore
we talk of such for their purity.

4. Such above all the Virgin Mother.   She therefore, as coming so near to God, is associated with His
titles—*sedes sapientiae, janua coeli, vita, dulcedo,* etc.

5. But on the other hand, when a soul has given
itself to sin, when it has lost its first estate or never
had grace—when it is in *bonds,* whether to be converted or to be reclaimed, what is to counteract
and antagonise to pride and pleasure ? [to compete]
with formed habits ?   What but a superior attraction ?   (St. Augustine in Pentecost.[1])

Hence *love* is the great instrument of conversion :
(therefore as purity is the emblem of the one
[the Innocent], *i.e.* it shows itself more, takes a
prominent place — so love of the other [the
Penitent]), therefore, as the love of the pure is
tranquil, so the love of the penitent is energetic,
zealous, active, belligerent, [full] of emotion, of
work, of passion—the one the love which is of peace,
the other which is of warfare.   [Examples of the
love of the penitent.]   (1) David in the Psalms ; (2)

[1] The reference is to a passage of St. Augustine [*Tract. In
Joann. XXVI.*] read in the matins of Wednesday in Whit-week.
It is quoted in *Sermons to Mixed Congregations,* p. 70.

St. Mary Magdalene—her energy, thrusting herself
into the room, tears in the room and in the garden ;
(3) St. Peter—loving more than the rest—walking
on the sea—John xxi. (contrast St. John's tranquil
'It is the Lord') rushed forward—weeping for his
denial—crucified head downwards ; (4) St. Paul,
'the life I now live in the flesh,' [1] 'the love of Christ
constraineth us,' [2] etc. ; (5) St. Augustine represented in pictures as loving ; (6) thus in the Confiteor
3, [Our Lady, St. Michael, St. John the Baptist,
the Innocent] then 2, [SS. Peter and Paul—
Penitents].

July 8
POWER OF PRAYER

1. INTROD.—If there is anything which distin-
guishes religion at all, which is meant by the very
word, it is the power of prayer. Yet wonderful at
first [sight] that prayer should have an effect.

2. The *order* of the world seems to forbid it—
sun rising and setting—everything uniform—laws
(causes and effects) [3]—winds, indeed, and atmosphere
and sea irregular, but a regular irregularity. All
things cause and effect, bound together like a steam-
engine ; would prayer to its Maker make it stop ?

3. Hence at all times the wise in this world have
laughed prayer to scorn : they have thought it was
a superstition.[4]

---

[1] Gal. ii. 20.   [2] 2 Cor. v. 14.

[3] Over these words is written an incomplete sentence : 'and
the more you inquire the more . . .'

[4] This sermon was not completed. Underneath it is pasted a
small scrap of paper with notes, apparently used in the pulpit.

July 22 [1]

CAUSES WHICH KEEP MEN FROM CATHOLICITY

1. INTROD.—Catholics often surprised that every one does not become a Catholic. And they have a difficulty, how any one can see the Church without acknowledging it.

2. Now this often arises from *invincible ignorance*, as almost all would admit ; viz. when the reasons for Catholicity have never been brought home to a man. Born in another religion—not come across the Church—never been a practical question. They are Protestant simply from Protestantism being in possession.

3. Prejudice, violent—yet some danger here that not invincible ignorance, because they cannot but hear other side in part.

4. The reason I shall here mention is a main one, viz. not liking to belong to a body. (1) Contrast of Church of England—taking a pew, etc. ;—they can believe what they please, they are not bound. (2) This applies in part to dissenting bodies. You will say ' I grant it in part.' Still a great difference, for the Catholic Church [is] a body, a society such as no body of men is.

Enumerate particulars.—(1) Not able to believe what they please, not knowing what they are pledged to ; strictness of confession, the Church having a *hold* upon them. (2) Pride—not liking to

---

[1] Note by the writer—' Not preached yet.'

condescend. (3) Human respect—not liking to be laughed at. It involves outward profession.

5. But this is the *strength* as well as the *difficulty*, for it is a body or society which has privilege from Christ. Men come for the sacraments—for pardon of sin—hence they feel *peace* on joining it. Communion of saints, of merits, of indulgences.

July 22

ON HUMAN RESPECT

1. On Magdalene's entrance to our Lord at the feast—circumstances of it ; the way the guests sat —custom of lying at table. The Pharisee would start from a bad woman coming in.[1] Not strange a woman should come in, but that she should anoint feet, not head, and weep. She chose a banquet, the very place where she might have been seen in splendour, not weeping—Maldonatus on Matt. xxv., p. 286.[2] How she was able to get in—*ib., in loc.* [Luke vii. 38], p. 167 ; neglectful of self—she did not think what others would say, because she saw Christ. Just allude to people not going to church with bad clothes.

2. Now I suppose no more urgent motive than ' what people will think of us '—fear of the world and human respect—extends from high to low. The feeling is tyrannical—fashion.

[1] The writer corrected this statement in note written in pencil and much of which is illegible: ' No, probably they mixed with them without thinking of converting them, but despising them ; only solicitous they should not touch them.'

[2] See Note 2, p. 334.

3. I am far from meaning that it is bad or useless; it is not *in itself* bad because it is natural. Nothing natural bad, for from God, except under circumstances—in excess, not so as God wills it, or to the exclusion of God.[1]

4. Nor useless—the contrary. A number of good things are done which would not else be [done], and bad avoided which would not else be [avoided]. We cannot go right without a *feeling of responsibility*. Now the mass of mankind do not realise God, and therefore human opinion makes them responsible, and makes them act *rightly*—a present *visible judgment* useful as far as true. *E.g.* (1) No public office would go on well without responsibility—abuses coming in. (2) When upper classes have been shielded from responsibility, we know what excesses. (3) In colonies and abroad society sinks down to an immoral level—even ministers of religion.

5. But while we acknowledge it *good on a large scale, we should be very jealous of it in our own case.* Insist on this contrast—it *usurps the place* of God— ' Loving the praise of men rather than God ' [John xii. 42]. (1) Instances with what I began with— Magdalene; not going to church with bad clothes— a little thing, but most expressive; it extends to all communions and religions, and to all but the higher classes who wear the same clothes on Sundays and other days. (2) A greater matter by contrast making propriety of appearance taking [take] place of virtue

---

[1] Written over in pencil: ' perfectly becoming we should have a regard for each other—" provide things honest in the sight of men." '—Rom. xii. 17.

—unchastity nothing so that you are not found out; infanticide; Spartan boy stealing fox; being ridiculed for religion; not daring to obey God; obliged to take part in bad discourse; ashamed of being known to pray—I do not wish to be hard upon them—St. Augustine before his conversion, *pudebat me*, etc.; *St. Alfonso's Sermons*, p. 172.

6. Hence saints have been so set against human respect. *St. Francis Borgia* carrying a vessel of broth to some prisoners met his son on horseback, etc., vide *St. Alfonso's Sermons*, pp. 175-6—hence strange penances of S. Filippo Neri.

7. We should not go out of our way, without direction, to do strange things, but one thing we *should* aim at—to substitute the presence of God for dependence on the world. Act in thought of God. How many things we do in private which it would be the greatest punishment possible we can conceive to do in public. Well, act as if God's eye were on you—fear Him more than man, etc.

CONCLUSION.—And, O my friends, if any Protestants are here, are you sure that *you* would not become Catholics but for the fear of men? Are you prepared to say, 'I will follow wherever God leads me. I do not, indeed, see my way to be a Catholic, but I will become one, in spite of the world, if I find it is my duty to be one, and if I *suspect* it is my duty, I will inquire and not give over.' The world passes; in a little time those only are blessed who, putting aside (*al.* thinking nothing of) the world's opinion (He that is ashamed of Me and of My words, etc.) like Magdalene, see Christ alone and gain His favour.

Note appended by the preacher to this sermon

QUERY.—This sermon would be more complete,
if not so short, if confined to the following :

1. As above (1) circumstances of St. Mary M.
   coming to our Lord.
2. On appearing before the Lord in the particular
   judgment—longing to see Him though He
   punishes.
3. Looking on our Lord in benediction which
   follows the sermon.

July 29

ON THE GOSPEL FOR PENTECOST IX. [CHRIST WEEPING OVER JERUSALEM]

1. INTROD. — Wonderful union of mercy and
severity in God, as in our Saviour weeping over
Jerusalem.   Who can have hard thoughts of Him ?
Yet who can presume ?

2. Take the case of the Jews.   St. Paul says ' these
things happened in figure ' [1] : they are a figure of
God's dealings with every soul.   Consider the fre-
quent judgments mentioned in the epistle—how
often He had to punish before He gave them up.
At last wrath came without remedy—He wept
while He denounced—it was over and there was
no hope.   He dried His tears—He rose up—He
executed wrath—He rejected them and burned up
their city.

3. And so in every age.   Consider what a wonderful patience—the same thing acted over and over

---

[1] Alluding to the epistle of the Sunday, 1 Cor. **x.** 6-13.

again—how *weary* the angels must get of the *history* of the world—every generation beginning with sinners, and then some turning to repentance—looking at individual souls, seeing them plunge into sin fearlessly—yet they are afterwards to repent—they must feel indignation that God should be trifled with. The very same poor souls who now sin will repent as the generation before them : they even take their fill of sin before they turn to God.

4. Then they see repentance—all so promising, such a good start; yet God sees that those very persons, who are beginning so well, are again to fall from Him—to profane and ungratefully treat all His gifts.

5. But so the world goes on. Numbers never coming back to God [at] all, numbers coming back then falling again, numbers repenting only in the end of life, numbers sinning against light and warning, again and again, till they are cast off without remedy. Observe how stern the words, ' *for now they are hidden from thine eyes.*'

6. Yet *how beautiful* the temple looked. Describe —goodly stones—how unlikely that it should be destroyed, yet it was doomed.

7. Blessed they who do not sin ; next blessed they who consider God's wrath and mercy—*not one of them* only, lest they despair or presume.

August 5

ON PRIVATE JUDGMENT

SUBJECT.—*Why* such opposition to Catholicity ?

1. Many reasons may be given, but this is one of

the chief : viz. (1) popularly and rhetorically (for they cannot speak calmly) Catholicity a system which conspires against the peace and liberty of man ; a tyrannical system which imposes a load of things upon the conscience, which terrifies the weak ; anathemas ; a grasping secret system ; and so they go on—and worse, till they rise to priestcraft, Babylon, Antichrist, man of sin, etc., etc.

(2) Really this (for almost all exaggeration is founded on truth : now the question is what truth there is in this) : viz. that it [Catholicity] is intrusive—interferes between a man and God. Religion [they say] a private matter ; every one has a right to judge for himself—I am quite able to teach myself ; I will never allow dictation ; I am a free-born Briton ; Britons never were slaves, and such like vulgar swaggering, etc., etc.[1]

2. How much truth ? We must sift it still further: viz. there is interference, but not by an individual, as if the clergy might bind the laity by their private judgment, but by a system, a system of laws, etc. This must be cleared up. (1) Mistake to suppose the Pope can order what he will to be believed. You say, Suppose the Pope were to say [this or that preposterous thing] we must believe it. Well, but suppose there were no God, etc. ? or again, what would you do with two and two making five ? (2) The confessor cannot do what he will : (i) a penitent chooses his confessor ; (ii) he need not be

---

[1] The following sentences are jotted down in pencil between (1) and (2): ‘Let us sift this, for it is spoken rhetorically. For nothing like prose—all rhetoric [and] declamation. An inspiring subject and controversial, it always rises into oratory.’

known to him, *e.g.* extraordinary missions on purpose ; (iii) the confessor goes by rule as a judge does ; (iv) the penitent may appeal to another confessor ; (v) the confessor may not speak out of confession even to the penitent ; (vi) a penitent may not introduce the name of others—detraction ; (vii) the confessor knows his penitent too little, not too much ; (viii) two confessors may not talk over a penitent. Account of Protestant who said the confessor looked like a God—how absurd ! a father and child [is nearer the mark]. How the penitent may tell, [while] the confessor can't defend himself, can't employ his knowledge in any way, not even to defend himself against poisoning ; therefore in this individual arbitrary sense, the reproach against Catholicity, as stated above, not true. Yet it is true that Catholicity, the Church, interposes between man and his God, teaching him, warning him, and judging for him. Now I have brought it down to what is true, and here I join issue with it.

3. Now the Protestant view [of no interference] is unnatural, irrational, unscriptural, etc. Now to show this—why Protestants cannot carry it out themselves ! If they were consistent they would not educate their children ; yet so eager for education, and against Catholics educating ! If every one should form an opinion for himself, children should be let alone. Some people have done so. But *you* take, not a common time, but the first time, and the most impressionable ; it is half, three-fourths of the battle to educate children [as Protestants virtually admit].

4. But you will say it can't be helped. If we

don't educate, others will—the devil will. Well, [that shows that] the nature, the state of things, is against you. This is just what I said, that your way [view of non-interference] was *unnatural*.

If then children, why not grown men ?

5. But you will say this is absurd, because they can judge for themselves. No. No proof that they *can* judge for themselves, only that they *will*. They can't in worldly matters : wouldn't it be better if they didn't in worldly matters ? Why then in spiritual ? Men are all their lives children as regards religion ; they can't in spiritual [things] judge. You know they can't in business and cares of life— this is what I meant by irrational—and in matter of fact they don't. You know they are influenced first by their education, next by the persons they meet ; to say they go by [their own judgment is] simply absurd—they go by counsels. Why not right of private judgment in children ? Simply because they are weak and depend on you.

6. Well then, you make every one a prey of every confident talker, as you do. God has provided the Church to prevent this very evil.

7. Now think how else you would get out of the difficulty, viz. the fact that human nature requires guidance, and will take the first that comes. Does not God's goodness point to a church ?

8. O my brethren, which is the more scriptural ? One church in heaven and earth—the saints— souls in purgatory—communication of merits—each depends on each—hand and foot—(explain). This why Englishmen so unamiable—coldness.

August 19

ON THE FITNESS OF OUR LADY'S ASSUMPTION

1. Recollect Luke xxiv. 26, ' Ought not Christ,' etc. ; Hebrews ii. 10, ' It became Him,' etc. ; Rom. xii., ' Analogy of Faith.' [1]

2. In like manner it *became* our Lord to raise His mother, and her so sinless. Let us think of this.

3. Doctrine from the first—that God was her Son, lay in her womb, was suckled by her, etc. She enjoyed His voice, smile, etc.

4. Esther vi. 6, ' What should be done to the man whom the king is desirous to honour ? ' . . . ' He ought to be clothed in royal robes,' etc. And so of our Lady—she should be the Mirror of Justice, the Mystical Rose, etc. Thus has King Solomon risen up to meet his mother.

5. Now go into details—sanctity and spiritual office or work go commonly together : (1) the angels ; (2) seraphim. Exceptions : (i) Balaam, Caiaphas, overruled ; (ii) many shall say in that day, ' Lord, Lord, have we not prophesied in Thy Name,' and He shall answer, ' I never knew you '; (3) They may have fallen away ; (4) *gifts* are [imparted] separately from sanctity, but gifts are not offices. On the contrary (5) Enoch, Noe, Moses, Samuel, David, etc.—except Judas. [These are instances where, according to the general rule, ' sanctity and spiritual office go together.']

[1] See Note 3, p. 334.

6. If such to whom the word was *made*, much more [does sanctity go with spiritual office] in [her, in] whom He was born. Was it not fitting ? Do human parents otherwise ? Do they give their children to suckle to common persons ? *Nature* says that the fount of *truth* should be *holy*. Here is the difference [as between] miracles and sacraments.[1] Prophets receive, beget, and bear the Divine Word. Scripture-writers different from each other, and so the Fathers.[2] As the tree, so the fruit. ' Beware of false prophets ' [says our Lord, and then He adds, ' from their fruits ye shall know them ']. Mary not a mere *instrument*—as the first-fruit, so the mass. The Word did not pass through [her]. He *took* a body from her, therefore she was worthy of the Creator—*full of grace*.

7. Hence doctrine of Immaculate Conception—grace before Gabriel [*i.e.* before the Annunciation], before vow of virginity, before Temple, before birth, before St. John the Baptist [*i.e.* at an earlier period in her existence than that in which it was bestowed upon the Baptist]. *She must surpass all saints*.

8. Again with her *co-operation*—this her merit. She was peccable ; she *grew* in grace, etc. Enoch merited, Noe merited, Abraham merited, Levites merited, David, Daniel [merited] ; how much more Mary since her reward was such !

---

[1] Speaking generally, a miracle is a testimony to some truth. Its worker therefore is a *fount of truth,* and therefore presumably holy. A like presumption does not exist in the case of the administrator of a sacrament.

[2] The fact that the inspired writer, or the Father, preserves his individuality, shows that he is something else than ' a mere instrument.'

9. Her glories were not simply from her being Mother of God : *it* implies something before it. The feast of Annunciation implies feast of Conception and of Assumption.

10. Come then (I would not weary you) to Assumption—more difficult *not* to believe Assumption than to believe it after the Incarnation. Human sons sustain their mothers. She died ; she saw no corruption, for she had no original sin. ' Dust thou art,' etc.

11. Therefore she died in private. Give history of Assumption.

12. What is *it* fitting that *we* should be with such a mother ?

August 26

ON WANT OF FAITH [1]

1. INTROD.—Many, as I said lately, wonder the beauty of Catholicity does not attract multitudes of people ' to see that great sight ' [2]—' come and see ' [3]—and join the Church.

2. They do not become Catholics because they have not faith. This no truism ; faith is a certain faculty, like justice, etc.

3. Describe faith—assent on the word of another —as coming from God, not by sight or reason, not as word of man, which is a kind of faith, but not firm. We take man's word for what it is worth, but [divine] faith is most certain.

4. This was faith in the apostles' time—certainty.

---

[1] See Note 4, p. 335.   [2] Exod. iii. 3.   [3] John i. 39.

The converts entered the Church in order to learn.
Could they have disputed with an apostle ? or
separated from them ? or believed them not in-
wardly ? or wait for further proof ? No, there was
no private judgment then ; they either believed or
did not believe. They could not say, I will
choose, I will believe a little, as I please, etc.,
etc.

5. And this is plain from Scripture texts—1 Thess.
ii. 13, *ib.* iv. 8, Luke x. 16—' know most certainly ' [1]
or ' believe and be saved,' the ' word of hearing.' [2]

6. What a contrast between this or deducing from
a book to master it ! The one is submitting, the
other is judging. Faith, then, in the apostles' age
consisted in submitting.

7. Plainly not a temper of the world now ; they
have not what the apostles meant by faith. Men
change to and fro now : this is opinion, not faith.

8. Again they laugh at faith as servile, the work
of priestcraft. Would they not have rejected the
apostles ? Would they not have died pagans ?

9. Object—the pagan did so laugh—quote 1 Cor.
i. 23 [3] ; Matt. xi. 25. [4]

10. They have not faith. How then do they
believe the Scriptures ? They don't ; it is a nursery
habit. When they think of their contents they
begin to doubt.

11. What faith [was] in the apostles' days [it is]
now. I have proved, then, the world has not faith.
Though many men may admire, may encourage, yet

---

[1] Acts ii. 36.   [2] 1 Thess. ii. 13.
[3] '. . . Christ crucified . . . unto the Gentiles foolishness.'
[4] '. . . Thou hast hid these things from the wise and prudent.'

they will say, 'O that we were Catholics!' and get no further.

12. Deplorable state! for faith so necessary; *e.g.* Heb. xi. 6[1]; Mark xvi. 16[2]; John iii. 18.[3] Christ might have saved by sight, but He saves by faith.

13. Let them try to put faith elsewhere if they can. Faith through grace.

14. Exhortation to Protestants to use existing grace.

September 2

PREJUDICE AS A CAUSE WHY MEN ARE NOT CATHOLICS

1. INTROD.—It may surprise those Catholics who live to themselves why so many Protestants are not Catholics, but it will not surprise those who go into the world. They will there find what will account for it, viz. a prejudice about Catholicism such that the wonder is not why men do not become Catholics, but why any do at all.

2. Such is the power of prejudice. What is prejudice? It is forming a judgment without sufficient grounds. We cannot help being prejudiced, because there are ten thousand things about which we can but have an opinion; but the fault is—and this is what we truly mean by prejudice—when we stick to it in spite of better information, or will not listen to other information.

3. Now as regards Catholicism. Men in child-

---

[1] 'Without faith it is impossible to please God.'

[2] 'He that believeth and is baptized shall be saved.'

[3] 'He that doth not believe is already judged.'

B

hood have always heard Catholics abused. They
are considered to be cruel; stories of torments
inflicted by them are circulated: (1) exaggerated
stories of individuals; (2) a horror of some particular practice; (3) viewing things separately, not
as a whole. One thing fixes in their mind, and seems
to justify all anticipations, for persons take fright
at some one particular doctrine or fact, *e.g.* about
the confessional, and at one bad priest, etc., etc.
This especially inconsistent in those who profess to
go by private judgment. Why do they go by what
they hear, and that casually perhaps ?

4. Not believing [that] (1) priests believe what
they say; (2) are continent; (3) [that] converts
are satisfied—looking out for some change in them.
The consequence of this deep prejudice is that from
the nature of the case there are no ways of over-
coming it. If Catholics are particular, devout, or
charitable, etc., they are said to be hypocrites; if
all things apparently simple, they think there is
something in the background; they call them
plausible; if nothing can be found against them,
how well they conceal things; if they argue well,
what clever sophists; if charitable, they have vast
wealth; if they succeed, not of God's blessing, but
of craft. I wish we had half the cleverness they
impute to us.

5. Hence they circulate lies about us, not inquiring the authority, and when they are disproved,
instead of giving over, circulate others which can't
be. When any particular lie is put out, they embrace it at once as being so likely, *i.e.* like their
prejudice. They take not this age and place, but

a thousand miles away and two hundred years ago. Catholics alone can suffer this, because they are in all times and places ; they could not, *e.g.*, treat Quakers so. Explain how far honest. They say to themselves, if this is not true, yet something else is true quite as bad.

6. But this cannot last, *i.e.* prejudice (whether they become Catholics or not) ; as the ice goes in Canadian sea in a week, so when prejudice once begins to thaw it will go quickly. Now the remedy for all this is to see us—(enlarge on this). They cannot keep up their theories against us, but they are afraid to be puzzled with something on our side. They have a sort of feeling that if they were to see us we should contradict their prejudices, so they do all they can to keep us out of sight.

7. Hence no person hardly who has been much abroad and lived with the people can keep up their prejudices ; no one who has read much history : the strength of prejudice is with those who are not informed.

September 30

FAITH AND DOUBT[1]

1. INTROD.—Those who are curious ask, ' May I doubt *when* I am a Catholic ? ' Those who object say it is a tyranny, violence on the mind, immoral, etc. ; *i.e.* they ought to hold that it is wrong to make up the mind on any religious subject whatever, however sacred. A liberty to doubt [is what they ask].

[1] See Note 5, p. 335.

2. First, doubt is incompatible with faith. Who would say a man believed the apostles' mission who added that perhaps he should one day doubt about it ? A real but latent doubt. ' I perhaps am excited,' or ' in a delusion,' or ' everything may turn out.' What men object to is *faith*. If the thing is *true*—that God became man—why must it be *doubted* ? Either they have faith now, and then, etc., or not, and then, etc. I may love and obey by halves, not believe.

3. And so when a Catholic [doubts] he has *already* lost it (*i.e.* faith). Persons converted to Protestantism by reading the Bible. Protestants only show by their objections that they do not know what faith is.

4. Secondly, love [rejects doubt] as well as faith. What would you think of a friend who bargained not to trust you ? who said he should be trifling with truth if he did not [so bargain] ? May I never have such a friend—jealous minds, etc.—[Give me] cordial, openhearted ones, etc. And so of God. If a man thought God might be unjust, or bargained to believe in, worship Him, only while his reason told him, he would be worshipping himself. And so of the Church. Fetters ! [Yes,] cords of Adam.

5. The world thinks faith a *burden*—cannot understand joy of believing. [It imagines] confession [to be] chiefly of doubts. On the contrary, *popule meus, quid feci tibi*, etc.

6. Third view. (Doubt does not destroy intellectual conviction, but) faith a gift of God. I may see I ought to believe, yet cannot. Conviction and acting, conviction and faith—faith not of necessity,

[*i.e.* the will not coerced] but of will—merit in faith.

7. Conviction may remain without faith. If we listen to objections without cause—case of those who fall away—they cannot answer arguments. Thus they either linger about the Church or go into atheism.

8. Fourth reason [why doubt is not permissible]. Inconsistent in the Church to do otherwise. St. Paul, St. John, Eliseus.[1]

9. No other body can demand faith—not Dissenters, not Church of England.

10. Be sure, before you join us. You must come to learn. Do not distress yourselves *whether* your faith will last.

11. Get *conviction*. Act when it comes; it comes differently to different persons. We are anxious about persons, not as wishing them to act without conviction, but because perhaps the time is past.

12. Oh the misery if you *have* not become Catholics! Oh the misery if we *had* not!

October 14

MATERNITY OF MARY [2]

1. INTROD.—When we look upon earth and sky we find everything connected together in a wonderful way—everything answering to each. Nothing could be altered—if there were one star less or more— and so of animal power—atmosphere and sea. The

---

[1] Eliseus prohibiting the search for Elias, 4 Kings ii. 16.
[2] See Note 6, p. 336.

like happens in the Catholic religion, and the more
a person examines the more he will find it, though
people have no time for examination. But concerning the doctrines of our Lady, apropos of the Maternity. (It seems fair to say, that if God would restore the world, she must be without sin. Yet [again]
one truth follows from another.)

2. When God intended to take flesh, He might
have taken a body like Adam or Eve (or from the
sky), but either men would not have believed He
was man, or not so readily. The notion of God
becoming man is so hard that the human mind will
evade it if it can. Hence, in order to *seal the doctrine*,
He took a human mother.

3. Hence the great doctrine that Mary is His
mother : the Mother of God has ever been the bulwark of our Lord's divinity. And it is that which
heretics have ever opposed, for it is the great witness
that the doctrine of God being man is true. The
making *much* of, the *prominence* of the doctrine is
the bulwark, hence she had her gifts—(1) to erect her
as a Turris Davidica, lest she should be forgotten ;
(2) to prepare her fitly, as a temple (no unclean thing
can enter heaven) ; (3) lest she should be puffed up
as Satan. She said, ' *Ecce ancilla Domini* ' ; thus she
ministers as a creature, and does glory to God.

4. The *first* mode heretics took was saying that
our Lord's body came down from heaven, or that
He was an apparent man, etc. They affected to be
reverent, and said the idea was shocking that a
born man should be God. Now you see how the
doctrine excludes *this* idea ; hence, in the creed,
' born of the Virgin Mary.'

The *second* mode was to say that Mary bore a man, and not God—mother of our Lord's manhood, etc.—but that God was in a particular way in Him, as He was in the prophets and good men.

The Council of Ephesus, about four hundred years after Christ, [decreed] the title of *Mother of God*.

The *third* ground was at the Reformation— bolder — that it [*i.e.* Catholic teaching about our Lady] was idolatry, etc., Satan hoping so to destroy the belief in our Lord's divinity. Here again false reverence, so they abolished the honour of our Lady out of tenderness to Christ's divinity ! Look at the issue. The truth is, the doctrine of our Lady keeps us from a dreaming, unreal way. If no mother, no history, how did He come here, etc ? He is from heaven. It startles us and makes us think what we say when we say Christ is God ; not merely like God, inhabited by, sent by God, but really God ; so really, that she is the mother of God because His mother.

Fourth, the tendency of this age to depress man, fancying the stars inhabited, etc. Why, then, should God think of us ? why should His son be incarnate ? Not so much meant. Now this doctrine *fixes* that so much is meant, *coelum animatum*.

November 11

PURGATORY

1. INTROD.—Not wonderful if God, who might have saved us without, yet saved us with Christ's passion—though He might have saved us without pain, [yet] saves us with pain.

2. Hence 'through many tribulations we must enter,' etc., either in this life or next. As Christ [suffered] without sin, so we for our own sins. Suffering in next life is in purgatory.

3. Now I shall best describe purgatory by first, 'He descended into hell.' What is meant by hell? Plainly the place to which *souls* go—as His body to the grave, so His soul to hell. So 'thou shalt not leave My soul in hell,' etc., Ps. xv. 10. Yet hell cannot mean the home of the devil, therefore it means something short of hell, though called hell.

4. Remarkable it should be so called. It cannot be called so without reason. A joyful place would not be called hell. Yet so also in the Mass, etc., 'de porta inferi,' 'de ore leonis et de profundo lacu,' '*ne absorbeat* eum'; and so again Phil. ii. 10 [1] and Rom. x. 6-7,[2] and Samuel, 'from the earth.'

5. Evidently then near hell, or in some respects like hell—*absorbeat*, like a whirlpool. Such is purgatory, and it is not wonderful that it should be a place of great punishment. Hence it is that, being near hell, the holy fathers say the flames are hell flames, like being scorched by a house on fire.

6. Still at least it cannot be a happy place, for it *is not heaven*. Pain of loss—(describe). God our good. We manage in this life to lean on creatures —our friends, etc.; our comforts, etc. The soul downcast, miserable, dreary, as being *hungry*, like

---

[1] 'That in the name of Jesus every knee should bow, of those that are in heaven, on earth and under the earth.'

[2] 'Say not in thy heart, Who shall ascend into heaven? that is, to bring Christ down. Or, Who shall descend into the deep? that is, to bring up Christ again from the dead.'

the feeling of sinking—fainting to the body. Such is purgatory, at worst flame, at best and always, desolation.

7. Different mansions in purgatory (as in heaven). This shown in the vision of St. Felicitas, and of St. Malachi.

8. Hence a received, or at least a pious, opinion that there is a region where there is no pain of sense at all. St. Bede speaks, as St. Felicitas suggests, of a meadow. St. Gertrude; St. Mechtilda. Such the place of the old patriarchs such as Samuel. Hence Abraham's bosom, though in sight of hell— and, ' with me in paradise '—a garden.

9. But since it is the place which, with all our penances and satisfactions here, we cannot escape from, I will add some consolations. First, they *do not sin*—no ruffling or impatience ; they are the *holy* souls in purgatory. (1) They hate their sin so much that they have greater pleasure in suffering than in not suffering with the feeling of sin. (2) No impatience; they *will* to suffer, for it is God's will. Thus every consolation—full resignation. A holy soul plunging into the place where it sent itself— rather feeling the pains of hell than the least sin.

10. Secondly, they *know* they have done with sin ; it was a phantom haunting them all through life, night and morning. Weariness—all at an end. Resignation in the storm ; ecstatic feeling ; nay, he rejoices to combat with the antagonist trial.

11. Assurance of salvation, as they know that each hour brings them nearer to the end.

12. Consoled by angels, etc. St. Francis de Sales. Transcendental state; not single bliss and single

pain ; nor mixed as in this life, but both together, pure and antagonistic.[1]

ST. FRANCIS DE SALES ON PURGATORY [2]

It is true that its torments are so great that the most extreme pains of this life cannot be compared with it ; yet, on the other hand, the internal satisfactions there are such that there is no prosperity or contentment on earth which can equal them. (1) The souls there are in a continual union with God. (2) They are perfectly resigned to His will, or, to speak more exactly, their will is so transformed into His will that they cannot will otherwise than God wills ; so that if paradise were opened to them, they would rather precipitate themselves into hell than appear before God with the defilements which they still recognise in themselves. (3) They are purified there voluntarily and lovingly, since such is the divine good pleasure. (4) They wish to be there in the manner which pleases God, and for so long as pleases Him. (5) They cannot sin, and cannot experience the least motion of impatience, nor commit the least imperfection. (6) They love God more than themselves, or anything, with a full love, pure and disinterested. (7) They are there consoled by angels. (8) They are there assured of their salvation, with a hope which cannot be confounded in its expectation. (9) Their bitterness, most bitter as it is, is in the midst of peace most profound. (10) Though purgatory be a sort of hell

---

[1] See Note 7, p. 336.

[2] This summary of St. Francis' teaching was written on a loose leaf, and does not belong to the sermon.

as regards the pain, yet it is a paradise as regards
the sweetness which charity spreads abroad in the
heart ; charity more strong than death, more
powerful than hell, the lights of which are all fire
and flame. (11) Happy state, more desirable than
formidable, since the flames are flames of love and
charity. (12) Formidable nevertheless, since they
retard the end of all consummation, which consists
in seeing God and loving Him, and by that sight and
that love, in praising and glorifying Him through
the whole extent of eternity.

December 9

ON MAN AS DISOBEDIENT BY SIN AS CON-TRASTED WITH MARY

1. INTROD.—Our Saviour came at this time of
year to bring peace on earth.

2. Prince of peace—leopard and lamb[1]—'on earth
peace ' ; hence, as type, peace in Roman Empire.

3. He reconciled man to man, God to man, but
especially the soul to itself. He made peace within
—this the great gift.

4. Man created at unity with himself ; his different powers, irascible and concupiscible—how are
they to be brought together ? Only by God's
grace. He is not sufficient for his own happiness.
Stoics have tried to subject the passions to the
reason, without subjecting the reason to God. Sin
is self-destructive.

5. Such the case, about eternal punishment—it
is not religion brings in the doctrine ; it is a fact

---

[1] 'The leopard shall lie down with the *kid*.'—Isaias xi. 6.

in prospect before us—for suppose no God, and man immortal, he would be his own eternal torment, and could not free himself.

6. Give a person riches, health, name, power, ability, let him live centuries here, would that be a gain, or the contrary ? Would not the very time show that these things had failed ?

7. Two great principles, the irascible and the concupiscible. Solomon in Eccles. ii.—indulgence of sensuality ; what does mirth and grasping profit ? Tired out—sated—the same dishes daily ; the same faces ; the same servants behind chairs—Lord Byron—the man who killed himself because he had to get up and go to bed. When such men get to the end of life they would not live longer ; they want rest, as the man in 'The Siege of Corinth '—' The Giaour.'

8. Satiety would make way for gloom—ill-temper. The misery of ill-temper—gloom ; eating the heart out. On kings with unrestrained power, what brutes they become ! Their furious passions. Youth is gay, age is crabbed—vain regret of first youthful feelings, gone for ever. Why, such feelings would tend to madness. Oh the awful misery of a man living an eternity in this world !

9. Yet they do not live on, but die. And then, what the additional agony of a soul left to itself ! with nothing corporeal ; no means of communicating with others ; thrown on itself ; voluntarily cut off from God, who is our only stay, comfort, then— and so for eternity.

10. Pain of the body great, but pain of the mind worse, though we do not know much of it here.

Scaring, bad dreams, hair turning white—what when it comes in its fulness ?   The wicked is like the troubled sea.   Here is your portion, my brethren, if you will not turn to God.

11. Oh, what dreadful thoughts for the future! This is how man, then, will appear before his Maker —covered with wounds, etc.   Suppose at the judgment God, without positive infliction, merely left a man to himself.

12. What a contrast our Lady to this—our Saviour is God and cannot afford the contrast. Immaculate in her conception—so sweet, so musical, etc.   She holds up to us what man is intended to be, as a type, the most perfect submission of his powers to grace.

13. Instinctive feeling in the Church that it is so.

14. Christ the source, Mary the work of grace.

December 16

ON THE LAST TIMES OF THE WORLD

1. INTROD.—Two Advents of Christ.

2. The difference between them : (1) the latter sudden ; the former, a long course of preparation, so that He could not have come sooner than He did—the latter, hardly any preparation—Antichrist alone—else it may come any day.

3. (2) An apostasy before the second—quote 2 Thess. ii. 3-4[1] ; yet this no infringement on its

---

[1] 'Let no man deceive you by any means, for . . . unless there come a revolt first, and that man of sin be revealed, the son of perdition ; who opposeth and is lifted up above all that is called God,' etc.

suddenness, for the apostasy began working even in apostolic times.[1]

4. On the contrary, since it is always working, the contemplation of it may be useful to us.

5. *Characteristic* of the apostasy—*not idolatry*, not presumption, as ' the Temple of the Lord,' etc.[2] Not despair, as ' why should I wait on the Lord,' 2 Kings vi. 33, but infidelity—quote 2 Thess. ii. 4, ' Shewing himself,' etc.[3]

6. Particular sins have *particular* punishments, as fire for Sodom and Gomorrah. (1) Parallel of flood, first destruction of the world : (i) An *apostasy* —*filii Dei ad filias hominum* ; a new state of things followed ; a sort of perfection—*viri famosi* ; (ii) St. Peter called it the world of the impious ; (iii) St. Paul, by *faith* Enoch and Noe *endured the world* ; (iv) St. Jude, Enoch's prophecy against the *impious* ; (v) remarkable ; Tubal-cain and Jubal— useful and fine arts [4]; and so ἄνομος, 2 Thess. ii., with *iniquitas*, Gen. vi. 13.[5]

7. (2) Description of the last apostasy in the New Testament : (i) St. Paul, ' depart (apostatise) from the *faith* ' ; (ii) St. Paul, ' wax worse and worse ' ; (iii) St. Jude, ' mockers,' etc. A still

---

[1] Cf. 2 Thess. ii. 7 ; 1 John iv. 3.

[2] ' Trust ye not in lying words, saying, The temple of the Lord, The temple of the Lord, It is the temple of the Lord.'—Jer. vii. 4.

[3] ' Shewing himself as if he were God.'

[4] ' Jubal the father of them that play upon the harp and the organs. . . . Tubal-cain . . . a hammerer and artificer in every work of brass and iron.'—Gen. iv. 21, 22.

[5] ' The end of all flesh is come before me : for the earth is filled with iniquity through them ; . . . I will destroy them with the earth.'

more remarkable passage, 2 Peter ii. 4-9,[1] where the state of antediluvian and last days (unbelief) are connected. They thought nature must go on as hitherto,—' Where is the promise of the coming ? ' etc. Nature all-sufficient, all in all, that it should come to nought—*an idle tale.*

8. This further illustrated by the miracles of Antichrist, in whom the apostasy will terminate, 2 Thess. ii., Apoc. xiii. 13. Now the devil cannot do *real* miracles, therefore they are miracles of knowledge. Knowledge is power—parallel of Tubal-cain above—and they say power is but knowledge, *i.e.* the revealed miracles are not real ones.

9. Hence so plausible, that even the elect might be deceived by the sophism.

10. Such the apostasy, and while it is brought before us by the season, it concerns us because St. Paul says, 'It already worketh.' It is in all ages, and surely not the least in this—open infidelity, specious objections, various kinds of argument from long ages, geology, history of civilisation, antiquities, etc.

11. You may say it doesn't concern us ; it does —specious objections. But let us ask our *hearts,* do not they speak for religion in spite of these ?

12. It is all founded on *pride.* Pride is dependence

---

[1] ' For if God spared not the angels that sinned, but delivered them, drawn down by infernal ropes to the lower hell unto torments, to be reserved unto judgment. And spared not the original world, but preserved Noe, the eighth person, the preacher of justice, bringing in the flood upon the world for the ungodly. . . . The Lord knoweth how to deliver the godly from temptation, but to reserve the unjust unto the day of judgment to be tormented.'

on *nature* without grace, thinking the *supernatural* impossible. Eating the forbidden fruit was pride and unbelief; thus the world will end with the sin with which it begins.

January 6, 1850

ON THE CATHOLIC CHURCH

1. INTROD.—To-day the birthday of the Catholic Church, for the Gentiles came to it.

2. From eternity in the councils of God. At length in time it began to be ; it was conceived and lay in the womb. Its vital principle faith, therefore with Abraham especially it began. It remained in the womb of former dispensations its due time ; long expectations ; burstings of hope, till the time came ; and was born when Christ came.

3. In the fulness and consummation of time. OBJECTION.—Why so late ? True answer, because unmerited. God may choose His time and place. Again, because He had to *work through* human wills, and therefore, so to say, *under* the present order *could* not choose His time. But here I say fulness and consummation of time, *i.e.* man is born after months in the womb. He is born in due time, not an abortion. So of the church.

4. When born, a robust and perfect offspring, fulfilling its promise—its promise that it was to be everywhere, and was *to be able* to be everywhere.

5. *Able to be,* for this is the difficulty which no other religion ever attempted. None but the Catholic has *been able* to be everywhere. *Local*

religions—whether Eastern mythologies or Protestantism.

6. But even earthly empires do not spread over the world so *widely as* this and so diversely—now from east to west, now from north to south. Mahomet by the sword.

7. But even empires of this world gained by the *sword* do not *last*. Not only is this a single religious empire, but it has lasted out earthly empires, and now shows as little decay as ever.

8. And in such tumults—the whole world broken up so many times—present revolutions nothing to former. The deluge ; describe waters—whirlpools, waterspouts, currents, rush of waters, cataracts, waves, yet the ark on them. This, the ark, *the greatest of miracles.* Well, it is but the acknowledged type of the Church : as this was the miracle (as we all confess) of the deluge, such that morally of the Church.

9. A house *not* divided against itself *does* stand—other religions specimens of the reverse. House at this moment less divided than ever. Protestants have looked : they felt the question was, whether we were in extremities ? not whether the Pope was alive, but whether nations acknowledged him ? (1) No jealousy about Pope's power. Pope never so powerful as now—perfectly good understanding ; jealousy at an end. (2) No heresies now. (3) Nay, *schools* at an end, [*e.g.*] Immaculate Conception.[1]

---

[1] All opposition to this doctrine had disappeared though it was not yet (in 1850) defined. It no longer divided the *schools*.

c

January 27

ON LABOUR AND REST

1. INTROD.—On Septuagesima, beginning a time of penance and penitential work. No more Alleluias. The colour purple.

2. Labour is the lot, the punishment of man. Bad and good labour, nay, evil labours and virtue labours.

3. It is otherwise as God made things. There is motion and activity in Nature, but it is *without effort* ; all creation is as it were hung upon wheels, and moves noiselessly and gracefully—the sun, the stream, the breeze, life.

4. And so in paradise. Adam's tending the flowers was but a specimen of divine labour without effort ; such, too, was his service of God ; such the angels' service—without effort.

5. But sin has made things otherwise. Henceforth labour changes its character. It is no longer Eden, but that vineyard into which the labourers were sent in to-day's gospel—to pull out stones, to destroy the weeds, worms, blights—and a wall round it—for there is a warfare. Labour is a war and aims at conquest.

6. Take bodily labour, labour of the field—preparing the earth, felling trees, making roads, canals —then building houses ; it is all penitential, all the punishment of sin—the mind does not come in, but a weariness.

7. And much more with *intellectual* labour and the labour of the mind—the mere wear and tear of

business; the necessity of providing for a family; anxiety, suspense, fear, failure, dreariness and hopelessness. But even when successful, one enterprise leads to another, till the mind is overburdened and overwrought, and is sucked into a vortex. Most engrossing; no time for the thought of religion; religion must take its chance, and that they feel.

8. Much more sin; the bondage and service of the devil most wearisome—the drunkard, the sensualist. (I knew one who was tempted to fatalism.) Wearing, restless feeling, even when they call themselves happy.

9. Nay, virtue here is too a toil, because there is war between good and evil. Read the saints' lives. Such is labour, and it wearies soul and body. The body shows it, whether it is manual, mental, or intellectual.

10. Oh! if we must labour, let us labour in the service of the Great Master of the Vineyard—that only pays, that only has hire. Then we shall labour that we may rest, then only. Sin never rests; there is no rest in hell. This is that penny which they one and all received, because nothing better or higher.

11. When the evening of life comes, then shall we know most fully the meaning of labour by being freed from it.

12. The blessedness of rest, of freedom from sin and toil, even though in purgatory. Purgatory is rest compared with this life.

13. And much more in heaven, where we see the face of God.

February 24

ON GRACE, THE PRINCIPLE OF ETERNAL LIFE

1. INTROD.—God, who had been the sole life from eternity, is the life of all things. He did not lose His prerogative or give to others or creation what He is Himself.

2. Nothing lives without Him ; nothing is. Animated nature, vegetables, nay, the very material substances, have their life, if it may be so called, their motion and activity in Him—the elements. What is called Nature, a principle of life, is from Him.

3. Moreover, the life He has given to Nature is but transient and fleeting. It is beautiful while it lasts, but it comes to an end. Nay, it is self-destructive ; thus the water and the fire, which are the conservation, have been and shall be the destruction of the earth. And so growth tends to decay. It is the same process ; all things grow to an end.

4. Thus this earth, as I have said, will be consumed. Thus the year, too, comes to an end—how beautiful spring, yet it doesn't last. The year runs a reckless course, like a spendthrift ; it cannot help going on till it is nothing. So it is with bodily health—' dust thou art,' etc. We see it again in animals, which are sportive and playful when young, but get old and miserable and sullen. Thus in Nature the best is first.

5. Nature, then, has no immortal principle in it. All natural things run a course ; and this is true of the soul, of the natural soul. The soul as it is

by Nature, by original creation, has no principle of permanent life in it. The soul grows old as anything else.

6. Describe the engaging manners of the young —fascinating, light-heartedness, cheerfulness; affections warm; imagination, conversation, wit; all pain shaken off—what can be better? Why is not Nature enough? Wait awhile.

7. Wait awhile, for the soul grows old as anything else—as the leaves turn yellow, as the animal frame grows stiff, so wait on a few years, the natural soul too grows old; the beauty decays as beauty of person; the soul contracts, stiffens, hardens, instead of being supple and versatile, and elastic and vigorous; its limbs are cramped; everything is a burden; it is a fear to it to be pulled out into new positions; it cannot take pleasure in what once pleased—not in poetry or works of fiction, not in friendship; it cannot form new friends; it is bereaved [of the old ones], and does not replace them; it cannot laugh; disappointment breaks it; it cannot recover. Hence relapsing into natural imperfections (as crabbedness, ill-nature, etc.) which a man had seemed to overcome, having ever struggled against them.

8. Oh terrible! old people hard-hearted, without affections, careless of the loss of friends—not from high motives—they have no faith—virtue seems a fancy—with hearts like stone, etc.

9. Follow such a one into the next world. What is to be his happiness for eternity?—immortal, yet dead, eternal death. Life of the soul is in the affections; he has no affections—a closed heart.

The devil cannot love God—*vide* St. Catherine of Genoa in *St. Alfonso's Sermons*, p. 335.

10. Such is the course of Nature in the soul as in the body. Nature ages; it has in it no principle of life. No, grace is the only principle of immortality. We must go beyond nature; we must go to something higher. Here, then, is one characteristic difference between Nature and Grace.

11. EXHORTATION, Eccles. xii. All saints have lived by love—the martyrs, confessors, etc., etc. St. Valentine,[1] who connects us with the first age, shows that the Church has kept, not lost, her first bloom.

March 24 (*Palm Sunday*)

ON OUR LORD'S AGONY

1. INTROD.—We naturally seek to be told something of the death and the deathbeds of those we know and love. We are drawn to the deathbed of the saints and holy people; and much more if anything remarkable about it, and much more if a man be our benefactor, parent, etc. How much more the death of the great God?

2. Thus, above all, our Lord's death—how sudden it was! One day brought into the city in triumph, the next plotted against, betrayed and seized.

3. God from eternity—the Holy Trinity. Each person all God; the Son the only God, as if only Person.

---

[1] Not the St. Valentine whose name is found in the Kalendar, but a martyr of the same name whose relics were found in the catacombs, and given to Newman by Pius IX.

4. God most happy ; Son all happy—bliss, peace, calmness, glory, beauty, perfection from all eternity.

5. And now look at that one only God, as we contemplate Him at this time of year. He is still one, sole, and alone. He was one in heaven ; He is one in the garden, one on the tree. He trod the winepress *alone.* When He went into the garden He took but a few with Him, and separated Himself from them ; and afterwards the disciples ' left Him alone,' and fled. Easy for the traitor to take Him, for He was alone.

6. But though one and alone, how different ! He who was glorious is become a leper ; He who was so peaceful has lost His rest.

7. It is said that nothing is so fearful as the overwhelming sorrow of man as contrasted with woman, of a hero or great and firm man overcome by adversity or bereavement ; for it being more difficult, it bursts more [violently] ; it is like a storm rending and shattering. What, then, in the most peaceful and serene ? What a conflict in the sinless !—(enlarge).

8. It is said that ' the wicked are like a boiling sea ' ; what means this in the innocent ? Yet so it is. He began to grow weary, sad, frightened. (Explain.) On the devil, who was foiled in the wilderness, to his surprise finding our Lord in the garden agitated as a sinner. He had gained his point—his eternal enemy vanquished. On the apostles sleeping for sorrow, but Christ praying more earnestly.

9. Pain of mind greater than that of body, though we are more conversant in bodily pain— grief, fear, anxiety, terror, despair, disappointment— *poena damni* of the lost greater than *poena sensus.*

On the effect of mental pain—hair turning white ;
Nabal.[1] So effect on Christ—agony of blood.

10. Let us gather round and look at Him whom
God has punished ; but in no idle way, for His
pain is from our sins. Address to sinners.

July 14

ON THE PARTICULAR JUDGMENT

1. INTROD.—Give an account of thy stewardship,
from the Gospel of Pentecost viii.

2. (A judgment will take place directly.) It
would be well if we could realise what our actual
position is. We *happen* at this moment to be in this
world, but *any moment* we may find ourselves in the
world unseen. We are now talking to each other ;
we see each other, etc. Yet just as walking we
may cross over a street, so suddenly we may cross
to the next world—' Thou fool, this night thy
soul will be required of thee,' etc.—a veil drawn
across.

3. It is difficult even for a Catholic who believes
it to realise. Thus a person who never was at York
could not realise that this time to-morrow he will
be there. Still, the more we meditate the more we
shall realise it ; and it is our duty to realise it more
and more. Saints realise it.

4. But a Protestant really has no notion of it.

[1] ' But early in the morning when Nabal had digested his
wine, his wife told him those words and his heart died within
him, and he became as a stone.'—1 Samuel xxv. 37.

This is proved by any *sudden* death—sudden deaths throw them off their balance and detect them. They at once betray by their words that, whatever they may say or wish, they do not really believe. They call it an *unknown* state; but though it is unseen it is not unknown. But a Protestant does not know *whither* he is going more than Adrian with his *anima blandula*, etc. He in his heart confesses it. He says, 'After all, we know nothing.' Whether he will lose consciousness, or be asleep; whether in heaven, or what is heaven. In a word, he is all abroad; the question is new to him, and he has not one idea about it, no more than a pagan. *What* has he more than a pagan?

I am not talking of heaven, or eternity, but of what will happen to him personally directly after death.

5. But a Catholic knows—particular judgment and purgatory—judgment on the very spot and time, expeditious like an inquest, as necessarily [following death] as an undertaker. 'After death the judgment': (1) Philip the Second to his courtiers, *St. Alphonso*, p. 249; (2) St. Mary Magdalene of Pazzi trembled in her sickness, *St. Alphonso*, p. 248.

6. Yet true as this in general, still none of us understand as we should what is meant by *stewardship*. What, have *all* stewardship?

7. [Bound to make our lives] conformable to the life of Christ—'if the just scarcely be saved.' Account [to be rendered] of (1) sins; (2) blessings and graces; (3) idle word—*ictus oculi*; (4) thoughts of heart; (5) *time*, recreations.

8. Let us live ever in the thought of judgment.

August 11

ON THE DOCTRINE OF PRAYER AS RECON-
CILING US TO THE CATHOLIC TEACHING
ABOUT OUR BLESSED LADY

1. In the course of Nature everything proceeds
in order; system of cause and effect proceeds
illimitably, so that we do not know where it stops.
It is a vast web. Hence all things seem fated.
This is what unassisted reason seems to teach :

2. and hence no religion proper, for God cannot
act upon us *directly*, but only through a system ;
and therefore it is a system only which acts. OB-
JECTION.—The laws of God will go on whether we
strive or not : *e.g.* how can prayer save from trouble,
give health, cut off a persecutor ?

3. Yet conscience, feeling, and the religious sense,
which are part of us, speak contrariwise, viz. of
particular providence.

4. Revelation confirms this. ' Not a sparrow
falls without . . . hairs of head,' etc. And specially it reveals the power *of prayer*.

5. Prayer in its effect, though the idea is so familiar
to us, is one of the greatest of mysteries and miracles,
yet it is the clear doctrine of Scripture.

6. Now I am going to use this without reference
to the subjects, which will be brought before us in
a few days in the Assumption.

7. Much is said by Protestants against our Lady's
power, but our Lady's power is nothing else than
the greatest exemplification of the power of prayer.
We don't give her power of atonement, etc., but
simply prayer, as we give ourselves ; we in a degree,

she in fulness. Now I can understand persons scrupling at the power of prayer *altogether* ; but why, that there should be one instance [*i.e.* great exemplification] of it ? We do not introduce a mystery, but realise it. The great mystery is that prayer should have influence. When once we get ourselves to believe the power of prayer, etc.

8. *E.g.* even Protestants say the strongest things about prayer—'prayer of faith'—'Satan trembles'— 'faith moves mountains'—'faith can do all things,' [1] that is, is omnipotent—this is just what we say about our Lady—omnipotent through prayer—'Let me alone' [Exod. xxxii. 9-11]—Amalec [2]—Jacob's wrestling [3]—'I cannot until thou come thither' [Gen. xix. 21, 22]—Luke xviii. 5—violent carry it away by force.

9. Perseverance. Again Amalec, Jacob's wrestling ; Luke xviii. 2-7,[4] the woman gives him no rest.

[1] *Written in pencil above,* 'faith can do. Prayer constrains God: well, this is the very thing Protestants think so shocking when we say it of our Lady.'

[2] 'And when Moses lifted up his hands Israel overcame: but if he let them down a little, Amalec overcame. And Moses' hands were heavy: so they took a stone, and put under him and he sat on it: and Aaron and Hur stayed up his hands on both sides.'—Exod. xvii. 11, 12.

[3] 'He remained alone, and behold a man wrestled with him till morning.'—Gen. xxxii. 24.

[4] 'There was a judge in a certain city who feared not God nor regarded man. And there was a certain widow in that city ; and she came to him, saying, Avenge me of my adversary. And he would not for a long time : but afterwards he said within himself, Although I fear not God, nor regard man, yet because this widow is troublesome to me, I will avenge her, lest continually coming she weary me. And the Lord said, Hear what the unjust judge saith. And will not God revenge his elect, who cry to him day and night ? '

10. Sanctity. ' God heareth not sinners.'

11. Now who can persevere as our Lady ? Who is as holy as she ? What wonder that in her [the power of prayer] should be fulfilled most perfectly ?

12. The more we pray the more we shall be reconciled to the doctrine.

13. Let us at this time make her both the example of prayer and its object.

October 6

ON THE NECESSITY OF SECURING OUR ELECTION

1. INTROD.—There are mysteries of revelation (most) which are beyond our experience ; we receive them only on faith, *e.g.* Trinity, Incarnation, etc., but there is one which we see, viz. the great mystery of election and predestination.

2. We see before our eyes the astonishing fact, that all are not in the same condition as regards religious truth. Some are born in heathen countries —of bad parents—in heresy. Again, of two men who sin, one is cut off, one lives to repent. Again, men who go on well for years suddenly fall away— how all are mixed together. The world and Catholics not distinguishable ; they dress alike, etc.

3. Now Scripture recognises this awful fact. It speaks about the elect being few, the flock being little. It says much of God's grace, of a choice, etc. This certainly is most wonderful, for it was a *prophecy* at the time, which every age has confirmed

since, and a curious *combination,* viz. that Christ's religion should at once surround and subdue the world, yet be thus small, and weak, and despised.

4. Such is the doctrine of Scripture, and it is put even more strongly. There is an awful text, 'If the mighty works,' Matt. xi. 20-24.[1]

5. Now in saying this, it is not (as I have many times urged) as if God did not give enough to all, but He gives more to one than another. Why, we know not. (Do not think I put it as a speculative mystery merely; it is most instructive; it is not only awful and mysterious, but on the other hand, a most profitable fact to consider.)

6. It arises from God's self-dependence, self-sufficiency. Eternally happy from everlasting. Creation did not make Him dependent. What is it to Him if thou art virtuous? You have no claims on Him except what He has given by pledging Himself. Beware of pride. He does not want you, etc. —you can do Him no good. In your own nature you are indefinitely removed from Him; it is only by superabundant grace that you come near Him.

---

[1] 'Then began he to upbraid the cities wherein were done the most of his miracles, for that they had not done penance: Woe to thee, Chorozain! woe to thee, Bethsaida! for if in Tyre and Sidon had been wrought the miracles that have been wrought in you, they had long ago done penance in sackcloth and ashes. But I say unto you, It shall be more tolerable for Tyre and Sidon in the day of judgment than for you. And thou, Capernaum, shalt thou be exalted up to heaven. Thou shalt go down even unto hell. For if in Sodom had been wrought the miracles that have been wrought in thee, perhaps it had remained unto this day. But I say unto you, That it shall be more tolerable for Sodom in the day of judgment than for thee.'

He is not bound to give grace, but He does give it to all. And as He is not bound to give at all, He is not bound in measure. He has full right to give so much as He pleases, more to one than to another.

7. Hence we cannot argue for certain that because He has forgiven our sins already, He will in future, if we sin. We cannot count that He will a second time give us the grace of repentance. Nor because He has forgiven others, therefore He will us. And so again, if we are external to the Church, we cannot rely on His always giving us the grace which He has given so far as He has, solely to bring us into the Church. And so again we have no confidence, because we are in a good way now, that therefore we shall persevere.

8. Do not think I am putting this as a harsh speculative mystery ; it is as a practical consideration. Beware of quenching grace. The grace of conversion is rare ; the grace of illumination is precious. You do not know but this may be the last grace given you, if you resist it. You have claim on nothing if you are external to the Church. You may have good feelings, dare not rely on them ; you may at present be in God's grace, do not conclude too easily that you will persevere. Watch against sin ; for what you know, the least wilful venial sin may act upon your deathbed, and subtract from the aid which would then have been given you.

9. The need of prayer. God sovereign, but prayer almighty. God has given to us as a means to overcome, as I may say, Himself. Let us never be satisfied with getting prayers for our perseverance.

10. Here is the special office of our Lady, and its

bearing on us. She does not predestinate, she does not give grace, she does not merit grace for us, but she gains it by prayer ; she gains perseverance by prayer. Thus she overcomes God, as I may say.

11. Suitable on Rosary Sunday. *Nunc et in hora mortis nostrae.*

12. May we die in peace.

October 18

ON EXTERNAL RELIGION

(*For St. Peter's, on the opening* [1])

1. Introd.—Gospel of the day, Pentecost xiii.— ' Glory to God.'

2. What is meant by glory ? We unprofitable, but we can *show* our worship, etc.

3. I am led to this, the natural subject of the day, now that the chapel, embellished, etc., is reopened.

4. How natural, you see from what every one of you does—children forming little altars, etc.

5. So the first Christians, even in caves [2] (which are most alien to Christianity), in catacombs, adorned them in times of persecution.

6. Whereas when an unreligious movement, the first business to destroy these [embellishments]— the Danes, the Reformers, the Huguenots, the French Revolution. As the devil delighted to destroy our Lord's beauty, so the beauty of His Church (even organ and surplice).

---

[1] Preached at St. Peter's, Birmingham.

[2] See Note 8, p. 337.

7. But it is exemplified in all religions. Look out into the first ages, patriarchal times, before religion was corrupted—a mountain top (beautiful prospect), or grove or rivers, where sweet smells and sounds of birds. No matter if afterwards corrupted—Garden of Eden.

8. Particularly in south, where scenery beautiful and weather fine—out-of-doors worship. Next, the first artificial part was processions, vestments, and music and statues.

9. Then came flowers and incense. Describe a procession—children with garments; the victim; no matter that superstition afterwards corrupted it to false gods.

10. Then they took it out of the open air—Jewish tabernacle. Then we come to furniture, as you read in Exodus—and so jewels, etc., marble, pictures; then painting, sculpture and music.

11. Lastly came architecture, which has to do with form. With it [is] so great a part of the beautiful. The dome represents the heaven, the arch the wood.

12. Thus at length all things—the eye, the ear, the scent—form, colour, music, incense.

13. One more characteristic in all this—costliness. Sacrifices. David spoke of ' that which doth cost me nothing.' [1] So also of the widow, ' She hath done what she could'—'two mites, which make a farthing,' Mark xii. 42, 43.[2]

---

[1] ' And the king answered him and said, Nay; I will buy it of thee at a price. I will not offer to the Lord my God holocausts free-cost.'—2 Samuel xxiv. 24.

[2] ' And there came a certain poor widow, and she cast in

14. 'The poor you have always with you; not me,' Matt. xxvi. 11; occasional call, as now, 'a stranger, and you took me in.' St. Peter and St. Paul—'shall receive a prophet's reward.'

December 1 (*Advent Sunday*)

ON DEATH

1. INTROD.—Again Advent. Christmas!—the day darkens; the year dies; all things tend to dissolution. It is the end; we have to think of death and all connected with it.

2. We are going on right to death; a truism, yet not felt. We are on a stream, rushing towards the ocean; every morning we rise nearer to death; every meal we take; every time we see our friends, etc.; nearer the time when we shall lose them. We rise, we work, we eat; all such acts are as milestones. As the clock ticks, we are under sentence of death. The sands of the glass run out; we are executed; we die.

3. And when it comes, what happens? We all know. This happens—we are no longer here. We see not indeed whither we go, but this we know full well, we are not here. The body which was ours is no longer ours; we have slipped it off; no longer

two mites, which make a farthing. And calling his disciples together, he said to them, Amen I say to you, this poor widow has cast in more than all they who have cast into the treasury: For all they did cast in of their abundance; but she of her want cast in all she had, even her whole living.'

D

a part of us. It is a mask, as a dress; but it is
not our instrument or organ. We who think, feel,
speak, etc., are not here. Where we are, nothing
that is here tells us; but this we know full well,
we are not in the body. We are cut off from all
here. This minute here, the next a wall impene-
trable has grown up; we are as utterly cut off as
if we had never been here; as if we had never known
any one here. We don't go by degrees—we do not
(as it were) lessen in perspective and disappear in
the horizon—we go at once and for all.

4. Where it is we see not; what it is we know not;
but what it is not we know, as we know where it
is not. The man is not what he was. He took
pleasure; he depended on this world. He depended for its enjoyment on the senses. That life
was not a burden; that it was dear to him; that
he enjoyed it; that he was unwilling to quit it,
was because he saw, he heard, etc., his amusements, his pleasures; he went to his club, or to
business, with his friends; he liked the warm fire,
the light; he liked his family, home comforts, his
dinner; he strolled out in summer, or he went to
places of merry-making and enjoyed the gratifica-
tions of sin—nothing supernatural: how many we
have known such! Why are people unwilling to
die? What is the one reason? There is no
pain in it. Because they leave what is known;
they go to what is unknown. They leave the sun,
etc.; they leave their families, their schemes, their
wealth.

5. Oh, how much is implied in this! Men witness
against themselves. They are afraid to leave this

life ; they own they are going to the unknown, yet they are unwilling to make that unknown known. Do lay this to heart ;—you are going to the unknown.

6. Now I will tell you what you are going to— not to creatures as here, but to God. Oh the dreadful state of the soul when this step is over ! Another world is close to us. It has taken the step, and is in that other world. Have you any relations with God ? Do you know aught about Him ? Do you know what He is like ? Have you tried to make Him your friend ? Have you made your peace with Him ? What madness ! If men are going on a voyage they take letters of introduction ; they inquire about the country ; they try to make friends beforehand ; they take money with them, etc. Yet you do not try to disperse the thick darkness ; on the contrary, you learn to be content, because you do not know.

7. Yet that acquiescence is an additional alarm, for it shows God is angry with you. Men lightly say : ' It is a matter of opinion.' No, it is a matter of punishment. This very discordance of sects is a sign of God's displeasure.

8. The longest life comes to an end. You may be young, you may be vigorous, but you must die. When it is over, the longest life is short.

9. Seek the Lord therefore ; this is the conclusion I come to ; this world is nothingness. Seek Him where He can be found, *i.e.* in the Catholic Church. He is here in the same sense in which we are.

December 29

ON THE OFFICE OF THE CHURCH—ST. THOMAS THE MARTYR

1. Introd.—This is the birthday of a great saint, one of the greatest of English saints, whose fame has gone out, etc.; a saint of the universal Church, especially known in France, North Italy, Roman States, etc.; nay, whose feast is embodied in the octave of Christmas.

2. His manner of death.

3. What did he die for ? If you ask a Protestant history, it will mention some minute ground, some question of detail, of course ; but, if examined, for *that* which is ever the cause of battle between the world and the Church. Parallel it to the early age, a grain of incense ; the present moment, calling bishops bishops of sees, etc. But all these are accidents—the ground, one and the same.

4. To explain this I must go into the subject. State of the world before Christ came—the world left to itself ; doubt and inquiry ; philosophers ; pagans ; yet no known truth. Philosophers felt it impossible to throw truth into a popular form. Hence they were tempted to believe there was no truth. Great difference between religious truth and scientific, etc. We can get to sciences of geology, etc., because we start from what we see, but who shall tell the designs of the Divine Mind ?

5. Prophecy of a Teacher—voice behind thee [?] —a law—a light (Isaias ix.)—Isaias xxv.—Thus a master, or guide, or monitor to be set up.

6. Such is the one province which Christianity was to fulfil.   Now Protestants think this fulfilled in the *Bible*.   But the Bible has not *in fact* been the means.   (1) The majority have not been able to read. (2) And now fifty years' experience shows it is not God's way.[1]   (3) Nor can it be, for a book does not speak ; it is shut till it is opened.   A law cannot enforce itself ; it implies an executive ; not a book instead of a physician, etc.   (4) It is nowhere said in Scripture that Scripture was to be the guide, but it is said what is to fight with the gates of hell, viz.

7. the Church—texts.   This is set up, and did exist before, etc., in all lands to appeal to high and low, to all ranks and callings—(enlarge).   To moderate, and in a certain sense to interfere, viz. with the conscience—on the misery of princes being made so much of from youth—to give the law and to teach the faith.

8. This is the quarrel—the world does not like to be taught.   (The Jewish kings did not like prophets.)   The Church interferes with it ; she lifts up a witness.   Men regret the old pagan times when each could say and think what he pleased.   Kings and ministers, etc., etc., don't like to be interfered with.

9. This, then, was the world's quarrel with St. Thomas.   Henry II. felt the Protestant ground just as the meetings now held do—it is the same spirit—therefore does the world persecute us now. When, then, men object that we interfere with conscience, etc., etc., we say ' yes.'   And if we did not,

[1] Does the preacher refer to the British and Foreign Bible Society founded in 1804 ?

we should not be the Church; if we did not, there would be no good in a Church.

10. And you may be sure that the Church will never betray its trust.

January 19, 1851

ON THE NAME OF JESUS

1. It has been from the beginning the order of Providence—nay, even *verbum*—not to create without giving a name. As grace is necessary to keep things together lest they dissipate, so a name is, as it were, the crown of the work, as giving it a meaning and description, and, as it were, registering it before Him. Henceforth it lives in His sight, as being in His *catalogue*.

2. Thus ' day ' and ' night,' ' earth ' and ' seas.' Hence Adam named his wife and the beasts, etc. Hence Abraham's name changed; Jacob's, Sarah's, Isaac's; Isaac's given, Jacob's changed; St. John Baptist; St. Peter and St. Paul. These names are descriptive.

3. Hence anxiety of men to know God's name. They are born in ignorance. They have a sense there is a God, but what is He ? The heavens and earth do not condense and concentrate His manifold attributes, etc. They give hints, glimpses, snatches, but what is He ? Hence He is the unknown God, and men are but ' feeling after Him ' by what they see. They are in God; He surrounds them, but they want to gaze on Him objectively.

4. Thus Jacob about the angel, 'What is thy name?' And to Manue, 'Why askest thou my name, which is *mirabile*?' Judg. xiii. 18. Moses bolder. God had been called 'God of Abraham,' etc. *Adonai.*

5. Hence you see a meaning why the Eternal Son would reveal this, that the Name of that Son was of consequence; it was a manifestation of the nature and attributes of God—Admirabilis, Isa. ix. 6 [1]; Emmanuel, Isa. vii. 14.[2] Still, however, the name was not told. At length Gabriel said it, Luke i. 31 [3]; circumcision, Luke ii. 21; angel to Joseph, Matt. i. 21,[4] His name was called Jesus. And hence the devils: 'Jesus the Son of God'; 'I know thee who thou art.' On the cross.[5] The first miracle of St. Peter and St. John, Acts iii.—'in the name,' 'this name,' 'no other name'—and St. Paul in Phil. ii. 8-11.[6] The two great apostles, the angels

---

[1] 'For a child is born to us . . . and his name shall be called Wonderful, Counsellor, God the mighty, the Father of the world to come, the Prince of Peace.'

[2] 'For behold a virgin shall conceive, and bear a son, and his name shall be called Emmanuel.'

[3] 'Behold, thou shalt conceive in thy womb, and shall bring forth a son, and thou shalt call his name Jesus.'

[4] 'She shall bring forth a son, and thou shalt call his name Jesus.'

[5] 'And the writing was, Jesus of Nazareth, the King of the Jews.'—John xix. 19.

[6] 'He humbled himself, becoming obedient unto death, even to the death of the cross. For which cause God also hath exalted him, and hath given him a name which is above all names. That in the name of Jesus every knee should bow, of those that are in heaven, on earth, and under the earth; And that every tongue should confess that the Lord Jesus Christ is in the glory of God the Father.'

from Gabriel, devils from the possessed, and men from the circumcision.

6. For in this the whole history of salvation, the whole creed—how God would save men, how He loved them, etc., recounting the Christian doctrine.[1] Thus when we would know who God is, we answer, Jesus. We see God in the clouds, in the mountains, etc., and who is He? Jesus. Who then rules? Who is looking, the ruler of bad men? Who is looking, the guardian of the virtuous? Who, etc.? and we answer, Jesus. He is the one word containing in itself all power, etc., because in it we thereby have in our minds the full description of Almighty God.

7. And in it an answer to all objections and difficulties. It surpasses all (this is the point of the sermon): whatever difficulties, whatever mysteries in religion, this comprehends and protects them. What is more wonderful than that God should become man. Real Presence, power of Mary, purgatory, eternal punishment, intercession of saints, election, original sin. The whole Catholic system bound up in it.

8. Hence, and since Protestants have the name of Jesus on their lips, it is the test whether or not they understand it, *i.e.* their taking Catholic doctrine or not. If they don't, if they stumble at it, they don't understand Jesus. On invincible ignorance, as alone hindering Catholicism.

9. Let us then rejoice in the fulness of this Name. Let us use it as the Name of virtue against devils, bad thoughts, evil men, the world, dangers and frights. It is our banner.

[1] *I.e.* the Holy Name sums up in Itself the history of salvation.

January 26 (*Third Epiphany*)

ON DISEASE AS THE TYPE OF SIN

1. INTROD.—When our Lord came His chief miracles were, not like Moses', etc., on elements, but on men, on diseases.

2. Why ? Because He was the Redeemer. The physical world had not to be redeemed, but men, and disease was a defect ; whereas the physical world was perfect after its kind, very good. He did work some miracles on the elements, to show He was the Creator ; most on the infirmities of human nature, to show He was its Redeemer.

3. He had to do with sin ; and bodily diseases are at once its symptoms and its representations (they represent sins both in their intensity and variety). When man fell, the grace which covered his soul and body was like a *skin* torn off and leaving him raw—(enlarge). Men would forget sin, but they cannot. Hence it is that all false views of religion fail—the views of the day ; a bright careless religion does in the sunshine, not in the shade. Here it is that Christ spoke to the heart. He comes to do that which false religions and infidelity *ignore*—to cure sin.

4. Nothing more awful than bodily pain, except mental ; but mental is a private matter, and can be denied, can be put off ; bodily is before us. Disease represents sin in its *intensity* and *variety*. Go through bodily complaints—fever, ague, sinking from weakness, oppression of breath, etc., cholera, restlessness, etc., paralysis, leprosy—here you have sin in its various forms.

5. And it suggests to us future punishment. No dreams of God's mercy can overcome the fact—and our Lord, most merciful though He is, requires it. ' Jerusalem, Jerusalem,' etc., ' Behold your house shall be left to you desolate,' Matt. xxiii. 37-38, Luke xiii. 34-35, and see His tears over Lazarus' grave, John xi. 35.[1] ' An enemy has done it,' Matt. xiii. 25-28.[2] It is necessary by the immutable laws of truth.

6. Nor can you say it is merely *remedial*, for why allowed, *i.e.* sin ? God could have hindered sin. Again, He need not have died for it, and yet might have pardoned it—' I will, be thou clean.' No, it is the beginning, not the no-ending of pain, etc., which is the marvel. When once it comes in, there is no reason why it should not continue, etc.

7. Come to the Physician of Souls, etc.

February 9 *(Fifth Epiphany)*

ON THE DESCENT INTO EGYPT

1. INTROD.—There is one subject not much thought of, the descent into Egypt, though belonging to this season, and it may be accounted one of

---

[1] ' Where have you laid him ? They say to him, Lord, come and see. And Jesus wept. The Jews therefore said, behold how he loved him.'—John xi. 34-36.

[2] ' The kingdom of heaven is like to a man who sowed good seed in his field, but while men were asleep his enemy came and oversowed cockle. . . . And the servants of the goodman of the house coming, said to him, Sir, didst thou not sow good seed in thy field ? Whence then hath it cockle ? And he said to them, An enemy hath done this,'

the Epiphanies of Christ. (1) Magi ; (2) purification ; (3) idol-breaking in Egypt, for as the Ark
levelling the walls of Jericho, and [overthrowing]
Dagon, so much more Christ.

2. Circumstances. How one journey to Bethlehem—then they got home to Nazareth—not enough,
must set out again. It is remarkable that these
first years were spent in a heathen country. There
till seven years old.

3. Now why ? I will give you a reason. He
would undergo every suffering ; He would be in a
heathen country to share the trials of His apostles
and missioners. In Jerusalem was the Temple of
God, in the Holy Land His religion ; but even
there He chose not the Temple, but Nazareth—and
the first years of His life Heliopolis, in heathen
Egypt.

4. Now it must not be supposed that our Lord
was too young to have a trial. (Explain.) Ignorance
came from the fall. He was as sensitive [in child-
hood] as [we] when we are grown. Thus He saw all
the evil of the place ; and as His body made Him
feel in the crucifixion, so His soul was exposed to
moral sufferings from the first.

5. And the suffering was greater than we conceive. To live among heathens is a misery, the
greater, the purer the mind—Lot in Sodom, St. Paul
at Athens—the world is everywhere, and we can
understand from a country which is not heathen,
such as this, how evil it is, though it would be a great
deal worse [among heathens].

6. Even in this country, I say, which is not
heathen, the misery of being in the world is great

to any holy mind. Take *e.g.* a city like this, and
fancy the thoughts of an apostle in it. Could he go
about it freely ? A continual service of the devil
here. How ? By sins of the tongue ; not like the
seven Catholic Hours coming at intervals, but in-
cessantly ; a continual light talk in a thousand
places, from morning to night, with scarce breaks.
Who is honoured like the devil ? Blasphemy and
immodesty, so that most men's mouths and all
men's ears are polluted from year to year's end.
And are not their hearts too ? Then imagination.
Alas ! *this* is why the devil loves the bad talk ; it is
the *pabulum*, the *silva* of corruption ; it sets the
heart on fire, as shavings round the wood and coal
for a fire. I don't know anything more awful.
Other sins men commit from time to time, but this
one now. The evil concupiscence boils over and
burns without exhaustion, and involves every one,
so that religious people are like the Three Children
[in the fiery furnace]—and how many, many fall !

7. Well this, bad as it is, is not so bad as Egypt,
as heathen Heliopolis, for this country has been
Catholic—remains of good, which have soaked in.
Grant that a modern city is a furnace of sin—yet
it [sin] was deified in Egypt. Vices canonised in
animals—heathen idolatry—all vices made gods—
the world lieth in wickedness, etc.[1]—the god of this
world, etc.[2]—the prince of the power of this air, of
the spirit that now worketh on the children of
unbelief.[3] O misery of the infant Jesus walking
in the streets ! St. Aloysius fainting at the mention
of a mortal sin—smell—saints detecting mortal sin

---

[1] 2 Cor. iv. 4.   [2] 1 John v. 19.   [3] Eph. ii. 2.

[by its smell].   As sick men cannot bear strong scent or sound, so purity here.   What a living martyrdom, etc.

8. I have said He did this for our sakes, to taste every trial, to sanctify every state, to sanctify the state of those who live in the world.

9. You who live in the world, resist evil.   On confraternities—third order of St. Francis, and so allude to the Oratorium Parvum.   Your confessors may, or may not, from not liking to put burdens on you, speak of these.

February 16 (*Septuagesima*)

ON LABOUR—OUR WORK HERE

1. INTROD.—Before Lent the Church begins by setting before us work as an introduction.

2. Epistle and gospel—beginning of Genesis. Even before the fall, and much more after—thorns and thistles.

3. This the contrast between before the fall and after.   The ground typifies our hearts—and now we have labour.

4. And this will show us the heinousness of the fall, for before it, the labour, the effort, was to sin— before as difficult to sin as now to be a hero.   Grace was so great.

5. But grace being gone, the lower nature rose against the upper [1] as the upper against God.

6. This then, I say, our work—labour of one kind

---

[1] Written above in pencil, ' Is this right ? '

or another. It has different names—self-discipline,
self-denial, penance, reformation, mortification—
all meaning the bringing under of ourselves. Don't
think it hard if you find a thing difficult ; it is your
work.

7. This implied in the subduing our 'ruling
passion,' so called.

8. Also exemplified in particular examination.

9. Also done in suffering. Suffering is a work.
On satisfaction and *satispassio*[1] ; on bearing pain
with sweetness or patience, with sweet faces, ways,
voice, etc., etc. On the discipline when associated
with the thought of Christ's sufferings, more meritorious ; for the mind goes with it and is not otiose.

10. Thus let us begin this sacred time.

February 23 (*Sexagesima*)

ON ST. PAUL THE TYPE OF THE CHURCH AS MISSIONARISING

1. INTROD.—This day seems especially set apart
for the consideration of the apostle St. Paul, in
collect, in epistle, in gospel, for he is the sower.

2. How he sowed in all places. How he preached.
He fought. The great soldier. David goes out
against a giant, but he against the world. What
a great ideal ! Patriots, Joan of Arc, etc., etc., but
this, not in one country only. To east and west,
north and south, he goes and forms a kingdom.

3. But this great portent is completed by the

---

[1] *Satispassio* is paying the full penalty—' the last farthing.'

history of the Church after him. It is not solitary, not an accident, not like one great man, as Buonaparte ; but he *intended* and the work has *lasted* eighteen hundred years, going on the same way.

4. Now the warfare goes on just the same, and with the same enemies. This again most extraordinary. The view of the battle is just the same. As a shadow may move onwards and presents the same outline over hills and dales, so as time has gone, this one grouping has gone on for eighteen centuries.

5. Look at it in St. Paul's day—zealots and indifferents, statesmen and philosophers. Describe them.

6. Zealots—Jews and pagans. Pagan, Acts xix., [tumult of silversmiths at Ephesus] : Jewish, Acts xxiii. 12 [forty men bound under a great curse neither to eat nor drink till they killed Paul].

7. Indifferents—magistrates. Gallio, Acts xviii. 12; Festus, 'Paul, thou art beside thyself,' Acts xxvi. 24 ; philosophers at Athens, Acts xvii. 18.

8. Application to the present times. Furious evangelicals and statesmen. Their different ground. The first call Rome Antichrist.

The second profess to care nothing for doctrine, but only go to political grounds.

9. Nay, our blessed Lord. Pharisees furious— 'The Son of God.' Then they come to Pilate (What is truth ?) with a different plea. 'Thou art not Caesar's friend,' etc. The emperor's supremacy, etc., denied.

10. This awful unity of the Church is our consolation. While it proves the Church comes from

God, it proves nothing comes strange and new to her.

11. No, our business to sow and to fight, and to leave the rest to God. It is never to be supposed we shall not go on doing the same as before.

March 9 (*First Lent*)

ON THE ACCEPTED TIME

1. INTROD.—Lent an apostolical observance.

2. And well did it become the Divine Mercy to appoint a time for repentance, who had in the fulness of time died for our redemption. For what is every one's business is no one's; what is for all times is for no time.

3. And even those who will not take God's time, feel a time there must be. They always profess a time; they quiet their conscience by naming a time; but when?

4. ' Go thy way for this time; when I have a convenient season,' etc., Acts xxiv. 24-25.[1] When the present temptation is out of the way. When the present business or trouble is got through. When they have enjoyed life a little more.

5. When ' a little more,' for there is no satisfaction in sin, each sin is the last. But the thirst

---

[1] 'And after some days Felix coming with Drusilla his wife, who was a Jewess, sent for Paul, and heard of him the faith that is in Christ Jesus. And as he treated of justice and chastity and of the judgment to come, Felix being terrified, answered, For this time go thy way, but when I have a convenient time I will send for thee.'

comes again ; there is no term at which we can quit it ; it is like drinking salt water—horizon recedes.

6. End of life, time of retirement. The seriousness will come as a matter of course ; passions will naturally burn out—*otium cum dignitate*—alas, the change of nature is not the coming of grace. We may change, but we shall not be nearer heaven. To near heaven is not a natural change, but a specific work, as much as building a house. It is not a growth till there is something to grow from.

7. Feeling then there must be a time, and having the conscience of men on this point with her, the Church appoints a time and says, ' Now is the appointed time.' She blows the trumpet ; proclaims forgiveness ; an indulgence—scattering gifts—inviting all to come and claim. Not sternly, but most lovingly and persuasively she does it.

8. Oh for those who have neglected the summons hitherto, year after year, conscience pleading !

9. Or perhaps we have repented just through Lent and then relapsed and undone, and more than undone, all.

10. And so we get older, older, and farther from heaven every year, till we come to our last Lent, and we do not keep it a bit the better.

11. Then we come near death, yet won't believe that death is near. Set thy house in order—packing up, and how many things left out. We cannot realise it. All hurry and confusion. Between illness, delirium, weakness, relations, worldly affairs, etc., we shall be able to recollect nothing—all in disorder. No real contrition. And so we die.

12. Ah ! then in that very moment of death

E

we shall recollect everything; all things will come before us. We shall wish to speak; it will be too late. We shall have passed from this life; the accepted time will have passed by.

March 23 (Third Lent)

ON THE STRONG MAN OF SIN AND UNBELIEF

1. INTROD.—' The strong man ' represents the sinner in his strength and security. It represents him fortified by his three friends—the world, the flesh, and the devil. ' The old man,' Eph. iv. 22,[1] the old Adam, the evil spirit who has taken possession of him.

2. He has a ' house.' It is a castle : nor is it the work of a day. How long it takes to build a castle ! and buildings grow up about it, fort after fort, treasure house after treasure house, viz. by habits. (Explain about habits.) No one remains without them ; they are intended to be a defence for the good. They also become a defence in wickedness. Supernatural habits and natural habits.

3. Absence of faith—' The light that is in them.' His standard of things—scoffs at things supernatural; does not think himself a bad man because he does not pray ; is in ' peace ' ; perfectly satisfied with his standard ; may not come up to it ; is firmly

---

[1] ' For our wrestling is not against flesh and blood, but against principalities and powers, against the rulers of the darkness of this world, against the spirits of wickedness in the high places.' —Eph. vi. 12.

seated. He may be educated, learned, able, etc.; this only increases the evil.

4. Enormous strength of a bad man. His *vis inertiae*, his *momentum*. In his black panoply, armed *cap-à-pie* like a knight in story, such the bad man. Then fancy a host of them, the rulers of this world, like a bodyguard of Satan, or his ' guards.'

5. Such are the enemies of Christ, described in the Gospel : ' We wrestle not against,' etc., Eph. vi. 12. Then Christ's grace more powerful : ' A stronger than he,' etc.

6. No one can come up to the strength of God's grace—stronger than the elements ; stronger than miracles. It bears up against anything ; it overcomes everything. On the wonderful way in which Christianity overthrew the establishment of paganism (*vide* Döllinger).

7. Let this be your comfort if you feel afraid, and have to do a great work. God's grace can convert ; it has converted from sin of whatever kind.

March 30 (*Fourth Lent*)

ON BEARING MOCKERY

1. INTROD.—Laetare Sunday. Joy, like a flower springing out of desolation and mortification, as Christ goes along the desert.

2. What flower shall be our offering ? We cannot do much in the way of fasting, or other bodily mortifications. Why, the time supplies one, and which the epistle suggests, viz. our bearing reviling,

etc. On the epistle of the day—Hagar and Sarah.
It was a strong boy bullying a small child—cowardly
and ungenerous. This animal nature. (Describe
Ishmael.) Sarah childless till Isaac. *Laetare*—the
mocking. 'Even so it is now,' says St. Paul. It is
the mark of the true Church, and the form of its
warfare—mockery. And so it is at this minute.

3. The scoffings, etc., which surround us not
exactly violence or suffering, but slander, etc. The
huge Protestantism of this land cannot keep from
grinning, scoffing, etc.

4. Now this has ever been the case with the
Church, as I have said, *e.g.* Isaac.

5. Joseph, Job, David, Jeremias, Daniel—Heb.
xi. 36.

6. Our Lord—(particulars)—bowing the knee, etc.
Christ's sensitiveness.

7. Something very irritating in mockery, irony,
etc. Indignation and anger natural, and not sinful,
yet to be restrained lest they become sinful. Slander,
misrepresentation, abuse of the good, blasphemy
of things sacred, ludicrous views, pictures, etc.
Nay, the people who throng the doors of a chapel
like this, with persons going to and fro, and insult
them.

8. All painful, yet *laetare*. Rejoice in your desolation ; let it be your Lent. Rejoice and leap for
joy, for great is your reward in heaven.

9. Rejoice if you are made like Christ and His
saints.

10. Rejoice, for it is a proof of your real strength.
Quare fremuerunt gentes. Our Lord's whisper terrifies this great country. His vicar, a feeble old

man, by a bit of paper frightens it—*vox Domini super aquas*. Can Wesleyans, etc., do so ? When did Protestantism ever raise a whole state as a small act of the vicar of Christ has done ? You see how the devils fear. Tall Ishmael is mocking in our streets ; a strong boy beating a small one.

11. Rejoice, for it is an augury for the future. The desolate has many more children than she that has a husband. So Protestantism is married to the state. Rejoice not against me, O my enemy, etc.[1]

April 6 (*Passion Sunday*)

ON THE PRIESTHOOD OF CHRIST

1. INTROD.—Go through the gospel of the day, showing the strangeness of our Lord's doctrine, and the surprise and contempt of the Jews, in detail—modes of expression, ideas, objects, different.

2. So it was : it was a different system. If the world was true, He was not ; if He, the world not.

3. They felt it obscurely and in detail, though He did not speak openly. How would they have felt if our Lord had said openly, ' I am the priest of the world ' ? What a great expression ! But this is the truth, as forced on us by to-day's epistle. What the gospel says obscurely the epistle speaks out.

4. What is a priest ? See how much it implies : first the need of reconciliation—it has at once to

[1] 'Rejoice not thou, my enemy, over me, because I am fallen: I shall arise; when I sit in darkness, the Lord is my light.' —Mic. vii. 8.

do with sin ; it presupposes sin. When then our Lord is known to come as a priest, see how the whole face of the world is changed. Describe the world, how it goes on, buying and selling, etc. ; then the *light* thrown on it that it is responsible to God, and has ill acquitted itself of that responsibility.

5. Again, it implies one the highest in rank. The head of the family was a priest—primogeniture. Hence Christ the Son of God.

6. Christ then, the Son of God, offers for the whole world, and that offering is Himself. He who is high as eternity, whose arms stretch through infinity, is lifted up on the cross for the sins of the world.

7. And He is a priest for ever. ' Thou art a priest *for ever* according to the order of Melchisedec.' The offering of the Mass. Say not it is an *historical* religion, done and over ; it lasts.

8. And as, for ever, so *all things* with blood. Why ? Grace of Christ, and Adam's grace before the fall. Men ' washed their robes in the blood of the Lamb ' ; ' the blood of Christ cleanseth,' 1 John i. 7.[1]

9. Now turn back and see how different from what we see—need of *faith*, so says our Lord in the gospel of the day.

10. And this awful addition, ' He that heareth the word of God is of God,' etc., John viii. 47.[2]

11. This a reason for these yearly commemorations, to bring on us the thought of the unseen world.

---

[1] 'We have fellowship one with another, and the blood of Jesus Christ his Son cleanseth us from all sin.'

[2] 'He that is of God heareth the words of God : therefore you hear him not, because you are not of God.'

April 13 (*Palm Sunday*)

ON CHRIST AS HIDDEN

1. INTROD.—At this season we veil our images. Why ? because the light of our eyes has gone from us. God is hidden. He showed Himself. He manifested Himself, but He is gone.

2. This is especially referred to in the gospels of the past week. Go through them ; there is only one, that on Thursday, which does not obviously refer to it.

3. He had shown Himself through His ministry for three years as all beautiful—' Blessed is the womb that bore Thee, and the breasts that gave Thee suck,' etc., Luke xi. 27 ; ' He has done all things well,' Mark vii. 37. But now a change. Hidden, bloody sweat, indignities, blows, etc., called a deceiver, Isa. liii. 3-4.[1] Ps. xxii. 6-7 [2] ; even the disciples doubting, etc.

4. Epiphany the beginning, Palm Sunday the end. From Passion Sunday till now He had been hidden.

---

[1] ' Despised and most abject of men ; a man of sorrows, and acquainted with infirmity. And his look was as it were hidden and despised, whereupon we esteemed him not. Surely he hath borne our infirmities, and carried our sorrows : and we have thought him as it were a leper, and as one struck by God, and afflicted.'

[2] ' But I am a worm, and no man ; the reproach of men, and the outcast of the people. All they that saw me have laughed me to scorn : they have spoken with the lips and wagged the head.'

5. He did not show himself after the resurrection 'to all the people.' Ascension, and now the Holy Eucharist, a hidden manna. John xiv. 19.[1]

6. Difference in the mode in which He has been hidden before and after—'Verily thou art a God that hidest Thyself,' Isa. xlv. 15—before, all men in ignorance ; now, 'the people that sat in darkness,' etc. ; but still, before, He would not be found ; now, men will not seek. John xvi. 16.[2]

7. 'The light shineth in the darkness.' Go through John i. and thus explain the gospel for Thursday [in Passion week].[3] Magdalene saw what the Pharisee did not see.

8. Hence He is at once hid and not hid, John xiv.-xvi. : xiv. 19-23 : xvi. 16. Plenty of Catholics in this country, yet how little they are known. Falsehoods circulated against them.

9. But let us beware how we refuse the light when it comes. State of the Jews on Palm Sunday. To-day's Mass implies they were visited by grace. A sudden great grace illuminated that day—(enlarge on the palms, procession, etc.). Alas, how soon it went !

10. Alas, it was like the 'stronger than he' taking possession of His house, and the evil spirit returning.

11. O may that not be the case of any of us. We look up at the cross now, and cannot see Christ's face. A veil, a thick veil is over it. O let us say,

[1] 'Yet a little while, and the world seeth me no more ; but you see me : because I live and you shall live.'

[2] 'A little while, and now you shall not see me : and again, a little while, and you shall see me.'

[3] Luke vii. 36-50.

'My Saviour, let it not be so really with my soul.
I know I cannot always enjoy Thy consolations, but
let not Thy face really be hidden from me.   It is my
eternal joy.'

April 15 (*Tuesday in Holy Week*)

MARIA ADDOLORATA

1. INTROD.—It is often said that men in trial act
well or ill, according to their previous life, which
then is brought out.   They cannot work themselves
up to be martyrs.   This applies also to the contemplation of the sufferings of the saints, and of
our Lord and His blessed Mother.   I should like
e.g. to bring before you the subject of the Mater
Addolorata.   But how am I to do so ?   It depends
on yourselves.   Are you familiar with her image ?
Is she a household word ?   If so, you will meditate
well ; if not, ill.

2. This comes on us at this time of year, when we
wish so much to meditate, and find it so difficult.
We shall keep this time well, according as we have
kept the year well.   As we have meditated through
the year, so shall we celebrate this season.   We
cannot force our minds into love, compassion,
gratitude, etc.

3. So as to matters of this world.   We hear of
deaths, losses, accidents, etc., with emotion or not,
according as we know the persons, according as the
name is familiar to us.

4. I cannot impress this knowledge upon you or

myself, and this makes me almost loth to discourse
on these great topics. The very sight of a crucifix
or holy picture, such as we have in our chambers,
should be enough. It is not a matter of words, but
of heart.

5. Think then of her, first as she was, as she had
been, and you will understand what she was in her
grief. Go through her character—so lovely, so
perfect, so glorious ; the ideal of painters and poets ;
yet superhuman, the flower of human nature—the
soul so beaming through her that you could not tell
her features, etc. ; so gentle, winning, harmonious,
attractive ; so loving towards others ; so pained
at sorrow and pain ; so modest, so retiring : her
voice, her eyes — yet still so chaste and holy
that she inspired holiness. Hence the fulness of
the sanctity of St. Joseph : it was inspired by
her.

6. And she had lived with a Son who cannot be
described in this way only, because He is God ; who
surpassed her infinitely, but in another order. In
the one the attributes of the Creator, in the other
the most perfect work. What a picture ! what a
vision ! Mother and Son.

7. Next, that Son has left her. And now the news
comes to her that He is to die, to be tortured ; that
He is to die a criminal's death of shame and torment ;
His limbs to be torn to pieces, etc., and He so
innocent. Why, it is worse than killing and torturing the innocent babe.

8. Under those circumstances, remarkable bold-
ness in coming to see Him die. Does a mother
commonly so act ? Here the perfection of Mary's

character. Hagar, 'Let me not see the death of my son,' Gen. xxi. 15-16.[1]

9. [She saw] Christ bearing the cross. Then at cross.

10. Our distress at seeing mother's grief, which we cannot help.

11. On mental pain. Greatest. Christ's mental pain would have swallowed up even His bodily, had He not willed to feel it.

April 27 (*Low Sunday*)

FAITH THE BASIS OF THE CHRISTIAN EMPIRE

1. INTROD.—Our Lord came to form a kingdom all over the earth unto the end of time. And to this end the commission to preach the Gospel, etc. [Mark xvi. 15.]

2. Now observe what a great problem is this. It had never been done before ; it has never been done since, except in the instance of that kingdom. Why, a large empire extending over many countries, *mole ruit sua !* On the four empires and others—but were by an effort and ephemeral.

3. Even the Jews, small as they were, could not keep together in one. Divisions of Reuben—

---

[1] 'And when the water in the bottle was spent, she cast the boy under one of the trees that were there. And she went her way, and sat over against him a great way off, as far as a bow can carry : for she said, I will not see the boy die. And sitting over against him, she lifted up her voice and wept.'

Benjamin slaughtered ; ten tribes ; various sects, Pharisees, etc.

4. (So in Protestants, though fain would be one, but cannot), but the Catholic Church has lasted one through all time, and is as much or more one now than ever she has been.

5. Now to-day's Mass tells us in the epistle and gospel how it is, and what means God took. It was by means of faith, which is not only the beginning of all acceptable service, but is the binding principle of the Church. John xx. 29, St. Thomas, ' Blessed are they that have not seen, and have believed.' 1 John v. 4, ' This is the victory which overcometh the world, our faith.' Now consider this attentively. It is a problem which has never been solved before. He did not take self-interest, worldly benefit, etc., because they would not last ; and it is what the world proposes to mankind.

6. When He would make a universal empire, He did not take a book or law for the basis. Some would have said the Bible, but the event, the divisions of Protestants show it would not do.

7. Not a law, nor a polity, nor episcopacy (as Anglo-Catholics say). *Quis custodiet*, etc. What shall make bishops obeyed, etc.?

8. Nor reason (as Liberals and Latitudinarians will say), for it only arrives at opinion.

9. Nor love (as religious persons may think), quoting : ' By this shall all men know that you are my disciples, because you have love one for another'; for concupiscence overcomes love,[1] and the good

[1] Written over these words—' love the heart, not the whole body.'

will never be the many. Some principle must be taken which all can have.

10. Therefore He took faith—a supernatural gift. Faith may be possessed by good and bad, and is most influential ; even the bad are made to serve His glory and praise. And it is the bond, for thus all have common objects. Faith is not easily lost.

11. Hence 1 Peter ii. 9, 'a royal priesthood as in yesterday's epistle—hence Jeremias xxxi. [33-34 [1]]—and 'our hearts enlarge.' They obey because they believe. It is not the Church enforces on them faith, but faith obliges them to take the Church—1 John ii. [20], 'know all things'; [*ib.* 27], 'no one to teach you.'

12. Hence the people never wrong (individuals indeed, and sometimes nations, may apostatise), but I mean the whole body. Unlike the Jewish Church. Aaron and calf. Pilate 'willing to content the people.' But the Christian people cannot be wrong. *Vox populi*, etc. Hence 'when the Son of Man cometh shall faith be found,' etc., because of the obscuration under Antichrist.

13. This is our consolation at all times. Our very sins do not overcome the Church, for faith is independent of sin.

---

[1] 'But this shall be the covenant that I will make with the house of Israel; After those days, saith the Lord, I will put my law in their bowels, and I will write it in their hearts; and I will be their God, and they shall be my people. And they shall teach no more every man his neighbour, and every man his brother, saying, Know the Lord : for all shall know me, from the least of them even to the greatest.'

May 1 (*Month of Mary* 1)

ON MARY AS THE PATTERN OF THE NATURAL WORLD

1. INTROD.—Why May the month of Mary ?

2. Consider what May denotes. It is the youth of the year ; its beauty, grace and purity. Next is its fertility ; all things bud forth. The virgin and mother.

3. See how the ecclesiastical year answers to it. Our Lord passed His time in the winter—born at Christmas, etc. He struggles on. We sympathise with Him. We fast in Lent—the rough weather continues. He comes to His death and burial when the weather is still bad, yet with promise— fits of better anticipations. He rises ; the weather mends ; but, as He was not known as risen, not all at once. But at length it is not doubtful. He is a risen king, and, still the weather gets warmer. As a climax May comes, and He gives His mother.

4. Such is the comparison. Nothing so beautiful in the natural world as the season when it opens. Nothing so beautiful in the supernatural as Mary. The more you know of this world the more beautiful you would know it to be—in other climates—beauty of scenery, etc., etc.

5. But this is not all. Alas, the world is so beautiful as to tempt us to idolatry. St. Peter said, ' It is good to be here ' [on Mt. Thabor], but ' It is not good to be in the world.' ' Say, hast thou track'd a traveller's round,' etc.[1]—All that is so beautiful tempts us. Hence all Nature tends to sin (not in itself), etc.

[1] See Note 10, p. 338.

6. Here then a further reason why the month is given to Mary, viz. in order that we may sanctify the year.

And thus she is a better Eve. Eve, too, in the beginning may be called the May of the year. She was the first-fruits of God's beautiful creation. She was the type of all beauty ; but alas ! she represented the world also in its fragility. She stayed not in her original creation. Mary comes as a second and holier Eve, having the grace of indefectibility and the gift of perseverance from the first, and teaching us how to use God's gifts without abusing them.

May 4 (*Second Easter*)

ON THE GOOD SHEPHERD AND LOST SHEEP

1. INTROD.—God is from eternity and ever blessed in Himself, and needs nothing.

2. On His, being such, taking part in things of time.

3. An office of ministration—one towards things physical ; a further towards things moral, *i.e.* which have free will.

4. A further still towards man fallen—on his waywardness, arising from concupiscence and ignorance —and even the just [not exempt]—of which ignorance remains more fully in all. Ignorance is the best estate. This is portrayed in sheep. Other animals [1] are fearful, etc., and represent sinners, but the innocent sheep, ignorant and helpless, is the fit type of the

---

[1] Written above—' animals,' ' or swine.'

just. What a picture this gives us ! We are tempted to laugh at sheep, who will not go the right way, start at every noise, do not know the meaning of anything, and are obliged to be forced by terror, as by the dog ; yet it is our best image. Our Lord, the Good Shepherd, is obliged to frighten us, etc., etc. Yet so patient.

5. O how patient towards us ! But more than patient—the lost sheep, and His laying down His life for it—the wolf [1]—nay, and that a *one*, though one.

6. What is meant by *one* ? Because any one must consider Himself the one. Every one is *worst* to himself : he alone knows himself.

7. On St. Augustine, this day St. Monica's day.

8. Does the Church lament over you, O *one* sinner ? Here we are in the happy time of the year —Christ risen and the month of May come—yet you have not been to your duties, or have not got absolution, or have fallen again into sin. Mater Ecclesia deplores you, our blessed Lord deplores you, etc.

May 8 (*Month of Mary* 2)

ON MARY AS OUR MOTHER

1. INTROD.—Our Lord from the cross said, ' Behold thy mother.' These words, spoken to St. John, have been considered by the Church to apply to us all.

---

[1] Killing the shepherd ? *or*, running away with one sheep ?

2. When our Lord went up on high, He supplied us with all those relations in a spiritual way which we have in a natural way. He is all of them—our physician, our teacher, our ruler or pastor, our father and our mother. Explain how our mother—as bearing us in pain. ' Shall a mother forget her sucking child ? ' and in nourishing us with the milk of the Holy Eucharist.

3. And as St. Peter the one pastor, as St. John, etc., and the prophets and doctors [as teachers], as priests His physicians, so He has left His own mother to be our mother.

4. ' Behold thy mother,' etc. Month of Mary.

5. Now consider what is meant by this—a mother's special gift—fostering care, tenderness, compassion, unfailing love, so that whenever we would express what is home, and a refuge, and a retreat, and a school of love, we call it our mother. Our country is our mother : our schools, colleges, universities, etc., etc.[1] Hence the Church.

6. This is what Mary fulfils to all who seek her care, and in a far higher degree than any mother can do ; for,

7. First, many lose their mothers, or have unkind mothers, etc. Everything of earth fades.

8. Second, a human mother's standard of things may be wrong : it may lead from God, hence human affections keep so many from the Church.

9. Everything human has a chance of fostering idolatry. What is always present hides the unseen.

10. Our heavenly mother cannot fail and cannot

---

[1] *E.g.* Alma mater.

F

err, cannot obscure her Son and Lord, but reminds of Him.

11. Let us try to get this filial feeling, though we can only learn it by degrees, and cannot force ourselves into it.

May 11 (*Third Easter*)

ORATORY OF BROTHERS—ON THE GENERAL SCOPE OF THE INSTITUTE

1. INTROD.—Perhaps some of you do not know what it is we are offering you in this association.

2. In one word, which, vague as it is, still is true, we are meeting together to do something towards saving our souls.

3. Difficulty of saving the soul. St. Philip's saying that no one could be expected to get to heaven who had not feared hell. Scripture texts, ' narrow is the way,' etc.

4. Grace most abundant. Till the last day, we shall not know how much.

5. But there is a most unaccountable waywardness in man. It is needless to speculate on it. Every one feels it. He cannot steady, command, direct himself—inefficacious desires. He is beaten about here and there at the mercy of the waves. Sloth, cowardice, anger, fretfulness, sullenness, vanity, curiosity, concupiscence, ever lead him astray.

6. Hence all serious men look out for a rule of life to defend them against themselves.

7. This leads many into religion for assistance, for sympathy, for guidance.

8. The Oratorium Parvum is a slight bond of sympathy and of mutual assistance.

9. Hence it matters not what we do, or whether you have anything definite in it beyond this end, if you secure it.

May 18 (*Fourth Easter*)

ON THE WORLD HATING THE CATHOLIC CHURCH

1. INTROD. — In the discourse of which the gospel is part, our Lord speaks of the world hating us.

2. This remarkable, viz. that we should be hated. That the Catholic faith is difficult and a stumbling-block is intelligible—but hateful ! Difficult to realise, for we are drawn to all, and cannot believe they hate us.

3. Consider its beauty—acknowledged by intellectual men—of its services ; of its rites ; of its majesty ; doctrine of our lady, etc., etc. Its connection with art, etc., etc. Paley on Romans xii., in *Evidences*.

4. Yet so our Lord has said—quote John xv. 18-19,[1]

---

[1] 'If the world hate you, ye know that it hath hated me before you. If you had been of the world, the world would love its own: but because you are not of the world, but I have chosen you out of the world, therefore the world hateth you.'

John xvii. 14,[1] and 1 John iii. 1.[2] 'Wonder not if the world hate you.'

5. And what is remarkable further, it is a prophecy. It has been fulfilled and is fulfilled to this day; it is literal honest hate. The world is not merely deceived; it has an instinct, and hates.

6. But more than this, or again, it is a note of the Church in every age; in the Middle Ages, when religion was established as much as now.

7. And none but the Church thus hated. So that our Lord's prophecy falls on us, and connects us with the apostles.

8. Others, indeed, by an accident and for a time.

9. For sects have (1) something true and good in them; (2) are extravagant; and these two things make them persecuted.

10. But it is for a time. The truth goes off, and the extravagance — they tame down; thus the Methodists and the Quakers.

11. But Catholics, nothing of this—sober—by token men of the world get on with us.

12. Yet the suspicion, irritability, impatience, etc., etc.—Demoniacs, and it is the devil's work.

13. This must not make us misanthropic, but cast us on the unseen world and purify our motives. This one benefit of the present agitation.

---

[1] 'I have given them thy word; and the world hath hated them, because they are not of the world, as I also am not of the world.'

[2] 'Behold, what manner of charity the Father hath bestowed on us, that we should be called and should be the sons of God. Therefore the world knoweth not us because it knew not Him.'

June 8 (*Whitsunday*)

THE LIFE-GIVING SPIRIT

1. INTROD.—We have what we have waited for.
Paschal time is not only a time of rejoicing, but of
waiting for a gift. The *whole creation groaning,* etc.
Hence, now being the end, we go no further, but
date our time from Pentecost.

2. The gift of to-day set up the Church, hence it
is said to be a vehement wind filling the house.
Solomon's temple filled with the glory, as the sweet
nard filled the house.

3. For up to this date the Church was not formed.
The multitude who followed Christ was but matter.[1]
They were not a body filled with Christ. Christ
was with them, but external [2]; they were not con-
firmed. They were all scattered abroad as sheep.
Hence as an individual may have first actual,
then habitual grace—so the *multitudo fidelium* all
Paschal time is begging to be the bride of Christ.

4. Now then the Spirit came down, to gather
together the children of God, etc., all those who had
fled away, etc.; returned—3000–5000.[3]

5. Like the resurrection of dry bones, Ezech. xxxvii.

6. Such is the power, the manifestation, of the
Spirit; thus sudden, thus gentle, thus silent. It is
life from death—what health is after sickness. It
makes young. Oh what a gift is this! Who would

---

[1] I.e. *materia sine forma.* A bold figure or comparison which
must not be taken too literally.

[2] 'External' is followed by some words which are nearly
illegible. They look like 'for was not a *form.*'

[3] 'There were added in that day about three thousand'
(Acts ii. 41). 'The number of the men was made five thousand'
(Acts iv. 4).

not wonder if a physician could make an old man
young ? See him, unable to do more than grope
about, his limbs stiff, his face withered, etc., etc.
But the physician comes, and health and comeliness
and vigour return, etc. This is what is fulfilled by
the power of the Spirit, in a measure in individuals,
certainly in the body.

7. And is it possible such is in store for England ?
—(explain). Nothing unexpected, nothing too difficult. It is grace, yet spreading not at once.

8. Prayer for it. Never so much prayer as now.

June 29

THE ROCK OF THE CHURCH—ST. PETER AND ST. PAUL

1. INTROD.—If nothing else could be said for our
holy religion than the topic of this day suggests, I
should think it abundantly proved.

2. At present we see a vast body with vast power
all over the earth. We know how great the British
power. Such (I don't say with the same weapons)
is the Catholic Roman Church, nay, far more fully,
because it reigns more directly—not through other
powers, as the British in India, etc.

3. Now look at the British Empire. What is its
peculiarity ? It has grown, as it happens, in the
course of a century ; but never mind that. The
Catholic Church has never grown ; it always has
been [what it now is].

4. Now one point is the great youth of all other
powers compared with the Catholic Church, but I
won't dwell on that.

5. What I wish to dwell on is, that whether they be young or old, they have had a growth—a beginning, a progress, and an ending like a tree—(enlarge). Look at the great Roman Empire; Gibbon has written its decline and fall.

6. No one can write, I will not say the decline and fall, but the growth of the Catholic Church—(explain). I don't say it has not developed in many respects; in consolidation, in temporal power, in definition of doctrine, in experience; but it is stationary.

7. Look back five centuries. Just the same—stationary. Look back ten, etc. No, it expanded at once in the apostles, and has ever since possessed the earth. ' Blessed are the meek,' etc.

8. But further. Suppose not only the British Empire had lasted long, that not only it was stationary, being just what it was in Alfred's time; but supposing Alfred declared it should last; suppose all the kings who ever were declared it would last—moreover, in consequence of an old prophecy in Julius Caesar's time, etc.

9. This fulfilled in the Church—St. Leo 1400 years ago. Our Lord's test—the rock—how exactly it fulfils it. ' The house upon the sand '—Protestantism.

August 10 (*Ninth Pentecost*)

ON THE DEATH OF THE SINNER

1. INTROD.—The gospel—our Lord weeping over Jerusalem. Particulars of it. The Jews so little

aware. They thought a great conqueror was coming to them. Their great infatuation. They had a vast future (they thought) before them. The Temple rebuilt. Our Lord saw through it all.

2. Application to the soul of the individual. Type of sinner in death. Our Lord looking and prophesying ill—(particulars). 'Cast a trench,' 'hedge them in.'

3. 'Hedge them in.' Yes, Satan will take possession of him ; keep God out ; keep him all to himself. What a portentous thought !

4. Christ foresees it, weeps over the man, but He leaves him.

5. But does He not give grace ? Yes, but it is ineffectual.

6. Why does He not give more ? What is that to the purpose ? He does not.

7. We cannot change things by asking questions. Why does He punish him ? Can you change it by disputing ? Your wisdom is to take things as they are, and submit and improve them. Is not this the way you do with this world ? You do not quarrel with the wind, the flame, etc., but use them. Our Lord with Judas. His denunciations of eternal woe. His own sufferings [are as if He said], 'I say not why, but I suffer.'

8. Well, then, the fact is this. The sinner generally is thus 'walled in.' *Vide* St. Alfonso on this day.

9. Saul. Antiochus.

10. Encircled—wild beasts. Sins as faithful friends who encircle you in their arms.

11. The priest's prayers in vain.

12. The sacraments in vain.

13. Our Lady not. Ave Maria! St. Andrew Avellino!

14. Let us ask her to intercede for us.

August 31 (*Twelfth Pentecost*)

ON CHRIST THE GOOD SAMARITAN

1. INTROD.—Go through the parable briefly, applying it in a secondary sense to the sinner and Christ.

2. In the parable the traveller was robbed against his will, the sinner with his will. Satan cannot conquer us against ourselves. Eve—temptation, etc.; it is a bargain.

3. Thus he gets from us justice, habitual grace, etc., nay, part of our mere nature, for he leaves wounds. Thus he may be said to suck the blood from us. A vampire bat sucking the blood out. All terrible stories of ghosts, etc., etc., are fulfilled in him who is the archetype of evil.

4. He has the best of the bargain, as is evident. What have we to show for it?—there are improvident spendthrifts who anticipate their money, and get nothing for it. What have we to show if we have given ourselves to Satan?

5. (1) Those who commit frauds—ill gains go. (2) Anger, swearing and blasphemy—what remains? (3) Sensuality is more rational, because men get something.

6. Yet in a few years where is it all? Let a man

enjoy life, let him be rich, but he gets old, and then !
Wisdom [v. 8]. ' What hath pride profited us ? '

7. Thus Satan has the best of the bargain, and
we lie like the traveller.

8. Nothing of this world can help us—priest or
Levite : there we should lie for ever, etc.

9. Christ alone, by His sacraments.

10. Mind He is a Samaritan — so Nazareth —
because the Catholic Church is hated. She is the
good Samaritan to Protestants. Observe again the
text, ' He who showed mercy to him.' Has the
Catholic Church or Protestantism done this for us ?

September 28 (*Sixteenth Pentecost*)

ON THE M. ADDOLORATA—THE SEVEN
DOLOURS

1. INTROD.—The usual representation which
painters make of our Lord and His mother is that
of virgin and child. Describe the peaceful virgin,
secure because she has Him, and He the Life and
Light. Hence she the Seat of Wisdom, etc., etc.

2. But let thirty years pass, and there is a great
change come over the picture. It melts into
something different. He is taken up from her soft
arms. He is lifted aloft. Something else embraces
Him. He is in the arms of the cross. There He
lies not easily, etc. He has grown to man's estate.
He has been scourged, etc. And she is standing
still, but it is at His feet. She can be of no use to
Him ; she can only lament. How the group is

changed ! He is covered with wounds ; she is almost killed with grief.

Such is the picture which the Church puts before us to-day, and that because, we may suppose, Easter is so long past.

3. Well, as to the sufferings of the Son of God, they are awful mysteries ; but they need not surprise us, for He comes to suffer. He indeed might have saved us without suffering, but it was in fact bound up in His coming. He was a combatant—combatants suffer. He was prophesied as a warrior and man of blood. He fought with the devil. He fought with sin, not indeed His own, but sin was imputed to Him. He came in the place and character of a sinner : no wonder He should suffer.

4. But there was one who neither sinned nor took on her the character of a sinner. What had she to do with blood, or wounds, or grief ? She had ever lived in private ; she bore Him without pain ; she had never come forward. She had on the whole been sheltered from the world, yet she suffered. This makes Mary's suffering so peculiar. She is the queen of martyrs.

5. Yet she too was to suffer. She is innocent, so harmless, not provoking the devil, etc. She was to suffer, and be the queen of martyrs. Joseph was taken away ; she remained.

6. It is true she was not to undergo that bodily pain and violent death which literally makes a martyr. He alone suffered all who died for all. He alone suffered bodily and mentally. Her tender flesh was not scourged, but His was ; her virginal form was not rudely exposed, but His was. All

this would have been unseemly and unnecessary. He was to save us by that body and blood which she furnished ; not she. He was to be made a *sacrament* for us as well as a sacrifice.

7. Yet she was privileged to share the *acutest* part of His sufferings, the mental, once she came into the midst, at His crucifixion.

8. Mental pain all in a moment, like a spear ; despondency, sinking of nerves ; no support.

9. Yet she stood.

10. Surely it quite changed her outward appearance to the end of her life.

October 26 (*Twentieth Pentecost*)

ON THE PATROCINIUM B.V.M.

1. INTROD.—This festival of our Lady [is] more immediately interesting to us than any, because by it we are made over to her and she to us. [In] the Incarnation, the Assumption, etc. [we celebrate more immediately her relations to Almighty God], but [in] this [feast we call to mind particularly her relations to ourselves].

2. It is like the divine works to turn things to *account*. Thus, though she subserved the Redeemer, she also subserves the redeemed. Hers is a *ministry* to us, and it was to Him originally.

3. As a pope makes a congregation over to a cardinal, or a king gives some one a ring, etc., saying, 'Whatever you want, send the ring and you shall have it.'

4. Thus she is the fount of mercy, as a magistrate of justice, etc.

5. Hence Protestant absurdity of saying [that] we rate her more merciful than Christ. Christ is the judge also. Show what is meant by it. Can a ring be merciful ?

6. As this [is] the feast most intimately interesting to us, so we hear much of this character and office in Scripture, in the Holy Fathers.

7. Gen. iii., Apoc. xii.—*Advocata* with clients ; mother of all living. ' Behold thy mother,' John xix. 27.

8. Hence first instances in history represent her in this character — St. Gregory Thaumaturgus — St. Justina — against unbelief, against impurity respectively.[1]

9. St. Gregory Thaumaturgus has a creed given him—St. Ignatius—St. Philip.

10. Experience of all saints.

11. Let us use it, for living, for dead, for young, for old. The two first instances [given] above are [of] a *young man*, a *young woman*.

1851

THE IMMACULATE CONCEPTION THE ANTAGONIST OF AN IMPURE AGE

1. INTROD.—The world always the same, and its history the same. It is always sinning, always going on to punishment. Judgments and visitations

---

[1] For the stories here referred to, see *Development of Christian Doctrine*, pp. 417, 418.

always [coming] upon it.   Christ always coming [in judgment].

Sin provoking wrath.

2. This is seen in the judgments on cities for their crimes—Nineveh, Babylon, etc., and above all, Sodom and Gomorrah—all figures of the end of the world.

3. And especially eras—the deluge—the Christian era [1]—the end of the world.   And they are compared together in Scripture, Matt. xxiv., etc.

4. *What* sin (provoking wrath) ?   Sensuality.

As the loss of vital powers brings on dissolution of [the] body, so when passion emancipates itself from conscience, the death of the world.

5. The truth is, that the flesh is so strong, it is always struggling against conscience.   It is like a wild beast in a cage, ever trying to get out, and but slowly subdued.   Heavy things fall ; steam rises up. So with concupiscence ; and hence St. Peter [speaks of] ' The corruption of that concupiscence which is in the world,' 2 Peter i. 4.

6. Now as this goes on in a state, reason becomes infidel and the conscience goes, and then there is nothing to restrain concupiscence.

7. Hence we are sure (*exceptis excipiendis*) that wherever there is not religion there is immorality. What is to keep a man from indulgence ?

8. Statesmen see this so well that they advocate religion.

9. Hence [came the] deluge—[the] Christian era [2]—

[1] The allusion must be to the destruction of the Temple and the rejection of the Jews.

[2] Cf. Romans i.

[hence will come the] end of the world, [*i.e.* when] infidelity [has] brought in sensuality.

10. This age [is] an impure age.

11. Hence [the] B[lessed] V[irgin] M[ary] [is] attacked.

12. Hence [the devotion to] the Immaculate Conception is so apposite.

1851

THE SPECIAL CHARM OF CHRISTMAS

1. INTROD.—[The] two chief festivals [of the Church are] Easter and Christmas ; [of these] Easter [is] the greater.

2. Yet somehow we adorn our churches more brightly and spontaneously, now than then. There is more of heart, apparently, in what we do. And there is an inexpressible charm over all. The midnight Mass, the three Masses. The special representations, whether the Stable or the Infant. [Again, the singing of] carols.

3. Why is this ? Christmas is easier to understand to the mass of men ; it comes home to them more readily, and imposes an easier duty on our worship.

4. It is the difference between coming and going. The apostles felt that sorrow filled their hearts [at the going of the Lord]. *Mane nobiscum Domine.*

Easter is the feast of the perfect. If we were perfect, we should rejoice in Easter the more [of the two festivals]. In the one Christ comes to us, in the other we go to Christ.

5. All our human feelings are soothed by Christ-

mas — Abraham had to leave his country.—We naturally do not like to move. We are allowed to remain at home : Christ comes to us as our guest.

6. And coming, He *brightens* everything. He does not take away, He adds. He adds grace to Nature. If at any time we might love the world, it is now. If at any time, [it is when He is come to be our Emmanuel].

7. He makes the world our home, for he deigns to be the light of it. He sanctifies families with the image of Mary and Jesus. And where there is no *home* in a family, then He brings us all together in one family in church. The midnight Mass is our holy celebration [of Christmas], eclipsing the world's merrymaking.

8. And we think of Him who put off all His glory, of which our celebrations are but a type. The priestly vestments a type of His glory, [which He put off in order] to come into this bleak prison and suffer for us.

9. Let us rejoice *in Him.*

December 28 (*Sunday in Octave of Christmas*)

ON CHRISTIAN PEACE

1. INTROD.—Peace is, as we all know, the special promise of the Gospel.

2. Isa. xl., Rom. xi., Isa. ix., ' Peace on earth.' ' Peace I leave with you ' [John xiv. 27]. ' Peace be with you,' and St. Paul ' making peace ' [Rom. xii. 18].

3. This is the great want of human nature. It is what all men are seeking ; they are restless because they have not peace. They always think the time will come when they shall be happy, yet it never comes.

The schoolboy — the young man — the soul in disorder.

4. Hence it forms to itself notions of peace and happiness, [such notions as we find in] novels, tales, poems ; [notions which are] imaginary.

And above all, [notions of] religion. It attempts to make religions for itself, where everything shall be beautiful, etc.

5. Thus it goes on, and then it looks down on Christianity. Christ Jesus (they say) does not bring peace.

This is the way of so many infidels now. They say they want a religion more beautiful, more comfortable than the Gospel. They point to the gloominess of Catholicity—nothing sunny and bright —confession, penance, mortifications of the senses and the will ; monks, etc., etc. ; and they say this is a dreary religion, and they could form a better one. They say they could form a better god than the Father of Jesus Christ—a god of their own dreams ; [they could form] a religion without sin and without punishment.

6. Thus they go on ; but what is this but to say, ' Peace, peace, where there is no peace ' ?

7. The more haste, the worse speed. Shrubs putting out their leaves too soon—the hare and the tortoise. ' The end is the trial.'

8. The truth is, once beautifulness and peace *did*

G

come first, viz. in the Garden of Eden. Since then there has been a fall. There must be a restoration, and it is painful.

9. Contrasting pantheism with true religion, recollect we are only in process, etc., and *therefore* we look to disadvantage.

Hence religion gloomy, because it is an intermediate state.

10. But we look forward for peace to the next world.

January 11, 1852

ON THE EPIPHANY, AS CHRIST'S REIGN MANIFESTED TO FAITH

1. INTROD.—On the peculiarity of this octave.

2. Viz. no saint's day in it. Contrast Christmas. Contrast Easter and Whitsun as not *perfect*,[1] [the latter containing] fast days. Contrast [octaves of the] Ascension, Corpus Christi, [the] Assumption.

3. Why ? Christ [is] a king, and we anticipate His reign. It is the season most nearly typical of heaven.

4. Now, how was this fulfilled ? His palace a stable, His throne a manger—(enlarge).

5. Here it was the three kings came. They came a long way to see, what ? The poor child of a poor woman—(describe). They entered. Mary drew off the covering cast over the sleeping Child. They gazed, etc. ; they offered gifts ; they adored.

6. What a remarkable scene ! And this was the

---

[1] The octave of Christmas is full of saints' days—St. Stephen, St. John, etc. Those of Easter and Pentecost are cut short by Low Sunday and Trinity Sunday respectively.

manifestation of His glory! For this they had travelled their weary way!

7. Describe what they had to go through—the wonder of their people—why were they setting off?—Then, they did not know whither they were going, etc.

8. Describe their state of mind. They *knew* they ought to go; they *knew* there was something to find.

9. Enlarge on faith and reason, and explain.

10. This is that faith which is the beginning of salvation in every age, and the greatest specimen [of it]. It is like St. Thomas's, with less evidence, 'My Lord and my God.'

11. Greater than, yet like that in the Holy Eucharist.

(*No date* [1])

SELF-DENIAL IN COMFORTS

1. INTROD.—Contrast between men and other animals, that they [the latter] are sufficient for themselves.

2. The Creator has so ordained things that everything is there, where it can flourish. External nature and the nature of animals correspond.

3. Thus warmth and air, abode and food given to all; and when external nature is likely to press hard, [there are given] internal means of meeting it, *e.g.* furs, or hardiness, or instincts, etc., etc.

4. But man an exception. Strange to say, if born in a state of simple nature, he would die.

---

[1] 'Not used as yet.'

His delicate frame ill-suited to the elements, etc. He needs clothes, a house, etc.

5. Revelation tells us it was [not] always so, not in his creation, for he was in Paradise ; but it is one of the consequences of the fall.

6. Hence man is ever striving to get out of this state of fallen nature (so far [as concerns the needs of his body]). *Curis acuens mortalia corda.*[1] Hence his arts, etc. Hence his loom and his carpentering, etc., etc. I may say the whole course of life is escaping from this state of fallen nature, i.e. *as regards the body* : for the worst penalties, viz. the wounds of the soul, he leaves untouched.

7. Till at length he surrounds himself with comforts. They are called comforts, and make the whole world minister to him, and make his home and his rest here.

8. Now it is startling how our Lord took just the reverse course. He threw away comforts—born in a stable, carried into Egypt, not a place to lay His head, etc.

9. WHAT AN AWFUL CONTRAST between Him and us—(enlarge).

10. Let us take a lesson from it. We have here no abiding city, etc.

January 25

ON THE CHARACTER OF THE CHRISTIAN ELECTION—ST. PAUL'S CONVERSION

1. INTROD.—A great principle—not many mighty, noble, wise, called.

[1] Virgil, *Georgics*, i. 123.

2. St. Paul—*exceptio probat regulam*.

3. Still, such is the awful phenomenon in every age. When Catholicism [is] national, then indeed *all* Catholics. But when the Church acts freely, then the same characteristic as at the first.

4. *E.g.* the Church now [is] what it was in the apostles' time—few learned, etc.

5. It is a most wonderful phenomenon how it goes on. Why it does not fall to pieces, [seeing there are but] just enough of learned, etc., men to keep it going.

6. And here we see the reason, viz. that it may be manifestly God's doing.

7. This [is] set forth in Epistle to Corinthians.[1]

8. Describe how riches, power, learning, nay, natural goodness, often prejudice [men] against [the] Gospel.

9. On self-sufficient virtue, on putting up our own feelings, etc., as the rule. These men *complete in themselves* . . .

10. Apoc. iii. [vv. 1, 2, 8, 17, etc.], 1 Cor. iv. [vv. 4, 7, etc.], and not thrown upon God.

11. But I have [not] got at the bottom of the mystery. I have been speaking only of the *called*, but [there is] a second [and] wonderful mystery perfectly hid from us — who are the *chosen* ?

12. The visible Church does not stand for the invisible future elect. Those rich men who are in

---

[1] 'For see your vocation, brethren, that there are not many wise according to the flesh, not many mighty, not many noble : but the foolish things of the world hath God chosen, that he may confound the wise,' etc.—1 Cor. i. 26-27.

the Church may be holier than the poor. So many of the saints [were both] rich and noble men.

13. [The] moral is, the necessity of waiting on God's grace, and not quenching it.

February 1 (*Fourth Epiphany*)

PRESENT STATE OF OUR ORATORY

1. INTROD.—This day, commencing with this evening, is a great day for our Congregation, for it is the anniversary of its establishment in England.

2. This day four years [ago in England], and again this day three, in Birmingham.

3. The Purification, though not the greatest feast, [is] a good day, suitable to those who are *beginning* a work in an heretical country.—

    (1) It is a forlorn day in winter.

    (2) Christmas gone, Lent coming.

    (3) A little child and a poor mother coming to the Temple.

    (4) Purification reminds us of necessity of purity of heart.

4. To me *especially* interesting, for it has been my great feast-day for thirty years. Thirty years this year since I was brought under the shadow of our Lady,[1] whom I ever wished to love and honour

---

[1] Elected Fellow of Oriel (*the House or Hall of Blessed Mary*) in 1822.

more and more. And thus, when I became a Catholic, it was the day of the Congregation, etc.

5. God has blessed us through her intercession for three years in this place (Alcester St.). We have gradually prospered, year after year, and now a more definite establishment at Edgbaston.

6. Everything has come naturally, like a tree growing, and we hope it will still [grow].

7. About the Achilli matter. When it first arose, I said, ' The devil is here. Look not on prosecutor, lawyers, friends, etc. They are all weapons of the devil.' A NET—pulling strings close. *Vide* Psalter.

8. Therefore the remedy was prayer. What showed this more, was the extreme difficulty [of the case].

9. Eph. vi. 12, ' We wrestle,' etc.

10. *Number* of prayers offered.

11. The sequel has shown it—a great noise ending in nothing, so as to disappoint—first a roaring lion, then a serpent slinking away ; so it is *now*. People will say, ' Oh, there was no great danger.'

12. If we fail, it will be because we do not pray enough.

13. Therefore commend ourselves to our Lady.

August 15 (*Eleventh Pentecost*)

ON OUR LADY AS IN THE BODY

1. INTROD.—*Question.*—Whether this feast, [the Assumption, is] not inconsistent with the Immaculate Conception ; for why should our Lady die if she did not inherit Adam's sin ?

2. *Answer.*—Because she was under the laws of fallen Nature, and inherited its evils, except so far as sin [is concerned]. Thus our Blessed Lord [suffered fatigue, pain and death]. Thus she had not perfect knowledge from the first. She had need of shelter, clothing, etc., not in a garden [as our first parents were].

3. Hence, since all men die, she died. Our Lord died.

4. Yet even as regards the body, our Lord observed a special dispensation about her. Hence she was not only protected from diseases, but from torture, wounds, etc.

5. It was becoming that she who was *inviolata*, *intemerata*, should have no wound.

6. The difference between men and women as to warfare. The women protected and sit at home. How many a wife, or sister or daughter, suffers in mind, and you hear them say, ' O that I were a man ! ' And they suffer in soul, [as the] saints about *the cross* [who were] not martyrs [suffered].

And hence Mary had a sword through her [heart]. Mental pains, like bodily. And this her pain.

7. And hence she brings before us the remarkable instance of a soul suffering, yet not the body.

8. She lived therefore to the full age of human kind. [In this she was] different from our Lord.

9. What a picture this puts before us! Fancy her thirty, forty, fifty, sixty, looking still so beautiful and young, not fading, more heavenly every year; so that she grew in beauty, and the soul always grew in grace and merit.

10. And then, fancy the increased pain at the absence of Christ, [for she lived] fifteen or sixteen years without Him!

11. On the long life and waiting of the antediluvian patriarchs—Jacob's ' I have waited for Thy salvation, O Lord '; Moses; Daniel; the souls in Limbo Patrum like Mary, though the time [of her waiting] shorter.

It was like purgatory, waiting for Christ's face; except with merit and not for sin.

12. Hence [it is] not wonderful [that] it is a pious belief that she died from love. This alone could kill that body. It was a *contest* between body and soul. The body so strong, the soul so desirous to see God. No disease could kill that body. What killed it? The soul, that it might get to heaven.

13. (1) By languishing; (2) by *striving* to get loose.

14. Hence [it was] fitting that, when she did get loose, her Son should not let the body be so overmatched and overcome, but at once that the soul had got the victory, He raised up the body without corruption.

15. Our Advocate in heaven.

December 8, 1853

ON THE PECULIARITIES AND CONSEQUENT SUFFERINGS OF OUR LADY'S SANCTITY

1. INTROD.—Genesis iii. We cannot be surprised at our Lady's Immaculate Conception.

2. The reason is so plain that it seems axiomatic, nor, though it has been a point of controversy, do I think any holy person in any age has ever really denied it ; if they seemed to do so, it was something else they opposed.

3. Has not God required holiness wherever He has come ?—(1) burning bush [1]; (2) ' Be ye holy, for,' etc.[2]; (3) priests' purifications ; (4) consecration of Temple and tabernacle ; (5) without sanctity, no one, etc. ; (6) Confession before Communion. If, then, our Lady was to hold God, etc.

4. Still more, if from her flesh, etc.

5. Hence, though the Church has never proposed it as a point of faith,[3] it is not difficult to conceive it should be one, and there has been a growing wish that the Church could find that it was part of the original dogma. Indeed, it is almost saying what has been said in other words, for if no venial sin, *must* there not be Immaculate Conception ?

6. Now to explain what the doctrine is. Eve, as Adam, had been not only created, but constituted

---

[1] ' Come not nigh hither : put off the shoes from thy feet, for the place whereon thou standest is holy ground.'—Exodus iii. 5.

[2] ' Sanctify yourselves, and be ye holy : because I am the Lord your God.'—Levit. xx. 7.

[3] See p. 116, sec. 6.

holy, grace given, etc. Eve was without sin from
the first, filled with grace from the first.

7. When Adam and Eve fell, this grace was removed; and this constitutes the state of original sin.
Describe war of passions, etc. This is the state
into which the soul of man comes on its creation.
Nothing can hinder it but a *return* of the great gift.

8. Now in the text *she* was to restore, and more,
the age of Paradise. She was promised upon the
fall. Eve has been deceived. *She* was to conquer.
How would this be the case, unless Mary had at least
the gifts which Eve had ?

9. We believe, then, that Mary had this sanctify-
ing grace from the moment she began to be.

10. This being the case, I wish you to contemplate
her state. First, her wonderful state *before* her birth.
She had knowledge and the use of reason from the
first. This [was] necessary for love, therefore she had
it. What knowledge ?—(1) supernatural, (2) not
physical, (3) of divine objects—[as] the Holy Trinity,
which commonly requires external instruction.

11. Not of sin. Here difference from our Lord,
by way of illustration.

12. Consequences—her idea of disobedience ; no
recognition of separate sins. It is only temptation
brings this knowledge home to ordinarily innocent
people. She would know she *could* disobey if she
would, but it was like willing to jump down a
precipice ; she was sure not.

13. She would not be able to comprehend *how*
people came to sin. And if the supernatural information told her the fact, she would take it of necessity simply on faith.

14. Let us suppose her passing out of her first infancy. She is taught external things. She is taught to read. She learns Scripture. She hears of the sins of her people. She has to take it on faith.

15. She is a little child, not three years old, but she cannot pass her mother's threshold but the very scent of the world overpowers her. It is a bad world : how is she to live in it ? She understands many things : she does not understand it.

16. At length she is taken to the Temple, and there she lives ten years—what a blessed change ! —in the presence of her God. But even then, though she looks at the priests as God's ministers, yet, alas, how is she to bear the world, even in its best shape !

17. Time comes that she must return. Alas ! she has a growing suffering ; she is thrown on the world. Do you not see that there cannot be a more insufferable penance than to be thus perfectly holy, yet in this unholy world ? I know she has full consolations, but she is in a sinful world, and has the *poena damni*.

18. She looks back on the happy mysterious time which passed between the creation of her soul and her birth.

19. What a comfort to find herself transferred to St. Joseph's charge ! This is the first alleviation, for a time, which God gives to her penance.

20. Then the angel Gabriel. Ah ! here is an alleviation indeed. She is no longer desolate for thirty years.

21. Prophecy of Simeon. Loss of Jesus at twelve years old. His ministry. His crucifixion.

22. O Mary, you were young, now you are old—old, yet not as other old people, dwindling, but increasing in grace to the end. But oh what a penance ! *O commutationem !* [1]

23. And to go about the world ! to go to Ephesus ! Oh wonderful ! Your journey to St. Elizabeth, to Bethlehem, was with your Son. Now you journey further without Him.

24. CONCLUSION.—The holier we are, the less of this world [can we endure].

25. Fitting to be the Feast of the Congregation [of the Oratory] since, especially in a country like this, we must begin with holiness.

July 23, 1854 (*Seventh Pentecost*)

[NATURE AND GRACE]

1. INTROD.—Text : ' Jesus loved him.'

2. Explain the circumstances. And then we come to this anomaly—that God loves *for something in them* those who will not obey His call.

3. Now this is a difficulty surely which we feel ourselves. People are (1) amiable, (2) conscientious, (3) benevolent ; they do many good actions, but are not Catholics ; or not in God's grace.

4. Explanation. Nature not simply evil. We do not say that Nature cannot do good actions without God's grace. Far from it. Instances of great heathens.

5. What we say is that no one can get to *heaven* without God's grace.

[1] See Note 9, p. 337.

6. Contrast of two states as on two levels : (1) moral virtues with ' their reward,' industry, etc., has a reward in *this* life.

7. (2) Spiritual state of grace. It has all these virtues and a *good* deal more, and especially faith.

8. This is why faith is so necessary. Explain what faith *is*, as a door. It is a sight, [power of vision]. It is looking up to God. When we *pray*, we have faith, etc., etc.

9. Now what an awful thought this is when you look at the world—if something *more than* Nature is necessary for salvation.

10. People say, ' If I do my duty '—' He was such a good father ' ; ' He was upright,' etc., etc. All this is good, but by itself will not bring a man to heaven.

11. When you think what *heaven* is, is it wonderful ? Think of *our sins*. Is it wonderful God does not give forgiveness to Nature ?

12. Is it wonderful that grace alone can get repentance ?

13. Let us turn this [over] in our hearts.

August 6 (*Ninth Pentecost*)

' NO ONE CAN COME TO ME EXCEPT THE FATHER,' ETC.

1. INTROD.—I said, a fortnight ago, that when we saw what is good in those who are external to the Church, we must say that it is from Nature, and did not prove that such persons were in God's favour.

2. This is true, but you may insist that Protestants, [as well as] those who do not believe that Christ is God, etc., etc., have an *appearance* of *religion* ; that you cannot deny your senses ; that as you believe them in other things, *e.g.* that they are honest, so you must here ; that they must have *grace* if they have *faith* and *love,* and therefore must be in God's favour and in the way to heaven.

3. I am going, then, to give a further answer. First, I *grant* they show often real faith, real hope, real love, and that it comes from grace, and that while they obey that grace, etc., they are in a certain sense in the way to heaven ; but still this is quite consistent with what I have said.

4. All men in God's wrath. How are they brought out of it ? By God's grace coming like a robe (the ordinary way in baptism, and afterwards by penance) and making them pleasing to Him. *Few* are in this state. It is called *the state of grace,* and it is the state to die in, and since we may die any moment, the state to live in, if we would be safe.

5. And though few are in this state, it is the state in which God wills *all* to be in, for Christ died for *all.*

6. As He sends out *preachers* all over the earth, and as still more, guardian angels, so *graces.*

7. To all He gives grace, even to those who are not yet in His favour, or *in* grace. He gives them this grace in order that they may *come* into a state of grace—heathens, idolaters, Jews, heretics, all who are not Catholics. All have grace without knowing it—' [even when they are] without God '—while they are *far* from Him.

8. When you see men, not Catholics, will good things, acknowledge it, but understand *why* they [these graces] are given, viz. like preachers, to bring them into the Church; and they are brought into the Church by obeying them, though not all at once.

9. Instances. A kindness to a Catholic [or to] any strangers—generosity—leads to hearing something about Catholicity. More grace [follows]. [The man] resisting [at first], but yielding [gradually], etc., etc., till he is brought in.

10. Again, purity may keep a person from bad company. This throws time on his hands. He passes a Catholic chapel, he goes in, and he is attracted by a picture of our blessed Lady, etc.

11. All the while these persons may be out of God's favour, not yet justified, though He has died for them and wishes to save them, and is gradually drawing them.

How [about] heathen? Sends angels?

12. And thus I answer the question with which I began.

13. I entreat all those who are in doubt or inquiring to be faithful to grace, and they will be brought in.

August 20 (*Eleventh Pentecost—Octave of the Assumption*)

[REJOICING WITH MARY]

1. INTROD.—This, we know, is one of the most joyful weeks of the year. Our Lord's Resurrection is, of course, pre-eminently [joyful] (and in like

manner His Nativity), as He is above all. But
this week is unlike most other feasts connected
with Him, and rather stands at the head of the
saints' feasts, and this is its peculiarity. I will
explain.

2. The one idea is *congratulation. Congratulamini
mihi, quia cum essem parvula.* Congratulation is
a special feeling. Not in Christmas, or [in] any
act of His economy [or of] His Passion, not in Pentecost [nor] Corpus Christi, nor in the Sacred Heart,
[do we congratulate]. We congratulate when some
great good has come to another. We do not
(strictly speaking) congratulate ourselves, though
we may each other. We congratulate martyrs and
saints, etc.

3. Now this life tells us what congratulation is.
We congratulate persons on good fortune, which
does not concern us [ourselves], on preferment, on
a fortune, on escaping danger, on marriages and
births, on honours, etc.

4. On Catholicity only [*i.e.* alone] *realising unseen*
things and carrying human feelings into the supernatural world. Hence care of those who [have]
departed—purgatory—heaven.

5. Now consider St. Paul's words. *Gaudere cum
gaudentibus, flere cum flentibus*—congratulation and
compassion, or pity [opposed to] two bad states of
mind, ἐπιχαιροκακία and envy. Congratulation and
compassion both disinterested and unselfish, but
congratulation the more. What is so beautiful as to
see in the case of brothers and sisters, (*e.g.*) where
a younger rejoices in the gain of an elder, etc.

6. Now we congratulate Mary at this time of

H

year, after her long waiting—sixty years. What a purgatory! This very circumstance that all her life was God's, made the trial longer. But now, as Christ ascended, so has she.

7. But again, even this congratulation has often something selfish in it ; men hope to get something for themselves through their promoted friend. This is true also in the supernatural order, but with this difference, that the one desire is good, the other evil.

8. We cannot *covet* unseen good. Again, we do not deprive another of it.

9. Hence we *may rejoice* selfishly in Mary's triumph.

10. We have a friend in court. She is the great work of God's love.

11. Foolish objection, as if [we asserted] she were more loving than God—a ring, *e.g.* a pledge of favour to a person, any favours will be granted.

12. CONCLUSION.

September 3 (*Thirteenth Pentecost*)

[DISEASE THE TYPE OF SIN]

1. INTROD.—About the ten lepers in the Gospel.

2. Description of leprosy as a disease. What it was.

3. It made the person (1) deformed—(describe) —swollen and disgusting ; (2) it was lasting, not like a fever ; (3) incurable.

4. Lepers were driven out of society, they were so loathsome ; and they became like beasts. Travellers describe them now as outside the cities in troops.

5. Now all this is *sin*. Go through the particulars, as the angels see it. Describe our souls.

6. Since we are one and all sinners, we do not understand it. But the angels must revolt from us, but for their love. We are an exception to the intellectual creation—except the devils.

7. Parallels : (1) a person with a bad temper ; (2) a vulgar person—we shrink from them.

8. Yet our Saviour loved us, in spite of all this.

9. Enlarge on this. Take the cases of saints : (1) tending the leper ; (2) sucking sores ; (3) Father Claver with the Blacks ; yet all this is nothing to Christ['s charity to us].

10. Here, to say nothing else, [is] difference from our Lady. She had never seen heaven.

But He came [from heaven] among us, and now gives Himself to us in the Holy Eucharist. You know how we shrink from dirt, etc.

11. Thus we have at once two thoughts—humility and thankfulness. How can we be proud of anything we are ? How can we not love Christ ?

December 25

[CHRISTMAS JOY]

1. On the special *beauty* of the narrations of the Gospel, especially as regards our Lord's birth, and of these Luke ii. So much so, that unbelievers have called them myths.

2. Luke ii. Describe the scene. It sends us back to Paradise and to Adam and Eve, and to the Canticles.

3. We might fancy [there had been] no fall. [We see] Christ, as if He did not come to die, and His immaculate Mother ; the angels ; the animals, as in Paradise, obeying man.

4. We all seem caught and transformed in its beauty—' from glory to glory '—as St. Joseph.

5. But, many Christmases as there have been, this has something peculiar. A crown given to Mary. The Feast of the Conception ever precedes Christmas, but this year something has been done.

6. This year, as you know, the Pope, in the midst of the bishops of the world, has defined the Immaculate Conception, viz. that Mary had nothing to do with sin.

7. We were sure that it was so. We could not believe it was not. We could not believe it had not been revealed. We thought it had, but the Church did not say it was, etc.

8. Not out of place here. As we sing to Mary when the Blessed Sacrament is exposed, so now on to-day.

9. And we of The Oratory have a special interest in it. For our Church is raised under the invocation of Mary Immaculate ; and, as queens give largesses on their great days, so now that this crown is put on her head, she has, we think, shown us especial favour.

10. You recollect, some of you, three years ago, our trials : the world flourishing (Achilli matter) ; my going to Ireland ; Lady Olivia Acheson's illness and death ; and the illness of three intimately connected with us. All this weighed us down. *The Christmas midnight Mass three years ago.*

11. The contrast now : benefactions to our house and Church.

12. Our state in the University through your prayers.

13. We may expect trouble again—joy as if sorrowing, sorrowing as rejoicing. But God is all-sufficient.

August 19, 1855

OUR LADY THE FULFILLING OF THE REVEALED DOCTRINE OF PRAYER

(*Vide above, p.* [21], *August* 11, 1850)

1. INTROD.—In this week we especially consider our Lady as rising to her doctrinal position in the Church. Her first feast and this. The Immaculate Conception and the Assumption, both doctrines.

2. She is the great *advocate* of the Church. By which is not meant Atonement, of course. We know perfectly that she was saved by her Son. But she is His greatest work, and He has exalted her to this special office.

3. Hence from the first, *advocata nostra*. St. Irenaeus, and pictures at Rome in St. Agnese, etc.

Now to understand this, we must throw ourselves back into the world as it is by nature. Everything goes by *law*. This order is the most beautiful proof of God, but it is turned against Him, as if it could support itself.

Hence Revelation is an interruption and contravention—all of it miraculous.

4. Now here we have a most wonderful doctrine of Revelation brought before us in its fulness, viz. the efficacy of prayer.

5. Nature uniform. *How* has prayer its power? Worship [we understand to be] right, and adoration and thanksgiving; but how petitioning and supplication?

6. This then is the marvel, and the comfort which Revelation gives us, viz. that God has broken through His own laws—nay, does continually.

7. This so much that prayer is called *omnipotent*.

8. Even Protestants grant all this. (Quote *Thomas Scott*.)

9. Now our Lady has the gift in fulness; not different from us except in degree and perfection. This is her feast.

10. Hence it is that the more we can go to her in simplicity, the more we shall get.

August 26 (*Thirteenth Pentecost*)

THANKFULNESS AND THANKSGIVING

1. The gospel of the day. Were not ten cleansed? etc.

2. Does not this event seem strange? Yet how thankless we are. We have all to condemn ourselves. There is nothing in which our guilt comes more home to us.

3. How we pray beforehand; how we petition again and again. Do we return thanks *even once*?

4. I think this feeling comes upon men, that they are not equal [to the task] ; that *words* will not do ; and so they do nothing from being overpowered. And this grows into a habit ; and thus, when we gain our object, we suddenly leave off our prayers and coldly accept the favour. But still we may show our gratitude by *deeds* and by recurrent remembrance. We might remember the *day* ; we might perpetuate our gratitude.

5. ' Where are the nine ? ' and he, the tenth, was a Samaritan ! (Other instances—woman at the well; good Samaritan.) It is a paradox which is fulfilled, that the less a man has the more he does. The centurion and the Syrophoenician.

6. When we have a number of blessings, we take them as our due. We do not consider that they are so many accumulated mercies. Thus the Jews especially, etc.

7. Now let us think what we can claim of God, and what He has done. Preservation perhaps implied *de congruo* in creation. But how much He has done for us ! for each one in his own way—yet so much to every one, that every one is specially favoured—favoured as no one else.

8. Survey your life, and you will find it a mass of mercies.

9. Hence the saints, three especially—Jacob, David, St. Paul—are instances [of thanksgiving].

10. Close connection with hope and love. This gratitude is the greatest support of hope, and hence those saints who have been patterns of gratitude were patterns of hope.

11. On setting up memorials.

12. Gratitude is even a kind of love, and leads to love. Against *hard* thoughts of God. Not [being] too proud to admit to *ourselves*, ' At least He is good to ME.'

September 2 (*Fourteenth Pentecost*) [1]

SERVICE OF GOD CONTRASTED WITH SERVICE OF SATAN

1. No man can serve two masters.

2. This is true, even *because* they are two, but much more if [they are] opposed. In all things we must throw *our heart* into our work. It is the only way in which any work is done well. This is how men succeed in any line.

3. Yet, though this is certain, men forget it as to religion. They think to serve God without taking His service *exclusively*.

4. What is meant by *exclusive* service ? Is it going out of the world ? No. There are persons so called—but it is not that.

5. But [it is] subordinating all things to God's service. Whether we eat or drink, etc.

Parallel of worldly matters. A worldly man carries his aim into all things. He is thinking of his business wherever he is.

6. So in religion. And this is what is meant by loving *God above all* things. And this is why such love alone keeps us in God's favour.

7. To be religious, then, is not merely to have a

---

[1] ' Not preached.'

respect for religion, to do some of its *duties,* to defend it, to profess it, but

8. It is to live in God's presence ; to know the whole economy of redemption.

9. Hence the necessity of meditation.

10. Warning, because the world is likely to *crush out* our religion.

September 9 (*Fifteenth Pentecost*)

LIFE OF THE SOUL

1. INTROD.—Gospel [Luke vii. 11-16—raising to life of the son of the widow of Naim].

Our Lord's miracles are especially typical—(1) leprosy—heresy ; (2) demoniac—cleansing the soul from the evil spirit ; (3) blind—John ix. ; (4) loaves—so this.

2. It brings before us the natural state of man— state of the whole world [typified in it].

3. What is meant is, *not* that man may not have natural powers, but [being lacking in] spiritual, that left to himself, he will know nothing of the unseen world. In one sense, then, the world is alive, in another dead.

4. It is in this sense that the soul is dead. Now if dead, observe the greatness of that death. (1) Dead men are without sense or feeling : so the soul as to heavenly things, motives, objects, etc. (2) [A dead body provokes] fear and odiousness : so the [dead] soul in the sight of angels and Almighty God.

5. (3) As to the outward form [of the dead] it is the same [as the living], and this suggests much.

(i) Imitation—Christianity in the world. (ii) Simulation, because they *know* more than they *do*, and pretend from shame. (iii) [Souls that are dead may still have] actual grace, [and] habits formed under it.

6. Yet in God's sight [they are] dead. Now consider Eph. ii. [see vv. 4 and 5].[1]

7. Now reflect on all this—the terrible state of the world—in detail ; here, there and everywhere. Yet, as dead men do not know they are dead, neither does the world.

8. On Christ, the sole source of life, from to-day's gospel—Gal. ii.

9. On the love which life implies.

September 16 (*Sixteenth Pentecost*)

SEPTEM DOLORUM—ELECTION

1. INTROD.—Nothing is, of course, so awful as the question of election, about which so much is said in Scripture. It is not to be supposed that I am going into any depths here.

2. The doctrine, as I shall take it, is this, and most practical ; and I will first illustrate it.

3. Take the case of some large and new institution in a nation, which requires a great many new hands, *e.g.* a new department of revenue, a new commission, some speculation abroad, the post office, railroads, the war.

---

[1] ' But God . . . even when we were dead in sins, hath quickened us together in Christ.'

4. Such an institution, especially if a speculation or expedition (1) promises great rewards to those who take part in it ; (2) it is not for every one to get, but he must make interest ; (3) no one will get part in, or receive the rewards of, if he does not join it.

5. Enlarge. As a question of justice. Suppose a man who went on with his own trade, etc., complaining that he had no part of the receipts of a speculation in which he took no part, etc.

6. Apply. Draw out the state of this world—its trades, occupations, aims ; its science, literature, politics, etc. People may acquit themselves well, and get the reward of their occupation, which is the reward of *this world*, *e.g.* such as wealth, fame, etc., etc.

7. But a new system comes in. Almighty God proclaims a different reward, viz. eternal life to those who take part in His objects, etc. You see it is quite distinct from Nature.

8. Enlarge on the *interest made* to get a place— no claim because [a] good father, a good subject, etc., etc.

9. Here, then, we have the election. If we want to take part in it, we must join it.

10. The cross of Christ puts a different complexion on the *whole* of life. If a man takes up any new course, his old ways are flat in comparison.

11. *Septem dolorum* in connection—we must take part with her.

September 23 (*Seventeenth Pentecost*)

LOVE OF GOD

1. INTROD.—The gospel is the second which we have lately had on the precept of the love of God.

2. Nature tells us we should love God. Nay, a natural inclination and leaning to the love of God.

3. Still, it never will lead us to love. It fails for want of strength, and the feeling comes to nothing and dwindles, as a tree of the south planted in the north. Grace essential.

4. On pure love of God—illustrate—single, real, for Himself, *e.g.* we are to love men *propter Deum*, thus *not propter* [*seipsos*], etc., which is Nature. If, then, we love God by association [*sic*], or merely for His benefits, etc., it is not enough.

Love delights in the name of God, likes to hear of Him, likes to think of Him, likes to act for Him, [is] zealous for His honour and a champion for His cause.

5. But this is not all. It is not merely looking at what does not notice us, as the Pantheists say. It is a friendship. Three things are necessary for friendship : (1) mutual love ; (2) mutual consciousness and sympathy ; (3) mutual intimacy—intercourse. Companions, walking with God, Luke xxiv.[1] Apply to confidence in God's loving us.

6. But this is not all—*dilectio* : choice. And no common choice, but *above* all things.

7. Thus it is pure, amicable, mutual and sovereign.

8. Now to see what it is, we may see what it is

[1] The journey to Emmaus.

not ; and parallel it to worldly principles. Take the course of men.

9. (1) They begin with self-indulgence and self-gratification. Here is something which is not love, yet acts as love does.

10. (2) Perhaps ambition, martial spirit. This possesses them—*this* not love.

11. (3) Love of home : [a man is] a good father, a good son, [devotes himself to such duty with] concentration of mind [1]—*this* not love.

12. (4) He gets wealthy, and is tempted to make wealth his *enough*—*this* not love.

13. (5) Love of consistency, character ; self his centre—*this* not love.

14. (6) Ease and comfort in old age—*this* not love.

15. *How* are we to gain love ? By reading of our Lord in the Gospels.

December 25

CHRISTMAS DAY

1. INTROD.—To-day a change in the history of mankind. Many important eras and seasons—this the most important. And it is described in various terms in the services [of the feast]. *Melliflui facti sunt coeli*, etc.

2. All things created good ; but man is fallen.

3. Man fell, and the angels fell before him ; but the case of the two is different. The angels were pure spirits, and have but one nature ; man has two

[1] *I.e.* without reference to God : not for His greater honour and glory.

natures.   Angels are spirit, but man is made up of
soul and body.   An angel is good or bad : if good,
[there is] nothing to resist the good ; if bad, nothing
to resist the bad.   If they fell, they fell once for all.
If man fell, there is a contest between the flesh and
spirit, reason and passion.

4. Man not simple [in his nature] ; [he is made up
of] two principles.   Illustration of these two formidable principles in man, by comparison to man and
beast.   In each heart of man there is what may be
called man's true nature and beast's nature.   Power
of wild animals.   The wild principle of man has
carried him away.

5. It first showed itself in the fall itself—passion
—then Cain and Abel.   Thence it swept over the
world.   Wars, murder, injustice, sensuality, crimes
of all sorts.

6. Thus things [went] continually from bad to
worse, and did Almighty God suffer it, there is no
depth to which man would not descend.   In 1600
years [he had become] so bad that [God sent] the
deluge.

7. The earth restored ; but how vainly !   Man
soon got almost as bad as before.   He cast off God ;
he set up idols ; he tyrannised over others.   He
went on to found states, and he impressed sin upon
them—idolatry mixed up with politics, with all
the usages of society — marriages, business contracts, births, deaths and burials, recreations and
institutions.   And the raising temples and stamp-
ing it on the great cities, and then misusing and
devoting the creature to idolatry, Rom. viii. [20].[1]

  [1] 'For the creature was made subject to vanity.'

And thus sin got so established as to exert a tyranny over each individual. Those who would have been better [were victims of] bad education, ridicule, persecution.

8. And then the struggles of the unregenerate and remorseful.

9. Who can estimate the entire establishment of evil ? In vain judgments, God's pleadings, etc.

10. Now this being so, was it not plain that if there was to be a change, God alone could do it ? If a Redeemer, He must be God. So this is the great event now [beginning].

11. Yet not at once a bloody combat, but a little child.

May 25, 1856 (*Sunday within the Octave of Corpus Christi*)

[DEVOTION TO THE HOLY EUCHARIST]

1. INTROD.—There is no feast, no season in the whole year which is so intimately connected with our religious life, or shows more wonderfully what Christianity is, as that which we are now celebrating. There is a point of view in which this doctrine [of the Body and Blood of Christ] is nearer to our religious life than any other. And now I will explain what I mean.

The Holy Trinity unseen. The Nativity, Easter, etc., past. But this is the record of a present miracle, a present dispensation of God towards us.

2. [In devotion there is always] one difficulty to

counteract. Our Lord came 1800 years ago. How shall we feel reverence of what took place 1800 years ago ? We are touched [with] pity, gratitude, love, by what we see. None of us have seen or heard even those, who saw those who saw those who saw Him.

How shall we learn to live under the eye of God ? Now we know how difficult it is to keep up the memory of things. Then again, books, how little can they do for us ! It is a great thing to be moved [even] once in a way by a book, but we cannot count upon their moving us habitually. Accordingly an historical religion, as it is called, is a very poor and inefficacious [*a word illegible*]. We see it in the case of Protestants. Their religion is historical, in consequence they speak of Christ as a mere historical personage—the titles they give Him, etc., etc.— there is a want of reality, etc.

This is one difficulty in the way of practical devotion.

3. A second difficulty. The world is in wickedness. Satan is god of the world ; unbelief rules. Now this opposition to us has a tendency to weigh us down, to dispirit us, to dull our apprehensions, etc.

These are two extreme difficulties in the way of religion.

Now observe,

4. How almighty love and wisdom has met this. He has met this by living among us with a continual presence. He is not past, He is present now. And though He is not seen, He is here. The same God who walked the water, who did miracles, etc.,

is in the Tabernacle. We come before Him, we speak
to Him just as He was spoken to 1800 years
ago, etc.

5. Nay, further, He [does] not [merely] present
Himself before us as the object of worship, but God
actually gives Himself to us to be received into our
breasts. Wonderful communion. Texts—Father,
Son and Holy Ghost.

6. This [is] how He counteracts time and the
world. It [the Blessed Sacrament] is not past, it is
not away. It is this that makes devotion in lives.
It is the life of our religion. We are brought into
the unseen world.

7. These thoughts are fitly entertained, and themselves increased at this season, when St. Philip's day
comes. Quote passages in his life to show his delight
in the Blessed Sacrament. He has died on this day.
We cannot have a better preparation for his, than
this, feast.

8. Let us rejoice in Jesus, Mary, Philip.

July 27 (*Eleventh Pentecost*)

[ON THE HEALING OF THE DEAF AND DUMB MAN]

1. INTROD.—We read these words in to-day's
gospel, ' They bring unto Him,' etc.[1]

2. The man is cured, and two things go to his
cure—Christ's word and act, and His disciples bring

---

[1] ' They bring unto him one deaf and dumb ; and they besought
him that he would lay his hand upon him.'—Mark vii. 32.

I

him to Him. Christ does not heal without His disciples, and they cannot heal except as bringing to Him.

3. So it is now—the great ordained system—Christ the Author of Grace, and His friends whom He brings round Him, and makes His family, the step towards obtaining grace *by prayer*.

4. Christ can do all things. He created, He redeemed without any one else; but He saved [saves?] through the co-operation of others—by the saints above and the Church below.

5. Christ can do all things—He *gives grace* too, and it is only by His ordained system—merit a promise—a contract, etc., etc.

6. Christ can do all things, and He does not confine Himself to [co-operation of] others, so far as this, that all over the earth, external to His Church, He hears those who call on Him. He has many ways. Every one has a guardian angel. Case of Hagar.

7. *But* He does this to bring them on into His Church, that *they* too may become His friends.

8. And it must be recollected that the Holy Church Universal is praying everywhere [for them]. Mass [continually offered].

9. Abraham and Moses. God reveals that His friends *may* pray, ' I say not that I will ask the Father,' etc.[1]

Therefore it is that we call our Lady our advocate, and the saints intercessors ; for our Lord has made

---

[1] ' In that day you shall ask in My Name : and I say not to you, that I will ask the Father for you : For the Father himself loveth you.'—John xvi. 26-27.

over this lower office to them, and stands in the higher, of the Giver of grace.

10. Thus the salvation of the world is in our hands, [*e.g.* of]

11. England—Birmingham.

12. Therefore let us *pray.*

August 29 (*Fifteenth Pentecost*)

[THE RAISING TO LIFE OF THE SON OF THE WIDOW OF NAIM—LUKE VII. 11-16]

1. INTROD.—The Holy Fathers are accustomed to derive a spiritual lesson from the miracle recorded in the gospel of this day. It was a miracle exercised on one, but it was a sort of specimen of what takes place by God's love so often. It was done once, but it images what occurs continually.

2. This was a young man borne out to his burial, and his mother is weeping over him.

The mother is the Church, who has borne him in baptism, when he was born again and became her child.

He has fallen away, and is dead in sin. He is here carried on his way, like Dives, to be buried in hell.

3. How awfully he is carried forth ! Slowly, but sure, as the course of a funeral.

Describe his odiousness—death so fearful, every one shrinks from the sight. Children in the streets turn away. Those only bear it who love the corpse, or have duties towards it. So *with the soul.* How angels must shrink from the dead soul!—the guardian angel bears it. How horrible it looks even [if in] venial sin, much more in mortal!

The mother bears it—the Church does not excommunicate.

4. Its bearers are four : (1) pride, (2) sensuality, (3) unbelief, (4) ignorance. We see these from Adam's original sin, and they are in every sinner, though perhaps in a different order in different persons. There are those who go on, through God's mercy, in the right way. But I am speaking of cases of sin.

5. Now I believe generally *pride* comes first— obstinacy of children ; disobedience ; quarrelling ; refusing to say prayers ; avoiding holy places, etc. Thus the soul being left open to the evil one, he proceeds to assault it with sensuality.

6. Sensuality. A person does not know when he is proud, but this [sensuality] need not be described, for every one who yields to it knows what it is. God has set a mark upon it, the mark of sting of conscience, because it is so pleasant; whereas pride is unpleasant to the person who exercises it.

7. Thirdly, unbelief. Pride and sensuality give birth to unbelief. A man begins to doubt and disbelieve.

8. Fourth, ignorance. At last he does not know right from wrong.

9. And thus a soul is led out to be buried, to be buried *in hell*. And how many reach that eternal tomb !

10. Wonderful electing grace of God, choosing

one and not another, coming without merit—the Church cannot do it.

11. We all have received it [this electing grace] without merit. Let us prize it when we have it.

September 7 (*Seventeenth Pentecost*)
[LOVE OF OUR NEIGHBOUR]

1. INTROD.—Sometimes it is said that there is one, sometimes two, great commandments. Charity is the great commandment. Though properly the love of God, it involves love of neighbour.

2. We have not seen God. How are we to ascertain that we love Him ? Feelings are deceptive. Thus, as by a test, by loving others, by love of *man*. And so St. John says, 1 John iv. [12].

3. First, we should love man *merely* as the work of God. If we love God, we shall love all His works. Undevout men walk about, and look round, and they never associate what they see with God ; but everything is the work of God. And though we should not be superstitious, we should destroy nothing without a reason. Cruelty to animals [is] as if we did not love God, their Maker ; nay, wanton destruction of plants.

4. Thus, even if mankind were of a different species, as fellow-beings [they would have] a relationship [to us].

5. But they are *of our blood*, Acts xiv. Adam [our one father].

6. And all involved in Adam's sin—the sympathy

of sin, as all in sin, in misery and transgression, and in danger of ruin.

7. Hence Gen. xviii.,[1] Ps. cxviii. 139.[2]   St. Paul, Rom. ix. [3],[3] Acts xvii. [26].[4]   Our Lord weeping over Jerusalem.   Missionaries to heathen countries, as St. Augustine who came here.

8. Of course, zeal for God *also* [moved these to heroism], but the sight of souls dying [more directly].

9. Still more if Christians, for then we are brought near to God.   He who dwelt in solitary light once, now has round Him a *circle* of holy beings, so that we cannot love Him without loving them.   Hence the glory paid to saints, as His garment.

10. Besides, we love the *divine* attributes and character *in* the saints : ' He who loveth God, loveth His brother also.'

11. This the condemnation of those who oppose the Church.

12. On the other hand—love of saints—love of our Lady as God's mother, [a] sign of predestination. She the great work [*i.e.* the greatest of God's works] and the glory of our race.   Let us at this season beg her to make us full of that love of herself, and of all those who have God's grace, and of all whom God has made.

---

[1] Abraham interceding for Sodom and Gomorrah.

[2] ' My zeal hath made me pine away : because my enemies forgot thy words.'

[3] ' I wished myself to be an anathema from Christ for my brethren.'

[4] ' He hath made of one all mankind.'

SEVEN DOLOURS

1. INTROD.—The most soothing of all the feasts
of Mary. What a contrast the first portion of the
Blessed Virgin's history is to the latter ! We sinners
have no sympathy with the first part of her life.
She had nothing but joy, increasing up to that day
which heralded its reverse. It was at the height
of her earthly joy that the reverse began—her seven
dolours.

We say seven, but that is a perfect number only ;
her woes were continuous.

2. Go through her life—Presentation, Annunciation, Visitation, the Nativity, Shepherds, Magi,
Purification—and then we hear of a sword. And
the flight into Egypt ; avoiding Herod ; loss of
our Lord in the Temple ; death of St. Joseph ; [our
Lord] leaving her to preach ; [His] crucifixion and
[her] bereavement.

3. Parallels of Moses, Deut. xxviii. Solomon at
dedication ; and Transfiguration with prophecy of
suffering ; and so riding in triumphantly into
Jerusalem, and ' Crucify Him ! '

4. Yet in truth it would seem that she knew it all
from the first, though we don't know *when* it was
told her. This is something which equalises the
two [portions of her life]—the knowledge beforehand
[of her woes]. And it is this which gives a character to her whole life. All through that first calm
time. she knew it was but the stillness before the

storm, and she could not enjoy what was so joyful.
All along there was the vision of One lifted on the
cross, and the sword pierces her heart.

5. Describe the cross—and she by it! This is
the key of her life on earth.

6. Ignorance is bliss—animals, men [even] do
not know what is to happen to them.

7. And this was the peculiarity of her life.
[Bodily] pain, trouble, etc., come at fixed times and
go, but it is otherwise with mental : foresight and
memory make them continuous. This is the sword
in Mary's heart, the peculiarity of it being that it is
mental.

8. And again she did nothing—only suffered—
did nothing indeed, except in internal acts. A
champion acts, and a martyr acts. Hers was mere
suffering.

9. And especially the sight of the suffering of
another which we cannot help. A mother seeing
her child suffer. Case of Hagar.

10. Many a wife, many a mother stands by and
says, ' O that I could take a part ! ' Martyrs declar-
ing themselves, and suffering because others were.
[Yet Mary suffered] not like Hagar,[1] but like the
brave mother in the Maccabees.

11. This is the *compassio* of Mary.

12. Suitable to us, most soothing of feasts : for
mental pain more widely spread than bodily, in this
age especially. Care, anxiety from difficulty of live-
lihood,—[those terrors of an] intellectual age—madness and heartache ; remorse at sin. In all Mary
is our sympathy and comfort, etc., etc.

[1] ' I will not see the boy die.'—Gen. xxi. 16.

October 12 (*Twenty-second Pentecost*)

THE MATERNITY OF MARY

1. INTROD.—There is no feast of our Lady which comprehends so much as this. It is a sort of central feast. It connects all that is taught about her in one.

2. A number of feasts look *towards* it—the [Immaculate] Conception, Birth, Purification, Visitation, Nativity. Her becoming a mother is the scope in which they end. For this all her graces, etc., *because* she was to be the Mother of God, and a temple set apart for Him.

3. What is meant by being the Mother of God ? Mother of the Person of the Son—God's blood—God's flesh, etc., and so God's Mother.

4. So high an office *required* a due preparation, as St. John the Baptist or the apostles, but much more.

5. And the reward and power [were in] proportion. *Monstra te esse Matrem.*

6. And thus we are brought to that other set of doctrines included in the Maternity. For she is our mother as well as God's. And thus this feast becomes not only one of the most wonderful, but of the most soothing.

7. Two natures in Christ—so she was mother of Him who was God as well as man. ' Behold I and my children,' etc., Heb. ii. 13.

8. Hence, ' Behold thy Son—[Behold] thy Mother,' John xx.

9. Here is its connection with the seven dolours.

Her first birth without pain ; her birth of us with
pain.

10. It became her who was to be a mother to us,
to be so far like other mothers as to have pain.

11. On the constant, unwearied affection of a
mother's love ; (on many not having experienced it)
but nothing extinguishes it. The father gives up
the son, brothers despair of him, but she remains
faithful to the end, hopes against hope, does not
mind slights, ingratitudes, etc.

12. Here you have the maternity of Mary. You
cannot weary her, she never reproaches, etc. Therefore do we pray her to help us in the *hour of death*,
for she will not leave us.

13. Especially as men get old and lose their earthly
relations and those who knew them when young.

14. Who are our constant friends but our guardian
angel, who has been with us since our youth, and
Mary, who will be with us to the end ?

October 19 (*Twenty-third Pentecost*)

PURITY OF MARY

1. INTROD.—If there is one thing more than
another which marks Christianity, it is the honour
given to virginity. We, who have ever heard the
doctrine, cannot fancy how it must come upon the
heathen at the beginning by the *contrast*.

2. And indeed the Holy Fathers appeal to it from
the first as a great miracle. When we consider
the state of the heathen, etc. So wonderful that

numbers of persons should be found who were willing
to debar themselves even of the marriage state,
living in chastity.

3. Moses, Aaron, the Priests, the Prophets.

4. Nay, the Jews—hardness of the heart, divorce,
polygamy.

5. Nay, celibacy was not held in honour even from
a religious reason. They each wished to be mother
of the Messias.

6. Hence the force of the prophecy, ' A virgin
shall conceive.' And when the time came, St. John
the Baptist went before Him a virgin. He Himself,
the Messias, pre-eminently such ; and His Virgin
Mother, and His favourite disciple, the other John,
St. Paul, and all of them, either gave up their wives
or had none.

7. Hence we see the force of the doctrine of the
Immaculate Conception. A new thing was coming
upon the earth. It was fitting that it should begin
with a new beginning, as Adam's at the first—of
grace before sin.

8. A new thing, though Joshua,[1] Elias, Eliseus.

9. The heathen philosophers, stern, proud, etc.,
whereas, St. Gregory insists, humility must be with
chastity, and our Lady a special instance of humility.

10. But further, the celibacy of false religions has
been negative—the *absence of love.*

11. This indeed is what is imputed to us—blighted
affections. The peculiarity of Christian celibacy is
that it is from love to God—' and followed Thee.'
St. Jerome in Breviary.

[1] See Note 11, p. 338.

12. The more we love God, the more we are drawn off from *earth*.

13. The Blessed Virgin's Purity arose from the excess of her love.

December 25 (*Christmas Day*)

OMNIPOTENCE IN SUBJECTION

1. INTROD.—(1) They say that love does not reason, *i.e.* so intent on [its] object that it does not regard itself or its own feelings ; and so of adoration and praise. Thus Christ was born in silence ; not a word from our Lady or St. Joseph, or the shepherds or the magi. The angels indeed, but very briefly.

And thus, I suppose, we all feel little disposed to speak to-day, as interfering with enjoyment. (2) A second reason is, because love has so *many* thoughts which reason cannot draw out fully and do justice to. Or, if we preach, we do it for the honour of the day.

2. If we speak, the first natural thought [is] that every feast, as it comes, is the *best*. Nothing like Christmas. But really we have reason to say so. Easter is the higher, but the sufferings of Christ, which we contemplated, are a shock which sudden reversal to good does not remove. And our own sin and penance [have preceded it].[1] But Christmas [is] as if we had never sinned. Some divines think that Christ would have come into the world though man had not sinned. Thus this feast has not necessarily the idea of sin in it, though in fact

[1] See Note 12, p. 338.

Christ came for our sin. Seeing the end from the
beginning, as Moses seeing the [promised] land,
through a valley of conflicts.

3. But if, for the honour of the day, I must take
one thought or lesson to put before you, it shall be
the adorable marvellousness of what may be called
the humiliation of the Divine Being, as at this
time of year. (1) Omnipotent—what He can do—
create and destroy worlds—He can do what He will,
therefore it would seem that God *could not* humble
Himself. (2) Idea that God is so high that He cannot listen to man. (3) For consider who He is. [He
has] no [obligation of] justice towards us, as none
on our part towards beasts. (4) If He only *attended*
to us (texts to the contrary, Isa. lvii.—' Inhabiteth
eternity ' ; ' Shall God dwell on earth ? ' [1] If ' Emmanuel ' only meant this). (5) But He has taken
our nature.

4. Now observe particulars. (1) Nine months in
His mother's womb ; (2) swathing bands ; (3)
infant—carried about, etc. : Simeon—Egypt ; (4)
subject to them, when He even displayed what
He really was ; (5) worked at trade ; (6) laid hold
of, as beside Himself ; (7) His Passion ; (8) His
Crucifixion ; (9) now in Tabernacle ; (10) in our
breasts.

5. Example to us. We are most of us in subjection ; why not sanctify it ?

6. This St. Philip [did] by sacraments, humility,
detachment, purity, and joy or peace, and cheerfulness.

[1] ' Is it then to be thought that God should indeed dwell upon
earth ? '—3 Kings viii. 27.

December 28 (*Sunday—Holy Innocents*)

SUFFERING

1. INTROD.—The three feasts about Christmas, as if to tame down its joy, bring before us suffering.

2. And so the events about our Lord's Nativity : (1) Circumcision, (2) Purification, ' [a] sword,' etc., (3) Epiphany—massacre of infants.

3. Remarkable that the children should suffer, because it is the age of innocence.

4. It suggests to us the doctrine of original sin— that man has fallen. Pain would not be, with man upright. Here then we have a proof that man is under God's displeasure—*pain* not death.

5. Sufferings of children : (1) from illness, (2) from cruel parents, etc. *Nothing worse than* to see a helpless child in great pain.

6. But, however, the Holy Innocents were otherwise circumstanced. This martyrdom was an [entrance] into the Church. Their sufferings meritorious.

7. St. Rose and other holy women, who inflicted on themselves penances extraordinary.

8. The Church like a joint-stock (all who share it must be cleansed).

9. Let us rejoice in this feast then ; particularly it is for mothers whose children suffer. *All the sufferings of baptized children merit,* and all innocent profit in suffering.

10. Let us thank Him who turned sufferings of children to account.

11. The merits of saints ever growing, of martyrs, and souls going from purgatory to heaven ; *of children suffering and dying in infancy.*

January 4, 1857 (*Octave of Holy Innocents*)

PASSAGE OF TIME

1. INTROD.—All times, all days are the beginning of a year, but especially when the date changes.

2. Time, as present, is momentary, as future, is unknown, as past, is irrevocable.

3. As present, momentary. No standing still. While we speak, it goes. We are all older when we leave this church than when we enter it. Whether it be joy or sorrow, it goes. We look forward to a great day ; we keep a great festival. It comes once in a year. [As] grains in an hour-glass, it is gone ere it is well come.

4. And on what road is this swift time driving ? On a road of darkness. We are every moment entering and driving along an unknown future—on a steam-engine on a railroad in the dark. Accidents may happen any moment. Unseen dangers waiting for us. Balaam and the angel. Hence Jacob asking God's blessing on his journey. St. Raphael. We are not merely journeying, we are rushing forward, and to what ?

5. To judgment. On the importance of time.

6. Thirdly, the past is irrevocable. What would we give to wipe out much !

7. On the necessity of taking good heed how we spend time. Counsel of perfection never to misuse time. Vow by some saints.

8. *Desideria efficacia et sterilia.*

9. Let us begin the new year well.

April 5 (*Palm Sunday*)

FALLING AWAY

1. INTROD.—Too awful a subject commonly, as leading [men] to despond ; yet useful sometimes, and natural at this season.

2. Now first let us lay down about nature and grace—[that] nature can do many things, but cannot bring to heaven. Grace is like a new nature, and joins us to the heavenly family ; and they are saved who die with this grace ; those lost who are without it.

3. This answers the question : Will good departed from avail ? As some Protestants say, ' Look how a man lives, not how he dies '—(explain).

4. Proof, Ezech. xviii. [24]. And rightly, for the sovereign Lord of heaven can prescribe His terms.

5. Now this chapter leads to a further thought, viz. that much as is said to encourage repentance, as much perhaps is said to warn against falling, as if the prospect, or chance, or issue on the whole were equal.

6. *E.g.* our Lord, ' I came not to call.' But on the other hand, recollect the number of passages such as ' Two shall be in the field'; ' Ten virgins'; ' He that persevereth,' etc. ; ' Many that are first,' etc.

7. So St. Paul, preacher of repentance : but Heb. vi. [4-6].[1]

8. So holy Simeon, ' This child [for the fall,

[1] ' For it is impossible for those who were once illuminated, . . . and are fallen away, to be renewed again to penance.'

and for the resurrection of many in Israel,' Luke
ii. 34].

9. This text of holy Simeon especially fulfilled
at Passion, when two special examples.

10. Multitude on Palm Sunday, *vide* their being
in grace [implied] in the prayers [second and last]
in the Blessing of Palms. Cp. our Lord's weeping—
disappointment of the foolish virgins.

11. Judas. Our Lord chose him when he was
in grace—trace about him—'the ten indignant,'
Mark x. 32, etc.[1]

12. Some fall away at one age, some at another.
Go through this.

13. On natural habits produced by supernatural
acts deceiving the old.

14. Our Lady. Prayer—pray *lest* we fall, if we
fall, and for others.

May 31

WHITSUNDAY

1. INTROD.—If we get to heaven, the wonderful
peace will be our great blessedness, the blessedness
of the end having come. And not only the end, but
the consummation, for not only will labour be over,
but our reward will have come.

2. To-day is the nearest approach we have to
such a consummation. Describe 'in one place,' etc.[2]
To-day we celebrate the day when Almighty God
exhausted His gifts upon us. They were long

---

[1] At the request of the sons of Zebedee.

[2] 'And when the days of Pentecost were accomplished, they
were all together in one place.'—Acts ii. 1.

K

promised, but on this day they were all poured out. He emptied the fulness of His mercy on us this day.

3. Long have we been following the course, from Christmas to Easter, etc. ; but now the end has come. We are called upon to be thankful for, and enjoy what we have been anticipating.

4. So was it at the first Pentecost, and more strikingly still. For ages had the Church been expecting this day, etc.

5. And again so different from their expectations. This happens to *us*. We pray, and we do not get our answer. Yet we do in a higher way. So the apostles. (1) They did not know their Lord was to suffer ; (2) that He was to go. Yet He said, ' If I go not away,' etc.[1] Yet the fulness, when it came, did not disappoint them.

6. All our infirmities, sins, etc., are reversed in the coming of the Holy Ghost. Sin is gone, fear is gone, etc.

7. All that we have of good comes from this day. All the sacraments from this day. If baptism gives, etc., it is from the day of Pentecost. If confirmation, if penance, etc. If [the Holy] Eucharist. If faith, if hope, etc. If chastity.

8. It is life for death. If we are dry, if cold, if defiled, if sickly, if wounded, etc. It is the sweet refreshing breath. If we are to overcome the foe, etc. If we have a refrigerium in purgatory. If at last we mount to heaven.

9. This day especially St. Philip's feast. He preached for fallen Christendom. We too.

---

[1] ' If I go not, the Paraclete will not come to you ; but if I go, I will send him to you.'—John xvi. 7.

October 11

DURING EXPOSITION FOR TROUBLES IN INDIA

1. When our Lord was on the Cross, He said, ' Father, forgive them.'

2. Now we know well what the obvious lesson of that prayer is. It shows the love of the Creator in compassionating His children when they were sinning; nay, sinning with the most awful intensity of outrage, for they were wounding, torturing, putting to death that nature which He had assumed.

3. But there is a further reflection perhaps, not so obvious, to be deduced from it, and which is very much to our purpose to consider, in reference to the great calamities which have on this day been so solemnly brought before our consideration by our bishop, and in consequence by us before the throne of grace.

4. He Himself, though ineffably holy in His human nature, still had that very same nature which in them who assailed Him was capable of such sin. If they were of His nature, on the other hand, He was of theirs. If they had the guilt of being His brethren, He had the shame of being theirs. We know how ashamed men commonly are when any one connected with them does anything wrong. The bad deed of any one of our blood is in a certain sense our own bad deed, and is an humiliation. Now our Lord, in His own proper nature as God, is infinitely separate from all beings whatever, but He

took on Him a created, a human, a frail nature, when He came on earth. He became a child of Adam. He took on Him that fallen nature which He had made perfect at the time that He created [it], but which had lost its perfection, and which anyhow was always [in] its own essence and by itself frail. If angelic natures have, separate from the grace of God, imperfection, much more has man's nature. Our Lord took on Him a nature which in any other (except His mother) but Him would be sure to sin. He took on Himself a nature which nothing but the grace of God could save from running into sin, from that inherent imperfection which attaches to the creature. He [His human nature] could not sin, but the reason why it could not was not because it was intrinsically higher or better than the nature of any other son of fallen Adam, but because the presence of Himself in it, of Himself who was God, rendered it utterly removed from sin and incompatible with it. Still, His human nature was such that, had it not been His, it might have sinned. But it never was by itself, it never had been without Him. From the first moment of its existence He had taken it up into Himself; He had created it for Himself, and thus it was absolutely and eternally secured from all sin.

5. But still He would know and understand, infinitely more than we can, the shame of having a nature which was in itself peccable. And therefore the sins of all His brethren weighed on Him, and were in one sense His, because He partook their nature, had a share in a common possession which was a very shameful possession. In this sense,

though most pure, He bore Him a body of death and the sins of the whole world.

6. At various times He shows this feeling : when He sighed and said ' Ephpheta ' ; when He wept at Lazarus's grave. These were the signs of the burden He was bearing, who, in partaking our nature, had *in solidum* the sins of that nature on Him. And so in the Garden, when He sweated drops of blood, it was the weight of that fallen nature which He had assumed which made Him weary even unto death.

7. And when He was on the cross, He had this additional woe, that the evil of human nature now showed itself in a new way, as rising up against Him who bore it. It was the climax of its depravity, that it turned against Him who for its sake had voluntarily put it on. And, while He felt its ingratitude, He felt perhaps equally its shame, as the father of a family is ashamed of his sons' acts against him, and though he feel them, dare not mention them, because they fall back upon himself.

8. And therefore, when He was lifted up upon the cross, He would not be angry with His torturers, lest it would seem as if it were His own act, for it was the act of that very nature in others which He bore Himself, and, as when we have a hand or a foot in pain, we are not angry with it, but feel a tenderness towards it, so He felt a tenderness to that fallen nature which was showing itself so awfully devilish in His persecutors, for it was His own.

9. My brethren, I do not know whether you see whither I am leading you by this train of thought.

We are on this day engaged, in obedience to the call of our bishop, etc.

10. Now I suppose most of us have heard something or other of those indescribable horrors which have been perpetrated by the revolted Hindoos and Mahomedans in the instance of our dear countrymen and countrywomen in India.

11. (Go through them.)

12. We are not only horrified, but angry. Dost thou well to be angry ? It is very horrible, but let us not ' think it strange,' 1 Peter iv.

13. Now I don't doubt the right of the Ruler. ' Vengeance is mine,' ' not the sword in vain.' But Catholics, of all people, have nothing to do with rule or responsibility in India.

14. What I am impressing on you is that these enormities belong to our nature, and that we ought to consider that we are of one blood with [those who did them], have one nature, and that that nature is such as might cover it. There is not any one of us but might in other circumstances have committed the same. (Hazael,[1] 'Thou art the man,' 2 Kings xii.[2] I assure you, my brethren, I speak in earnest when I say that, much as you pity the persecuted, yet should [you] pity the persecutors more.)

15. Instances to show it in every age and country.

[1] ' Their strong cities thou wilt burn with fire, and their young men thou wilt kill with the sword, and thou wilt dash their children, and rip up their pregnant women. And Hazael said, But what, am I thy servant a dog, that I should do this great thing ? '—4 Kings viii. 12-13.

[2] 'And Nathan said to David, Thou art the man.'—2 Kings xii. 7.

16. Therefore I say to any person who indulges in any bitter feeling about these dreadful trans-actions, that the question is whether that feeling is not the same in kind, though different in degree, with that which at this minute is making our soldiers in India, according to the confession of their officers, *demons*.   How do we make matters better by sharing and propagating the savageness of human nature ? 'Thou art the man.'   Hazael.

17. I turn to a truer view. These sufferings, certainly of children, are martyrdoms [*vide* sermon, December 28, 1856].   And how many brought to repentance.   The long suspense described by a lady in a letter from Cawnpore.   Her little child restless and nervous, etc., etc.   Priests and nuns have suffered.

18. May Our Blessed Lady, whose Maternity this day is, protect them.

19. Let us pray that it may all be overruled to our country's good.

Instances.

1. The savage conquerors in the East—Zingis, Timour, etc.   ' Zingis depopulated the whole country from the Danube to the Baltic in a season, and the ruins of the cities and churches were strewed with the bones of the inhabitants.   He allured the fugitives from the wood under a promise of pardon, got them to gather in the corn and grapes, and then put them all to death.   At one place he put to death 300 noble ladies in his presence.   He divided cities into three parts.   He left the infirm and old,

enlisted all the young men into his army, made the
women, the rich, and the artisans his slaves.   Almost
fabulous his slaughters : at Maru 1,300,000, at
Herat 1,600,000, at Neisabour 4,647,000.'   ' Timour
at Delhi massacred 100,000 prisoners, because some
of them showed exultation when the army of their
countrymen came into sight.   At Ispahan 70,000
human skulls, at Baghdad 90,000.'

2. The Persian shah about fifty years ago, in
Morier's *Zohrab* : three bushels of eyes at Asturabad.

3. Herod with the innocents.   Persians and Rome
savage persecutors of Christians.   Tortures.

4. Middle Ages. (From the newspapers of the
last week.) When the Norman barons conquered
England, they persecuted the poor English in the
most savage ways to gain money or their submission.
The *Saxon Chronicle* says : ' The men were hung by
the feet and by the thumbs, and thus smoked over
a smouldering fire.   Knotted strings about their
heads and pulled tight till they pierced the brain.
They were put into dungeons with adders and toads ;
they were put into chests too short and narrow to
hold them, and thus were crushed.   They were
attached by sharp iron collars to a beam, so that
they could in no ways sit, nor lie, nor sleep, but
they must bear the iron.   Thus many thousands
were exhausted by hunger.'

5. Guicciardini and Muratore.

6. The German and Spanish soldiers of Charles v.
in Rome, just before St. Philip's time, on getting
possession of Rome, put to death 4000 soldiers and
inhabitants.   I will not stop to speak of their
plunder of the great riches which it contained, but

I am speaking of their savage cruelties. They got
all the cardinals, bishops, prelates and nobles they
could, and put them to the torture to extract money
from them. (St. Caietan.) They carried off the
noble Roman ladies, and the nuns from all the
convents, and treated them to the most horrible
outrages. Their shrieks resounded on all sides.
And this went on for days. Many died in their
torments, and soon afterwards. It was worse than
the Goths. Only a few years ago, as many as sixty
priests are said to have been shot by the triumvirs
at Rome.[1]

7. Not much more than a hundred years ago,
there was an attempt in Scotland to place the old
royal family upon the throne, and a rising of the
people. After the English had got a victory, they
put the wounded Highlanders to death in cold
blood. They dragged them out of the huts or
thickets and shot them, or dispatched them with
the stocks of their guns. One farm-house with
twenty wounded men in it, they burned to the
ground ; and all this though the Highlanders had
been behaving in the most noble and generous and
merciful way to the wounded English. Moreover,
they brought together into heaps all the wounded
from the field of battle, ran them through with their
swords, and cut the throats of those who were found
sick in bed.

8. And a century before that, Cromwell and his
English soldiers had committed as great, or greater,
atrocities in Ireland. When he took Drogheda,
he offered quarter to all who would lay down their

[1] In 1848.

arms. And when they did so, he broke his word, and began an indiscriminate slaughter. The massacre lasted for five days, so that the streets literally ran with blood. They killed not only the soldiers who were in arms against him, but the inhabitants of the town. A thousand fled for safety to the church, and he killed them all in it. He then marched to Wexford, and did the same. He killed here, too, the inhabitants as well as the soldiers. Three hundred women gathered round the great cross of the place ; they were all put to the sword. Some writers say that the slaughter at Wexford amounted to 5000, and Cromwell himself confessed that it was as much as 2000.

9. Nay, what is the state of feeling of our own soldiers at this minute in India ? You will say they have reason ; but who has not a reason ? The Hindoos have thought they had. Now what do we read ? One of the officers before Delhi writes : ' We must have blood. The streets of Delhi will be a fearful sight. Our men are mad for revenge.' Another says : ' I only trust all the women and children will have been removed (by the time we take the place), for when we are once inside few will be spared.' Another says : ' Our men cannot be restrained, and they are *like demons* let loose.' Another says : ' I believe the city will be given up to three days' plunder. I fear it will make our Europeans very undisciplined. Heaven knows, they are hard enough to control here ; but when they have once gone in like bloodhounds, and been allowed to plunder, they will be downright demons.' These things are perhaps going on now.

April 11, 1858 (*Low Sunday*)

[THE CHURCH]

1. INTROD.—Last week I spoke of one of those
great and august works with which our Lord followed
up the great Act of Sacrifice, viz. the foundation of
His Church. Nor can there be a more suitable time
than this season to speak of it, considering it was
the chief concern, as far as we know, of the forty
days ; *vide* the gospel of this day.

2. Now in this we differ from all other religions
about us. They all profess to have the truth as
well as we profess it, but there is one thing they
do not profess, viz. that their religious society is
founded by Almighty God. We do of ours.

3. And since they do not profess it, they will not
let *us* have what they have not themselves.

4. State the doctrine. We profess, not only our
religion, but our society to come from Almighty
God ; we profess it to be divine. We profess it to
have a multitude of privileges, etc.

5. Now you may be asked sometimes by a serious
objector, sometimes by an inquirer, how it is that
we know that the Church comes from God ? I
answer that it bears the proof of it to all serious
men on its very face, if they will but be patient to
examine ; and I will say how.

6. I said on Good Friday concerning the world
that its strength is in the *look* of things. Men
associate together, say the same thing, and seem
strong. They keep up appearances. But there is
an *inside* to things as well as an *outside*. And here

is the weakness of the world as a prophet, that it does not touch the inside.

7. Men cannot live for ever on externals. They have heart, affections and aspirations, and the world cannot satisfy these. They have a conscience; they sin, and need direction.

8. Now this is what our Saviour, when on earth, did for His disciples; and thus He attached them to Him. He was a living object of worship—(1) He gave pardon; (2) He gave direction.

9. When He went, He said He would not leave them orphans.

10. This was fulfilled in the Church: (1) pardon, (2) direction, (3) presence—(enlarge).

11. Hence suited to our *need*—(enlarge).

12. Faith only requisite.

April 25 (*Third Easter*)

[THE HOLY EUCHARIST]

1. INTROD.—Passage in to-day's gospel: 'Yet a little while.'[1] *Vide* also John xiv.

2. This brings before us the thought of the Holy Eucharist, in which it is so wonderfully fulfilled.

3. (This great marvel or miracle, describe generally. Some remarks on it.)

4. Now first, the doctrine of the Resurrection. How wonderful this is. Describe it. It is as stupendous a miracle as any, though luckily Protestants retain it.

---

[1] 'A little while, and now you shall not see me: and again, a little while, you shall see me.'—John xvi. 16.

5. Another marvel. The risen Body shall ascend to heaven and live there for ever and ever.

6. Now see what this implies. We cannot suppose that our present gross bodies shall be in God's presence for eternity. Accordingly St. Paul says that ' we shall all be *changed* ' [1]—' animal body and spiritual body.' [2]

7. Now our Lord as the first-fruits is already gone to heaven, therefore His Body would be altered.

8. Now we know in a way what great changes matter goes through—ice, melting iron, gas. On the butterfly as an emblem.

9. Four great properties [of a glorified body]— impassibility, activity, brightness, subtlety. Again (1) doors being shut (subtlety), (2) appearing and disappearing (activity) : another form [of activity], ascending up on high, (3) brightness, Apoc. i. [14-15].

10. Two others : (1) in many places at once, (2) at a point. As to the second, how did He get through doors ? Child increasing, growing, etc. As to the first, God a spirit. His appearing to St. Paul.

11. These two in the Holy Eucharist.

12. Let us adore.

13. How wonderful, by making it a miracle, He has kept it secret, for the *world will not believe*, John xiv., xvii. And so when He was on earth, John i. [5].

---

[1] 1 Cor. xv. 51, 52.

[2] 'Seminatur corpus animale, surget corpus spiritale.'—1 Cor. xv. 44.

May 30 (*Trinity Sunday*)
[THE BLESSED TRINITY]

1. INTROD.—This is the everlasting mystery. All other mysteries arise in *time*, this in eternity.

2. No words of man can explain it. Three are one. Now soul and body are one, all the faithful are one. The soul, when enveloped in the Divine Essence, hereafter is one with it. But no illustration of earth can give the faintest shadow of the truth.

3. Yet though so difficult for the reason, it is not difficult for devotion, and thus is fulfilled the saying, ' Thou hast hid these things from the wise and prudent, and revealed them to Thy little ones.'

4. For each truth concerning the Holy Trinity is easy. It is their *combination* is the mystery. Exemplify. That there should be one God—that God should be called or be the Father—that He should be the Son—that He should be the Holy Ghost—but that all three propositions [four] should be true.[1]

5. Explain more fully. The Father is absolutely the One God, as if no Son and Spirit, etc. All the attributes, etc. belong to the *Father*, and to the Son, etc. Whatever the Father does or is, that the Son does or is—not as two, but One.

6. But they divide offices in mercy to our infirmity.

7. Now for devotion. The Father, the Creator, the Preserver, Governor, Judge. Source of all good; the harbour of our rest ; heaven, etc.

8. The Son has taken on Him our nature, etc.

9. Holy Ghost Sanctifier, etc.

10. Now while we address each in *devotion* as the

[1] See Note 13, p. 340.

One God, we may leave it to the next world how Each of Three can be the One God.

11. The joy of heaven, when all mysteries will be removed.

January 30, 1859 (*Fourth Epiphany*)
BLESSED SEBASTIAN VALFRE

1. INTROD.—The day. Blessed Sebastian born about thirty years after St. Philip's death.

2. General resemblance between the two : (1) St. Philip's early devotion to God ; no mortal sin ; hard life, long life, and hidden life. (2) Blessed Sebastian the same.   More is known of his boyhood —(give instances).   Like St. Philip, he labours till the day of his death.   Circumstances of his death.

3. Differences from St. Philip : (1) St. Philip without object [in life at first].   *Others* go to Rome for preferment.   He did not aim at being priest ; he did not aim at founding a Congregation—like Benedictines, no great *work*,[1] but [like] St. Vincent of Paul, e.g. *works*.   (2) Blessed Sebastian had the definite object of being a priest.

4. Hence Blessed Sebastian's particular character—of priestly, pastoral work of every kind—(go into details).   *He* differed from other priests [of his time] in his *incessant* work.

5. Well is it that his feast is this year on a Sunday, for we have just set up an altar to him.

[1] 'These early Religious [*i.e.* the first Benedictines] . . . had little or nothing to do with ecclesiastical matters or secular politics ; they had no large plan of action for religious ends ; they let each day do its work as it came.'—'The Mission of St. Philip,' *Sermons on Various Occasions*, p. 225.

6. And well is his feast at this time of the year, for it is the time we came to Birmingham.

7. We have been now ten years in Birmingham, and when I thank God for what He has allowed us to do, I can suitably do it, for I have had less to do with it than others. You know how many of us have devoted ourselves to missionary work.

8. Pray then for us—(details).

9. And pray for The Oratory at Turin—(details). Subscribing to the Achilli fund ; our going there— [their] simplicity of life, etc. Their present troubles. Little to choose between one country and another. All good men persecuted.

August 19, 1860 (*Twelfth Pentecost*)

GOD THE STAY OF ETERNITY

1. INTROD.—The gospel says, ' What shall I do to inherit ? ' etc. Here this man, whatever his own character, asks an all-important question.

2. He implies the soul will live for ever.

3. What is eternity ? Why, it is awful. I cannot call it good in itself. Some good and wise people have said so, but for me it is the most awful thought in the world.

Consider it. Time breaks to pieces everything ; much more does eternity. Our soul can never die, but it can get older and older. Fancy this—older and older, colder and colder, so that the longer we lived the more miserable [we should become]. Therefore, when I look at eternity itself, it is a sort of living death to creatures such as man, and no good. Who can bear the weight of eternal years ?

4. The scribe, then, does not ask for 'living for ever,' but for 'eternal life.' Life is something more than living; it is to live vigorously, to be always young, etc., etc. Many have *no* youth, as some years have no spring. It is therefore to be happy, and happier and happier as time goes on.

5. This being the case, it is plain also that nothing but what is infinite can sustain eternity. We read in romances of two persons determining to die, and die together, and care for nothing else, not even God —vain thought! We want something more than ourselves, something more than the creature. We must be associated then, and one with the Creator.

6. God then, the Almighty and the Infinite, is the only stay of eternity.

7. Now then we see the meaning of our Lord's answer to the scribe, of loving God, for He alone is eternal, and unless we are conformed to Him, we shall be miserable in eternity.

8. Let us learn to love. We know what it is on earth to love a person. Signs of love—liking the presence, speech, etc., of the loved person; taking up his opinions, etc., etc.

September 2 (Fourteenth Pentecost)

[THE HOLY ANGELS—I]

1. INTROD.—This month leads us to think of the holy angels. It is a far larger subject than I can get through this evening. There are two points of view in which they are to be considered—in nature, and in grace. And this evening I will speak of what they are in their nature.

L

2. God created them in the beginning of all things, with all other things which He created. When He created the heavens He created them, and He created them *in* the heavens. Here is the vast difference from earth; for man was created *on earth*, in order that in time he might attain to the heavens.

3. Simple spirits—hence no form—angels *with wings*. Mere appearances—as in the Holy Eucharist.

4. No shackle of body. We too are spirits, but in bodies (bodies *part* of us, disembodied saints *desire* their bodies). Hence we are *sluggish, passionate,* etc. Hence *we sleep,* not they. We cannot move about quickly ; they in the twinkling of an eye from heaven to earth.

5. *Most perfect of creatures*—the *image of God's attributes.*

6. Their knowledge most comprehensive. They do not *learn,* they do not discover, but at once from their nature they know intuitively all things of the world ; whereas the greatest philosophers with pains only knew a little.

7. They know God and His attributes by nature, even without grace. They understand His attributes, etc. They see God in all things, never being seduced by the creature, as separate from Him.

8. They have a natural love of God, from the perfection of their *reason.* They love Him above all things.

9. They love each other—and each order of angels, in its own degree, fittingly.

10. Three points which they have not by nature : (1) knowledge of the future ; (2) of the heart ; (3) of the mysteries of grace.

CONCLUSION.—Many wonderful things in this world, but an angel more wonderful than all. If a creature so wonderful what the Creator ?

September 9 (*Fifteenth Pentecost*)

THE HOLY ANGELS—II

1. INTROD.—Recapitulate. The Creator might make ten thousand worlds, each more perfect than the preceding, all more perfect than this. We know of but one besides this—the universe of angels. This may be otherwise. The angelic world differs from this, in that each part is perfect and independent of any other part.

2. Differences, but they *all* excel in two things naturally—(1) strength, (2) purity.

3. Purity—' As the angels '[1]—no bodies. Strength —Exod. xii.[2]; 2 Kings xxiv.[3]; 4 Kings xix.[4] Their voice—Apoc. x. [3][5]; 1 Thess. iv. [16].[6] Number— count the lowest—everywhere guardian angels— one to every man, though at one time a thousand millions of men.

4. Their differences. Some think no two [are]

---

[1] ' In the resurrection they shall neither marry, nor be married, but shall be as the angels in heaven.'—Matt. xxii. 30.

[2] The destroying angel—death of the firstborn in Egypt.

[3] The angel of the pestilence whom David saw by the thrashing-floor of Areuna the Jebusite.

[4] The angel that slew the host of Sennacherib.

[5] 'He [the angel] cried with a loud voice, as when a lion roareth : and when he had cried, seven thunders uttered their voices.'

[6] ' The Lord himself shall come down from heaven . . . with the voice of an archangel. . . .'

alike, but differ specifically, as eagle, dove and nightingale. Indeed, it is difficult, as I have ever thought, to consider pure spirits other than specifically distinct, because since no parts or whole in the angelic world, there are no logical laws in it (except virtue). But, leaving this question, [there are] nine orders in three hierarchies—(enumerate).[1]

5. Such by *nature*, now by *grace*. From the first instant of creation endowed with grace—habitual—faith, hope, charity. Knowledge of Holy Trinity, etc.

6. All of them holy, but in *proportion* to their nature. All have all virtues, but each order rises, having not only *all* virtues in greater perfection, but a characteristic virtue.

7. (1) Angels—contentment ; (2) archangels—imitation of the perfection of all the other orders—absence of all pride and rivalry ; (3) principalities—simplicity of intention.

8. (4) Powers—tenderness and sweetness ; (5) virtues—courage ; (6) dominations—zeal.

9. (7) Thrones—submission and resignation ; (8) cherubim—knowledge ; (9) seraphim—love.

10. Honour due to the angels, Exod. xxiii., Josh. v., Judges vi., xiii., Daniel x. Explain Apoc. xix. 10, that St. John was so great that he was not to adore.

11. Let us honour them in the best way, but imitating, like the archangels, the virtues of each order.

[1] See Note 14, p. 341.

September 16 (*Sixteenth Pentecost*)

THE [HOLY] ANGELS—III

1. INTROD.—Recapitulate.

2. The angels were all created perfect and gifted with supernatural holiness. Even Lucifer, etc.

3. They were first of all put on their trial. They did not see the face of God.

4. The time of this trial—no natural term like *death*—shorter than men['s] because of their spiritual nature, as it was so penetrating, etc., might stand or fall for good in a short time. (Why not in an instant ?)

5. Who fell ? [Some] out of all the orders. Lucifer a seraph.

6. The numbers. Some think a third—Apoc. xii. [4].

7. The sin of the angels, one and the same in all, from imitation. Lucifer led them.

8. *What* [was] the sin ? All [sins] in one doubtless, but especially pride. What *kind* of pride ? Obstinacy, ambition, disobedience, arrogance ?—all doubtless, but especially and initially reliance [on] and contentment in *natural* gifts, with despising *supernatural*.

9. Additions to this pride : (1) a sort of *sensual* love of self ; (2) presumption, ambition, hatred of God ; (3) jealousy of man who was to be created.

10. Battle in heaven. (Michael—'Who as God ? ') Each party trying to convert the other to its own side.

11. Cast into hell—fire in their spirit—though they are now out of it [till the day of judgment].

12. Allusion to matters going on in Italy. Good and bad not so keenly divided as in angels, but still it is the devil against Michael.

September 30 (*Eighteenth Pentecost*)

THE HOLY ANGELS—[IV]

1. INTROD.—About guardian angel.

2. The different works of angels. The word ἄγγελος denotes work and service.

3. What orders of angels have to do with this universe? The lowest, *i.e.* the *angels*, are the ministers. Mundane or exterior, and heavenly or domestic works. Extraordinary missions—the cherubim of Eden [Gen. iii. 24]—the seraph [in] Isaias [vi. 6, purifying the prophet's lips with living coal from the altar]—Gabriel and Mary [the Annunciation]. One [angel] making charge over to another to execute.

4. First work—' rolling the heavens '[1] [*i.e.* directing the movements of the heavenly bodies]—science need not [be supposed to have] superseded this—see my sermon, Parochial, etc., vol. ii. [The Powers of Nature. Feast of St. Michael, etc.]—John v. [Pool of Bethsaida].

5. Second work—guardians of nations, provinces, cities, bishopricks, churches. 'Let us depart hence.'

6. Of individuals. Every one from the time of the soul's creation to death. And every one. Judas, Antichrist.

---

[1] Probably a quotation from some poet.

7. St. Frances of Rome.

8. (1) Odiousness of the charge, *e.g.* St. Paul linked to a soldier ; (2) condescension, etc. ; (3) encouragement to us, and comfort.

October 7 (*Nineteenth Pentecost*)

CARDINAL VIRTUES—PRUDENCE

1. INTROD.—Apparently the greatest. It is called prudence, wisdom, judgment or discretion. ' Be ye prudent as serpents.'

2. For to resist self (or temperance), the world (or fortitude), and to be in grace (justice), is obviously necessary for all, but why prudence ?

3. Again, a man on looking back will often say, 'By the grace of God I overcame myself—the world —and I generally served God and my neighbour, but alas ! all my troubles have come from want of prudence.'

4. St. Anthony (in Cassian), when all the monks assigned different virtues as the greatest, said prudence—because it hinders virtues from becoming vices. This partly lets us in to what prudence is. Let us take different instances of imprudence.

5. (1) Virtue being in a man, prudence is the directing principle ; what is virtue in one man is not in another.

6. (2) On *turning-points* in life—as men mistake their way in the mountains and come to precipices.

7. (3) On avoiding occasions of sin—temptation nearly always comes before sin, as bad food, air, lodging, etc., before illness. If we avoided tempta-

tion, how little sin we should do ; but prudence is the directing principle.

8. (4) Command of tongue—sudden words, what harm they do ! Our Lord when they attempted to entrap Him—Joseph—David.

9. (5) On avoiding scandals. We ought ever to have our eyes about us lest we do others harm.

10. But how are uneducated men to do what seems a virtue of the *perfect* ? At least they may take advice.

11. And they may pray. Two passages in Scripture : Proverbs ii. 3-5,[1] Ecclus. li. 11.[2]

October 14 (*Twentieth Pentecost*)

CARDINAL VIRTUES—JUSTICE

1. INTROD.—Justice a name for *all* virtue. The robe of justice—justification. How great then must be the virtue proper so-called.

2. And so the beatitude : ' Who hunger and thirst after justice.'

[1] ' If thou shalt call for wisdom, and incline thy heart to prudence ; If thou shalt seek her as money, and shalt dig for her as for a treasure ; Then shalt thou understand the fear of the Lord, and shalt find the knowledge of God.'

[2] ' I remembered thy mercy, O Lord, and thy works, which are from the beginning of the world. How thou deliverest them that wait for thee, O Lord, and savest them out of the hands of the nations. Thou hast exalted my dwelling-place upon the earth, and I have prayed for death to pass away. I called upon the Lord, the father of my Lord, that he would not leave me in the day of my trouble, and in the time of the proud without help.'

3. The attribute of God enhances this, for the *first* attribute we know Him by is justice ; viz. in con-science—*before* experience, before the knowledge of providence, before we look out into the visible framework of the world.   Justice and all-knowledge the two ; and in Christianity it is the two, love and justice.   And where should we be without Christ's justice ?   Merits of saints founded on the covenant.

4. What *is* justice ?   Giving to all their *due* ; text in the Romans, ' Honour to whom honour,' etc. Hence it is synonymous with the habit of ' doing one's duty,' whether to God or our neighbour.   To God adoration, devotion, etc., and to the holy angels, etc., but I shall not *insist* on this part of the subject.

5. To man it is summed up in the maxim, ' Do as you would be done by.'   This is placing conduct on the basis of justice.   This basis of justice, for not ' as others would *like* you to do,' but ' ought to wish you to do.'   And so ' forgive us our trespasses, as,' etc. ; Matt. xviii. 23, parable [1] ; ' If I have washed your feet,' John xiii. 14.

6. Parts of justice : (1) truth, (2) honesty—resti-tution ; the terrible onus of restitution shows how important a virtue justice is.

7. (3) Faithfulness, and (4) gratitude, *e.g.* to parents.

8. (5) Liberality—detachment from money as being the opposite to rapacity and avarice.

9. (6) Courtesy in manner and act.

10. (7) Equity, consideration, kindness in judging,

---

[1] 'The servant who owed ten thousand talents.'

putting oneself into other person's situation. Not 'swift to wrath,' James i. 19; Ephes. iv., last verses.[1]

11. Application *on the contrary*—our only notion commonly of justice, is justice to ourselves, hence anger διὰ τὴν φαινομένην ὕβριν, etc., etc.

12. CONCLUSION.—At the judgment this is the attribute God will exercise. Our justice will then have a peculiar claim, while we are invoking God's promises.

October 21 (*Twenty-first Pentecost*)

CARDINAL VIRTUES—FORTITUDE

1. INTROD.—Fortitude and temperance (unlike prudence and justice), and fortitude especially, virtues of warfare in a fallen world. Cowardice the opposite. We know about bravery and cowardice in human matters. How our warfare spiritual, Eph. vi. 12.[2]

2. ' Overcometh the world,' 1 John v. 4 [3]; overcometh the devil, Apoc. xii. 10-11.[4]

3. Hence the Old Testament puts it forth as the characteristic virtue. The spies of the Lord, Deut.

---

[1] ' Let all bitterness and anger . . . be put away from you,' etc.

[2] ' For our wrestling is not against flesh and blood, but against principalities and powers, against the rulers of the darkness of this world, against the spirits of wickedness in the high places.'

[3] ' Whatsoever is born of God overcometh the world.'

[4] ' The accuser of our brethren is cast forth, who accused them before our God day and night. And they overcame him by the blood of the Lamb, and by the word of the testimony; and they loved not their lives unto death.'

xxxi. 7 [1]; Josh. i. 6, 7, 9 [2]—Gideon, David; Aggeus ii. 4.[3]

4. In the new covenant, martyrs, active courage as well as passive—St. Ignatius. St. Barlaam—his hand burnt off. All the children of the city coming to the governor saying, ' Kill us,' and he saying : ' O cacodaemons, have you not precipices and halters ? '

5. This is how Christianity was set up—a whole epistle, the Hebrews, not to say 1st of St. Peter, on the duty and virtue.

6. But you will say this is beyond us. How is it a cardinal natural virtue ? Well, I can give instances, *e.g.* ' because iniquity shall abound,' etc. [4]; cowardice—' lest they be discouraged ' (*ut non pusillo animo fiant*).[5]

7. Cowardice in telling the truth.

8. Cowardice in resisting evil, in not going after the way of sinners in act and deed.

9. Impatience of ill-usage from others.

10. Impatience at continued evils ; disgust—giving up.

---

[1] ' And Moses called Josua, and said to him before all Israel, Take courage and be valiant : for thou shalt bring this people into the land which the Lord swore he would give to their fathers.'

[2] ' Take courage and be strong. . . . Take courage and be very valiant. . . . Behold I command thee, take courage and be strong. Fear not and be not dismayed, because the Lord thy God is with thee in all things whatsoever thou shalt go to.'

[3] ' Yet now take courage, O Zorobabel, saith the Lord ; and take courage, O Josua, son of Josedec, the high priest ; and take courage, all ye people of the land, saith the Lord of hosts, and perform : (for I am with you, saith the Lord of hosts).'

[4] ' Because iniquity shall abound, the love of many shall grow cold.'—Matt. **xxiv.** 12.   [5] Coloss. iii. 21.

11. This brings me to perseverance. It is difficult to persevere in any course, though no positive obstacles or opposition. How great this cardinal virtue then, as connected with the end of life.

12. If the merits of the martyrs are to assist us, let us merit that assistance by some portion of their bravery.

October 28 (*Twenty-second Pentecost*)

CARDINAL VIRTUES—TEMPERANCE

1. INTROD.—Temperance contrasted with fortitude, as within with without, and the pleasant with the painful.

2. Now to explain it. Our soul may be said to have in it two natures, and at variance, and so opposed that peace and unity implies the subjection of one to the other—as two combatants will fight till one or other is thrown.

3. Reason and passions—grief, joy, anger, desire of having, fear—all going into extreme manifestations, and needing a controller. We see it in brute animals. When they cease [?] it is not that reason governs them, but the object [that excites them] is removed.

4. Comparison of a child on horseback. On the other hand, a rider who has perfect command—the Tartars, who live on horseback.

5. Now in the case of the warfare of the soul the struggle more serious and the dangers greater, because (1) the passions have *instruments*, as being united to the body ; (2) objects sensible ; whereas

the object of the reason and conscience, Almighty God, is *unseen*.

6. Therefore a certainty of the subjection of the soul, unless for a remarkable virtue, viz. temperance, or self-government, or control. It is the very critical, or cardinal, or most essential and directing virtue.

7. This self-rule is what *makes a man* ; without it a man is a slave, etc.—laments and curses himself, etc.

8. Hence not heroic, but we see what it is in the saints. It is the characteristic of the saints, and thus is inflicted [*sic*] on us, that in its degree it is the characteristic of a man. You may have wondered why a saint is characteristically mortified.

9. In saints we specially see how it subserves the soul ; their fastings, etc., etc., are to make them pray better, etc., etc.

10. I need not give instances as in the former virtues, but I will mention specially—

11. The necessity of temperance in *thoughts* and in *words*.

12. If we would have the saints assist us, let us cultivate that virtue which was their distinction.

February 24, 1861 (*Second Lent*)

STATE OF INNOCENCE

1. INTROD.—State of our first parents. Image and likeness.[1]

2. Image in nature. All things are in a way in

[1] 'Let us make man to our image and likeness.'—Gen. i. 26.

the image of God, as being His creatures. Man in a special way.

Soul (1) a spirit; (2) immortality; (3) knowledge illimitable [1]; (4) free will; (5) Godlikeness, as Satan said.[2]

Body—beautifulness, perfection of form, etc., etc. but still defects.

Soul—passions against reason; body—mortality.

Thirdly, war of soul with body, as having different ends. Strange the body cannot be without the soul, nor the soul well without the body; yet they cannot agree together.

3. Almighty God knows what He has created, and therefore He did not leave man thus, but gave him a supernatural gift.

4. Likeness—(explain)—sanctity. In fact [also] health and strength, viz. three subjections : (1) Soul to God, (2) passions to reason, and (3) body to soul.[3]

5. Hence a knowledge of mysteries. An absence of passions, only good affections.

6. Yet we need not lament paradise—on account of the future glory promised to us.

7. ' *Lest he take of the tree of life.*'

March 3 (*Third Lent*)

STATE OF ORIGINAL SIN

1. INTROD.—State of original sin. Deprivation of grace; consequences, the ' wounds.'

2. Stripped of God's supernatural gifts or grace.

---

[1] Note he does not say *infinite.*

[2] ' You shall be as gods.'—Gen. ii. 5.

[3] These ' subjections ' pertain to the gift of *Integrity.*

He might never have given it, and then no punishment. But since we were intended for heaven, it was a great punishment. Take the case of a person born to wealth, etc., of cultivated mind, etc., banished to a desert island.

3. And as a spendthrift involves all his descendants, so here.

4. But worse. I described last week the triple subjection. Well, when man cast off God, his passions and affections rebelled against his reason, and his body against his soul. Case of a strong man or child on horseback. Daniel in the lions' den.

5. This great calamity constitutes the wounds of human nature—parable of the Good Samaritan—*first* stripped, *then* wounded.

6. Now here I shall view them as three—the absence of three subjections—sloth, selfishness, sensuality.

7. Describe sloth—that deadness, blindness of soul, dislike of prayer, disgust at religion, liking to ridicule it. Dislike of ruling our mind and heart, etc., etc.

8. Therefore selfishness—making self the centre, etc.

9. And therefore sensuality—idolising the creature.

10. And then these may be considered sins against God, our neighbour and ourselves. Contrasts—love of God, love of our neighbour, and self-command.

11. They branch into the seven deadly sins : (1) sloth ; (2) pride, avarice, anger, envy ; (3) gluttony and luxury.

12. They tend to utter death. Are you to live after this life ? What is your state then, and is God

in heaven ?   Again I say, what is your state then, with the world swept away ?

13. What is your duty ?   As a ruined man might try to repair his fortunes.   Children of this world labouring to regain an ancestral estate.

14. Two great graces : illumination and *excitation*.

15. ' Now is the acceptable time.'

March 10 (*Fourth Lent*)

[RESTORATION]

1. INTROD.—All rational creatures find a need in their nature, and are insufficient for themselves.

2. But man especially.   We see this contrasting him with the inferior animals.

3. He has a body as they have, but observe the difference.   They are suited to their *habitat* by nature, he not.

4. Brutes need no dwellings, no clothes, no prepared food, no cooking.   Bread and wine both manufactures, etc., etc.   Caves, skins and furs, teeth and claws, stomachs.   Armour too and arms ; flight.

5. Again, if they need anything, Nature supplies them with instinct, *e.g.* changing colour in the north, etc., nests, holes, care of young, etc.

6. But consider man.   He is not adapted to this world in which he finds himself, and would die if left to himself.   Arts are necessary, dwellings, etc., etc.

7. Hence again he has to live in a society—for each needs the aid of many others—so many trades, etc. Then again language.   This not by nature, but by imitation.   Education, books, etc.

8. In like manner, as he is thus dependent in body and mind, so he is in *soul*, in religion. Insist on the analogy, but with this difference, that for body and mind he can get help from other men, as by education, but this change (*al.* addition) in the spirit comes *from God alone.* When man fell everything went, but with this difference, that he had powers within himself in course of time to remedy the evil in all matters of this world, but *not of his soul.*

9. In paradise he was healthy, etc., etc. He needed no habitation, etc. However, in process of time he could by his own powers find out food, medicine, dwellings, etc., hence societies, kingdoms; *but not religion.*

10. Nay, worse still, the very advancement in society, in civilisation, is antagonistic to religion. Society viewed on its religious side is *the world*, one of our three enemies.

11. (Analyse.) Each man condemns himself, but if another does the *same*, the example is a safeguard, defence, and excuse. How when a multitude [does the same], the world becomes a prophet antagonist to conscience.

12. Also the pomp, glory, etc., of the world becomes an idol.

13. And the more society grows, the worse the world.

14. I said last Sunday the man got worse and worse as time went on, much more society.

15. Explain ' progress.' [1]

16. Yes, in worldly matters.

17. But in religious, not.

---

[1] See Note 15, p. 341.

M

18. Worse and worse—judgments, flood, etc.
19. Only true progress in the individual, in the heart.
20. Let us at this season follow it out.

November 2, 1862 (*Twenty-first Pentecost*)

ON THE GOSPEL OF THE DAY—[THE PARABLE
OF THE SERVANT WHO OWED TEN THOU-
SAND TALENTS—MATT. XVIII.]

I consider this parable, and the other passages of
our Lord's teaching which are parallel to it, of a
very awful character. I think all of us will say so
who seriously turn their minds to consider them.
(Go through it.)

It is introduced by a question of St. Peter, which
itself may be viewed in connection with another
declaration of our Lord's on the same subject, which
is recorded in the 17th of St. Luke, vv. 3-5.[1] (Quote.)
Apparently in allusion to this, or in some connection with it, St. Peter asked: 'Lord, how often,'
etc. Matt. xviii. 21-22.[2]

---

[1] 'Take heed to yourselves: If thy brother sin against thee,
reprove him; and if he do penance, forgive him. And if he sin
against thee seven times, and seven times a day be converted
unto thee, saying, I repent; forgive him. And the apostles said
to the Lord, Increase our faith.'

[2] 'Then came Peter unto him, and said, Lord, how often shall
my brother offend against me, and I forgive him ? till seven
times ? Jesus saith to him, I say not to thee, Till seven times:
but, Till seventy times seven times.' And thus our Lord takes
the opportunity to follow out and complete the great evangelical
doctrine which He had begun to declare in the passage recorded
in St. Luke. St. Peter asked if seven times would be enough,
and our Lord answered, 'I say not,' etc., etc.

In the same way in the sermon on the mount, Matt. v. 22-24.[1] And He has introduced it as one of the seven petitions of His own prayer, which is the first element and type of all our devotions, and which we say every day. Forgiveness of injuries then bound up in the very idea of prayer in the evangelical law; and our Lord in a passage in St. Mark seems distinctly to say so ; for after speaking of the faith which will move mountains, He proceeds, Mark xi. 25-26, ' And when you shall stand to pray, forgive, if you have ought against any man : that your Father also who is in heaven may forgive you your sins. But if you will not forgive, neither will your Father that is in heaven forgive you your sins.'

Now this great Christian precept is often expressed in these two words : viz. that when injury is done to us, it is our duty to forgive and forget. Let us dwell upon these.

Now, at first sight, we shall all of us allow that it is a very beautiful precept, especially when we are young, when our hearts are light and open, and our tempers generous ; we shall on the one hand think it admirable and great, and, not having had to practise it in fact, we shall be drawn to it, think it easy, and resolve to observe it as life goes on. I

---

[1] ' I say to you, Whosoever is angry with his brother shall be in danger of the judgment : and whosoever shall say to his brother, Raca, shall be in danger of the council : and whosoever shall say, Thou fool, shall be in danger of hell fire. If therefore thou offer thy gift at the altar, and there thou remember that thy brother hath anything against thee ; Leave there thy offering before the altar, and go first to be reconciled to thy brother, and then coming thou shalt offer thy gift.'

can fancy young people drawing before their minds pictures of injuries done them, of their forgiving the injuries, and returning good for evil. And when they read accounts of men who have done so, and instances of generosity, magnanimity, patience and nobleness in this respect, they are greatly moved and filled with a love of the virtue. Nor is it only a beautiful precept, it is of a most useful and expedient character too. Every one must confess who turns his mind to the subject, that the world would go on far better, that all men would be happier, if this precept was universally observed. For what is a greater or wider scourge of man than war, dissensions and litigation ? and though these miseries arise in a great measure from covetousness (James iv.), they arise still more from passion, from a sense of injuries, from a fierce determination to retaliate, from a thirst for revenge. James iv. 1-2, 'From whence are wars and contentions among you ? . . . you covet, and have not; you kill, and envy, and cannot obtain.'

To forgive and forget, then, is (1) at first sight a beautiful, an admirable precept, and (2) one which on long experience leads to the greatest benefit to mankind. All men are interested in its recognition and observance ; yet it will be found not at all easy in fact, but a very difficult precept, one which is but rarely obeyed and very partially, where it is not altogether neglected ; and further, one to which many plausible objections may be made, and many arguments in favour of a contrary course, which become formidable when they are brought to defend that unwillingness to obey it ; and the difficulty of obeying it, which in matter of fact will be found in human nature.

Now I will first set down what I conceive the precept to be, and next consider how the objection to it arises.

(*I was interrupted, or I meant to have written a sketch of a whole sermon. I have forgotten now my arrangement. I put down some isolated* τόποι.) (1) Not to forgive is even contrary to justice, a *higher* kind of justice than natural justice, for we should do as it has been done by Almighty God to us. (2) Forgetting, yes, as God forgets, for He forgets by putting aside, behind His back, our sins. (3) We should put aside also, for a reason special *to us*, for the thinking of injury is a temptation to avenge it. (On distrust necessarily remaining after forgiveness.[1]) (4) Mere emotion is not revenge. (5) Though we must put aside the injury, we must not put aside the injurer, for that would be hatred—this the *cardo* of the difficulty of the precept. (6) On being obliged to *speak* to persons with whom we have quarrelled. This has *exceptions, e.g.* if they are likely to tempt us to sin, which perhaps *was* the injury ; but such exceptions must be determined by a *director*. (7) It seems to be contrary to justice if injuries are not punished. This is true, but we must not judge in our own case. (8) Contrary to nature to forgive. Yes, but sin and redemption (see above, 2). (9) This is what this age *forgets* when it speaks in favour of revenge. (10) Men do not believe in redemption, nor that they are sinners. Hence Mahomet. (11) Do

[1] These words were added in pencil. It is not clear whether they belong to (3) or to (4).

I put forgiveness [merely] as a *condition* [of obtaining forgiveness for ourselves] ? No, one who believes in what Christ has done has no *heart* for revenge. (12) Onesimus—Christ says ' forgive me ' by the lips of the fellow-servant. (13) Man's duty to pray for injurers. (14) Pray *to meet them in heaven*, (15) when all angularities will be rubbed off, and we shall be able truly to love them. (16) We and they are sinners ; let us help each other.

April 5, 1863 (*Easter Day*)

[SILENT JOY]

' I sat down under His shadow whom I desired, and His fruit was sweet to my mouth (*gutturi*).'[1] So says the Spouse in the Canticle.

Aggeus ii. 8, ' The desired of all nations shall come, and I will fill this house with glory.'

Malachias iii. 1, ' And presently the Lord whom you seek, and the angel of the testament whom you desire, shall come to his temple.'

And therefore the Bride sat down, *as Mary at His feet*. And so it is, whether in great joy or sorrow, we are silent. Each emotion, when profound, produces a calmness. Thus Job's friends, Job ii. 13, ' And they sat with him on the ground seven days and seven nights, and no man spoke to him a word : for they saw that his grief was very great.'

Thus in Christ's death and resurrection.

Look in the gospel and you will see that it is no peculiarity of ours, of our race, of these times, but

[1] Cant. ii. 3.

it is a deep characteristic of our nature. Who is it
that speaks in the gospel, from the time when Mary
poured the alabaster box to the time when Jesus
ascended into heaven ? [1]

And so as regards our Lord—read the whole
account—it is not the disciples who speak, it is Jesus
—Jesus in the supper, *the Last Supper*, the garden,
the Passion, the Cross, the Resurrection.

It is the wicked who speak—they speak who
speak to sin—Chronista, Christus, Synagoga [2]—all
[speakers except Christ] grouped under that word
[Synagoga]. Judas, chief priest, false witnesses,
Pilate, the multitude.

Exceptions : Pilate's wife, centurion.

Even apostles—as Peter who denied Him.

Two speakers alone—(1) when proper ? (2) who
is it ? [3]

Thus fulfilled, Psalms xiii. 3.[4]

Nay, a time came when even the wicked were
silent—'that every mouth should be stopped '—
and the Lord alone spoke. He spoke His seven last
words amid the silence : only one exception—the
penitent thief.

Thoughts good and bad. . . . His resurrection.
'My Lord and my God.' 'Lord, what shall this man
do ? ' And Acts i.

---

[1] The rest of the sermon is from a slip of paper pasted in the
book, apparently the notes which the preacher took with him
into the pulpit.

[2] The three deacons of the Passion on Palm Sunday.

[3] The meaning of this is not clear.

[4] 'Their throat is an open sepulchre : with their tongues they
acted deceitfully ; the poison of asps is under their lips. Their
mouth is full of cursing and bitterness.'

April 12 (*Low Sunday*)

[FAITH]

1. INTROD.—In to-day's epistle and gospel which I have just read, we have brought before us what is one of the great lessons of this sacred season, viz. the necessity of *faith* as the foundation of the Christian life.   Last week we considered the Passion and Resurrection, to-day the faith by which we receive them as by a channel.

2. Contrast faith and reason.   No great work done by mere reason, even in this world.

Not that they are opposed, but faith has the power of anticipating, and arrives at first at what reason scarcely guesses at at last—St. Peter and St. John in Keble's poem.[1]

3. Therefore, since Almighty God works by human means, He chose faith as the faculty which does great things.

4. Natural and supernatural faith.   It is often what we mean by genius in Nature, which sees what others see not, etc.   We believe in the existence of God, though it can be proved also ; and so of Christ, etc.

5. Hence the multitudes converted, etc., etc.

6. Quote passages from epistle 1 John v. 4-9.[2]   Cf. 1 Peter ii., then the gospel of yesterday [John xx. 1-9 ; St. Peter and St. John coming to the Sepulchre];

[1] See Note 16, p. 342.

[2] 'And this is our victory which overcometh the world, our faith.   Who is he that overcometh the world, but he that believeth that Jesus is the Son of God ? . . . If we receive the testimony of men, the testimony of God is greater.'

then gospel of the day, John xx. 19-31,[1] in which faith and reason are contrasted and the superiority given to faith.

7. And lest faith should be confused with enthusiasm, general notes are given to steer us, viz. the very effect of faith, ' Who is he that overcometh the world ? '—and so, ' Who is he that overcometh the flesh ? ' ' Who is he that overcometh the devil ? ' etc.

8. This *first, before* faith we see on a large scale in the world.

9. After faith we see the effects in our heart—the justifying by reason what we have done by faith.

January 3, 1864

ST. JOHN THE SAINT OF THE TIME, OF THE NEW YEAR, ETC.— OLD YEAR ENDING, NEW YEAR BEGINNING, ETC.

1. ' Canst thou drink of the chalice ? '[2] etc. ' What shall this man do ? '[3]

You see how little they knew, as we. The prospect quite dark.

---

[1] 'Jesus saith to him, because thou hast seen me, Thomas, thou hast believed : blessed are they that have not seen, and have believed.'

[2] 'Then came to him the mother of the sons of Zebedee with her sons adoring, and asking something of him. Who said to her, What wilt thou ? She saith to him, That these my two sons may sit the one on thy right hand, the other on thy left hand, in thy kingdom. And Jesus answering said, You know not what you ask. Can you drink the chalice that I shall drink ? They say, We can. And he saith to them, My chalice indeed you shall drink : but to sit on my right or left hand is not mine to give, but to them for whom it is prepared by my Father.'—Matt. xx. 20-23.

[3] 'Peter, turning about, saw that disciple whom Jesus loved following ; who also lent on his breast at supper, and said, Lord,

2. So sanguine and eager to serve his Lord, yet how differently from what he thought ! The throne on right hand and left were deferred till the next world. So we, and we shall find at the end that God is faithful and gives us our wish, but how differently from what we expect ! 'Commit thyself to God, and He will give thee the desires of thy heart,' yet in His way, not ours. Thus Jacob who said 'few and evil,'[1] yet speaks of the Lord who had been with him from the beginning to this day, etc.[2] So Solomon naming God's mercies, 'Thou hast not failed,' yet how differently !

3. He is the saint of the longest lived ; he covers all length of life. He is the saint of the young, the middle-aged and the old. Hence the appropriate addresses, 'Little children,' etc. : 1 John ii. 1, 'My little children, these things I write' ; ib. 18, 'Little children, it is the last hour'; ib. iii. 7, 'Little children, let no man deceive you' ; ib. 18, 'My little children, let us not love in word, nor in tongue ; but in deed and in truth,' etc. And what is his experience ? 'The world lieth in wickedness.' 1 John ii. 15-16, 'Love not the world, nor the things which are in the world. If any man love the world, the charity of the Father is not in him. For all that

who is it that shall betray thee ? Him therefore when Peter had seen he saith to Jesus, Lord, what shall this man do ? Jesus saith to him, So I will have him remain till I come, what is it to thee ? follow thou me.'—John xxi. 20-22.

[1] 'The days of my pilgrimage : . . . few and evil.'—Gen. xlvii. 9.

[2] 'The God that feedeth me from my youth until this day.'—Gen. xlviii. 15.

is in the world is the concupiscence of flesh, and the
concupiscence of the eyes, and the pride of life.'

July 24 (Tenth Pentecost)
[THE PHARISEE AND THE PUBLICAN]

1. INTROD.—' God be merciful to me a sinner.'

2. In these words is contained the essence of true
religion.

3. *Why ?* Because they refer to conscience as
leading the mind *to God.*

4. All men have a conscience of right and wrong,
Rom. ii. 14-15 [1]—*the conscience accusing*, etc. But
it does not lead them, when they transgress it, to
God. They are angry with themselves. They
know they are wrong, and are distressed, but it does
not lead them to religion ; at the utmost it leads
them to understand a sin against their neighbours
—as cruelty, etc. But when it leads the soul to
think of God, then that soul may be very sinful, but
at least it has something *of true religion* in it.

5. 2 Cor. vii. 10-11.[2] And so ' to Thee then only
have I sinned, and done evil before Thee.' Ps. l.

[1] 'For when the Gentiles, who have not the law, do by
nature those things that are of the law, these, having not the
law, are a law to themselves : who shew the work of the law
written in their hearts, their conscience bearing witness to them,
and their thoughts between themselves accusing or also defend-
ing one another.'

[2] 'For the sorrow which is according to God worketh penance
steadfast unto salvation : but the sorrow of the world worketh
death. For behold the selfsame thing, that you were made
sorrowful according to God, how great carefulness it worketh in
you, yea defence, yea indignation, yea fear, yea desire, yea
zeal, yea revenge ! In all things you have shewed yourselves
undefiled in the matter.'

6. Hence in the text the reason why the publican was *more justified*, because he understood that his offences were against God.

7. But see what comes from this. Directly a man realises that what he does wrong is against God, then he feels how much more extensive it is, viz. of the thoughts.

8. And how much more intensive, viz. as against the Highest. He calls it *sin*.

9. Then he grows in his notions. As blows don't pain at first, so sin may pain hereafter.

10. Thus he sees it is an offence against the moral nature of God.

11. Hence all diseases are but types of sin.

12. Hence idea of guilt.

13. Hence need of a cleansing.

July 31 (*Eleventh Pentecost*)

[ON THE GOSPEL OF THE SUNDAY—THE HEALING OF THE MAN DEAF AND DUMB]

Various maladies which our Lord cured, typical of various sins.

1. Blind.—Those that have not faith, and do not apprehend doctrine.

2. Deaf.—Those that are without devotion and cannot hear the songs of angels.

3. Dumb.—Those who through cowardice or pride do not confess the Gospel, though they believe in it.

4. Without taste (and smell).—Those who have a dull, unsensitive conscience.

5. Lame.—Those who are slothful.

August 7 (*Twelfth Pentecost*)

[LOVE OF GOD]

By contrast—love of God. Luke x. 27, ' Thou
shalt love the Lord thy God with thy whole heart,
and with thy whole soul, and with all thy strength,
and with all thy mind.'

Love of God—emotion not necessary ; straw
burns out quicker than iron.

1. Desire of His exaltation.

2. For His own sake, not ours : (1) *complacentia*,
(2) *ad majorem* [*Dei*] *gloriam*.

3. Yet with our own personal interest in it, as a
mother or sister follows the history of a son or
brother with sympathy, though without *personal*
gain, etc.

Loving God for His own sake.   None can be saved
without love.

August 7

THE ONE SACRIFICE

1. Christ a sacrifice.   We keep the feast at Easter :
' Christ our Pasch,' etc.

2. What is meant by sacrifice ?—offering, killing,
eating.   Objects—(1) worship, (2) thanksgiving, (3)
propitiation, (4) impetration.

3. Heathen sacrifices, 1 Cor. x. 20, ' The things
which the heathen sacrifice, they sacrifice to devils,
and not to God.' *Taurobolium*, etc. ; human sacrifices, etc.

4. Jewish sacrifices, Lev. ix., x., xvi.

5. Fulfilled in Christ. Two things—death and intercession. Therefore the Aaronic priesthood and bloody sacrifice fulfilled in one act and time by our Lord in the flesh. Scripture speaks of our Lord as not only fulfilling a bloody sacrifice (which is once for all), but besides this of a sacrifice according to Melchisedech, that is, bread and wine.

6. Superiority—once for all ; all sin.

7. His mercy in continuing the sacrifice, that it might not be a mere matter of history.

8. This is the Mass ; which is His sacrifice reiterated, represented, applied, as He continues it in heaven. Mal. i. 11.[1]

9. Order of Melchisedech.

10. One priest, one victim, one sacrificing, everywhere.

11. From the first—various liturgies—points in common. Detail of rites as in the bloody [sacrifice on Mount Calvary]—as our Lord taken before Pilate, etc., etc.

12. Arguments for apostolicity of the Mass.

August 14 (*Thirteenth Pentecost*)

[LOVE OF GOD]

1. INTROD.—I said last week that no one can be saved without *love of God*. This the awful truth.

---

[1] 'For from the rising of the sun even to the going down, my name is great among the Gentiles, and in every place there is sacrifice, and there is offered to my name a clean oblation : for my name is great among the Gentiles, saith the Lord of hosts.'

2. In fact this is plain, but considering the state of the case—the immortal soul—how tired it will get of everything in eternity, except of something which is infinite. God in Himself a world; His attributes infinite.

3. *Yet how can we love Him?* See how much against our nature it is. We take delight in things of the world, etc., etc., in science, in literature, etc. These are our aims; but to love God is *an aim* above our nature.

4. Granted *it is so*. However, God does not command impossibilities.

5. Therefore He gives us grace to raise us above our nature. Even angels need grace.

6. What is grace? and what does it do for us?

7. Let us pray God for it.

August 21 (*Fourteenth Pentecost*)

[THE LIFE OF GRACE]

1. Nothing is more common than to think that natural virtue, what we do by nature, is sufficient for our salvation.

The state of most men is sin, but as to those who go the highest [it is] natural virtue. Put it in the way of an objection. Why is not this enough? Two things confused with each other—the improvement of things in this world, which natural virtue can do, and the salvation of the soul by grace.

2. What most men consider enough is this—if they follow what they think right, if they do the

duties of their station, if they do what their conscience tells them, and so live and die. As to prayer, the best prayer is to do their duty here ; they think the next world may take its chance.

3. Now most men do not get so far as this. They live in sin ; but the utmost they think of is to be saved mainly by their own strength, and by doing the common duties of life without thinking of religion, though they may acknowledge that on great occasions God helps them, within or without, but is it when *dignus vindice nodus*.[1] They do not see the necessity of thinking of God, but they say that the best service is to do those duties which come before them.

4. Particularly at this day. When men think that religion is unnecessary, that the world will advance merely by its own powers.

5. On the other hand, *the life of grace*—virtues through grace.

6. Natural virtues bring on the world—doubtless social science, political economy, science of government, etc., etc.—but *I want to be saved.*

September 18

[THE MASS]

The Mass is to be viewed in two aspects—(1) as it regards our Lord ; (2) as it regards us. As it regards Him, it is the great act of sacrificial atonement. As regards us, the great act of intercession. Texts,

---

[1] 'Nec Deus intersit, nisi dignus vindice nodus
Inciderit.'—Horace, *Ars Poet.*, 191-2.

Rom. viii. 32 [1] ; Heb. vii. 22-25,[2] ix. 15 [3] and *passim* ; 1 Tim. ii. 5-6.[4]

1. He is the great High Priest who is ever offering up His meritorious sacrifice, and the Mass is but the earthly presence of it.

2. While He offers it above, the whole Church intercedes. (1) Mary on high, and the saints with her. Thus a heavenly Mass is now going on above. (2) Below—not a light benefit that we may intercede.

We have indeed a hope within us that God will hear us for ourselves, but will He hear us for others ? It is only through His wonderful meritorious sacrifice that we have this power, and therefore fitly in the Mass is the intercessory gift exercised. Therefore the very privilege of Catholics above others is intercessory prayer ; it is the imputation and the imparting to their prayers the merit of the sacrifice. Therefore St. Paul says, ' Pray without ceasing.' St. James, etc. All intercessory prayer all over the whole world, *e.g.* litanies, the priest's office, the

---

[1] ' He that spared not even His own Son, but delivered him up for us all, how hath he not also with him given us all things ? '

[2] ' By so much is Jesus made a surety of a better testament. And others indeed were made many priests, because by reason of death they were not suffered to continue : But this, for that he continueth for ever, hath an everlasting priesthood, whereby he is able to save for ever them that come to God by him : always living to make intercession for us.'

[3] ' And therefore he is the mediator of the new testament, that by means of his death, for the redemption of those transgressions which were under the former testament, they that are called may receive the promise of eternal inheritance.'

[4] ' For there is one God, and one mediator of God and men, the man Christ Jesus ; who gave himself a redemption for all.' . . .

N

breviary, is as it were in presence of the Mass. It is the great act of communion, etc.

January 1, 1865
[ETERNITY]

1. All days are the beginning of new years, but we have especially reason to place the first day in this time, for the season in which it comes is the beginning of a new year, because it is the beginning of a new revolution in this world's course. The earth is asleep, and I may say dead ; and as man's extremity was God's opportunity, when things are at their worst they begin to mend. The sun stays in its downward course—it turns back, the days become longer, etc., etc. The year awakens, and human thought and activity with it—the farmer because of the ground ; the navigator looks for favourable weather and the right wind ; the warrior opens his campaign ; parliaments, etc., etc.

2. MOTION.—Such is this wonderful world, in which all is motion—begins, goes on, increases, and dies again, year after year, and man in detail, day after day, goes on to his work and his labour till the evening.

3. CHANGE.—Such it is with us, and with an end. What does it end in ? We pass in the course of 365 days the day of our death—like walking over our gravestone. What does it end in ?—a state in which time ceases, or rather time, it may be said, stops. Time in this world is marked by motion. Motion, or what is commonly called change, is the very fulfilment of this state of things.

4. END OF CHANGE.—But the day will come when

time brings with it no changes—(past, present, and future because [there is] change)—when all is the same—day after day, age after age—in short, when time stops—*an eternal now*. This we call eternity.

5. TIME WITHOUT CHANGE IS ETERNITY.—Properly time cannot stop ; it runs on as I am speaking. There is nothing to end it ; but as soon as there is no change in it, it is eternity. All our thoughts, ideas, etc., will stop : they will be fixed and one and the same. As they are good or bad, it will be heaven or hell.

March 5 (*First Lent*)

[SIN]

1. INTROD.—At this time of year, ' Come let us reason together ; argue with me, saith the Lord.'

EXPOSTULATION.—Isa. i. 2 [1] and xliii. 21-26,[2] Mic. vi. 1-2.[3]

God, most blessed from eternity, created us, not for any good that we could do to Him. He would not be happier, stronger, etc., by creating us. On the other hand we are wholly dependent on Him.

[1] ' Hear, O ye heavens, and give ear, O earth : for the Lord hath spoken, I have brought up children and exalted them, but they have despised me.'

[2] ' This people have I formed for myself ; they shall shew forth my praise. But thou hast not called upon me ; neither hast thou laboured about me, O Israel. . . . I am he that blot out thy iniquities for my own sake, and I will not remember thy sins. Put me in remembrance, and let us plead together : tell me if thou hast any thing to justify thyself.'

[3] ' Hear ye what the Lord saith ; Arise, contend thou in judgment against the mountains, and let the hills hear thy voice. Let the mountains hear the judgment of the Lord, and the strong foundations of the earth : for the Lord will enter into judgment with his people, and he will plead against Israel.'

The axe does not depend on the carpenter for beginning of [existence], nor the son on the father for continuance of life, but God made the dust, out of which we are, out of nothing, etc. He sustains us, etc. We are entirely His work and property, and should do *His service*. Yet we have *cast off His yoke*.

2. But again, He made us in order *to bless* us. He knows of what we are made. He knows what will make us happy. Yet we have refused to be blessed ; we have sought our own happiness.

3. Two claims—duty and interest. Let us confess. We have preferred to be our own masters ; we have refused to believe that sin is an evil. We will not believe what an evil sin is ; we have no loathing or horror of it.

4. But now consider what sin is. God is infinite. It is the one thing which may be said to be of an infinite *nature* besides God. It is inexhaustible, irremediable ; it is greater than angel or archangel, a rival infinity to God—' against thee only have I sinned.' According to the person injuring [injured ?], so is the injury, *e.g.* insulting a superior. Sin is the lifting up the hand against the infinite benefactor.

5. He will leave me to myself. What will become of me ?

6. Save me from myself.

December 2, 1866

[OMNISCIENCE OF GOD]

1. INTROD.—Omniscience and omnipresence of God—*knowing the heart* ; incomprehensible ; millions

of men, yet He knows all that goes on in the heart
[of each one] and *remembers*.

2. [Incomprehensible] yet familiar to children.[1]

3. Scripture—1 Kings xvi. 7,[2] 1 Paralip. xxviii. 9,[3]
2 Paralip. vi. 30,[4] Jeremias xvii. 10,[5] Apoc. ii. 23.[6]
Future judgment—Rom. xiv. 10,[7] 1 Cor. iv. 4-5,[8]
Heb. iv. 12-13.[9]

[1] See Note 17, p. 342.

[2] ' And the Lord said to Samuel, Look not on his countenance,
nor on the height of his stature ; because I have rejected him :
nor do I judge according to the look of man ; for man seeth those
things which appear, but the Lord beholdeth the heart.'

[3] ' And thou, my son Solomon, know the God of thy father,
and serve him with a perfect heart and a willing mind : for the
Lord searcheth all hearts, and understandeth all the thoughts of
minds : if thou seek him, thou shalt find him ; but if thou
forsake him, he shall cast thee off for ever.'

[4] ' Hear thou from heaven, from thy high dwelling place, and
forgive, and render to every one according to his ways, which
thou knowest him to have in his heart ; (for thou only knowest
the hearts of the children of men).'

[5] ' I am the Lord who search the heart, and prove the reins ;
who give to every one according to his ways, and according to the
fruit of his devices.'

[6] ' I am he that searcheth the reins and hearts : and I will give
to every one of you according to his works.'

[7] ' For we shall all stand before the judgment seat of Christ.
Therefore every one of us shall render an account to God of
himself.'

[8] ' For I am not conscious to myself of anything ; yet am I not
thereby justified : but he that judgeth me is the Lord.   Therefore judge not before the time, until the Lord come, who will both
bring to light the hidden things of darkness, and will make
manifest the counsels of the hearts.'

[9] ' For the word of God is living, and effectual, and more
piercing than any twoedged sword, and reaching unto the
division of the soul and the spirit, of the joints also and the
marrow, and is a discerner of the thoughts and intents of the
heart.   Neither is there any creature invisible in his sight : but
all things are naked and open to his eyes.'

4. Suitable to this time of year—the particular and general judgment.

5. The keenness of the judgment—as above, Heb. iv.—magnifying-glass, the wonders of the microscope, a new world, diseases. Hence we must feel we do not know ourselves. *Therefore* 1 Cor. i., 'judge nothing before the time.'

6. Most awful, but different way in which good and bad take it.

7. The bad dread it. Adam and Eve in the garden. 'And then shall they say to the rocks, Fall upon us,' etc., etc., Luke xxiii. [30],[1] Apoc. vi. [16].[2]

8. The good desire it—to be known to God, Ps. cxxxviii.[3] Purgatory—willing victims.

9. This is one test whether we can bare our hearts before God.

March 20, 1870

ON THE GOSPEL OF THIRD LENT

1. INTROD.—The diseases which our Lord cured were typical of sins. The dumb spirit, who is he? One who will not go to confession, or who cannot, who has not the opportunity. I wish I could describe him and his misery.

2. Time was, before the Gospel, there was no personal individual confession. It is one of the great gifts of Christ's coming.

[1] 'And they shall begin to say to the mountains, Fall upon us; and to the hills, Cover us.'

[2] 'And they say to the mountains and the rocks, Fall upon us, and hide us from him that sitteth on the throne, and from the wrath of the Lamb.'

[3] *Domine, probasti me,* etc.

3. Christ came to fulfil all the needs of man—to give him hope, peace, strength, joy, and all virtues and blessings. Now let us see what is one special need of his nature.

4. Man is a social being. The instrument of society is the great gift of speech.

Begin thus [*2nd scheme*].

(1) Man is a social being.

(2) Speech the great tie and bond of society; dumbness and deafness generally go together. It is said that blind men are more cheerful than deaf and dumb, because society is *a truer world than the physical*.

(3) No man is sufficient for himself—the voice is an outlet. No greater misery than to be shut up in oneself—*speech* is the *great relief*. How dull it is to see beautiful things without companions to speak to. We must say all that is in our heart. As the pleasant things, so also the painful. Difficulty of keeping a secret, or of not speaking to others when we have been ill-treated.

(4) Nay, Almighty God not by Himself, but with His Son and Spirit. From eternity love, and not power.

5. The devil alone is solitary—and evil spirits— this the worst misery of hell.

Begin thus [*3rd scheme*].

(1) From this dumbness we may gain a great spiritual lesson.

(2) Social nature. Whatever we feel we bring out. Praise and prayer.

(3) And so all angels. One society in heaven. Praise and prayer.

(4) And so God Himself.

(5) Evil spirits and evil men on the contrary.

(6) On all our affections and passions relieved by words.

(7) Keeping secrets, etc.

(8) Confession one kind of speech.

(9) Those who from want of opportunity, from pride, from despair, do not confess.

(10) Comfort of confession.

(11) Those who don't are like the evil spirits.

(12) Happy all Catholics, if they knew their happiness.

April 3

GOSPEL FOR PASSION SUNDAY

1. INTROD.—We veil our crosses.   On the various gospels descriptive of our Lord's hiding Himself.

2. He hid Himself from the Jews because they had refused the light.

3. He is the light of the world and the light of the soul.

4. Abraham had first 'seen' Him—on Moriah— and the other prophets, as if mounted on high. And all the Jews, though they had not seen Him, had heard of Him and expected Him.   He was the 'expectation of the nations.'

5. At length 'He came unto His own,' etc.   'The light shineth in the darkness.'

6. A warning to all of us lest we receive the grace of God in vain.   A *yearly* warning.

7. We cannot be as others.   We have had great

opportunities. We mix with Protestants. They have their own views. They argue and conclude on their own basis. They are sharp and clever men of business; good politicians; on *their own* principles right. No wonder they think so differently, for the great bulk of them have not seen what we have seen. But Luke x. 23-24.[1]

8. O let us beware lest we ever get blinded. Isa. vi. 9-10.[2]

9. 'Strive to enter the strait gate : for many, I say to you, shall seek to enter, and shall not be able,' Luke xiii. 24.

April 24 (*Low Sunday*)

[FAITH]

1. INTROD. — Hope — Christmas ; love — Pentecost ; faith—Easter.

2. Because there was at first so much doubt, etc. (1) The first blow was that our Lord should die— this seemed impossible. (2) That He should rise from the dead.

3. Hence on Low Sunday epistle and gospel.

Now under these circumstances it seemed reason-

---

[1] 'Blessed are the eyes which see the things which you see : for I say to you, that many prophets and kings have desired to see the things which you see, and have not seen them ; and to hear the things which you hear, and have not heard them.'

[2] 'Go, and thou shalt say to this people, Hearing, hear and understand not ; and see the vision, and know it not. Blind the heart of this people, and make their ears heavy, and shut their eyes ; lest they see with their eyes, and hear with their ears, and understand with their heart, and be converted, and I heal them.'

able that our Lord should give them the testimony of sight, touch, etc., for, unless some one saw Him again, how were the apostles, how was the world to know it.

4. But a deeper lesson. Sight could not be given to all, because our Lord was going to heaven, and those who did not see must believe on the witness of others. Now the Gospel was to last to the end of the world. Therefore He in His love determined that one of the apostles should be away and not see Him.

5. This was Thomas, who, being in the state of confusion which they all were in before they saw Him, persisted in that unbelief which at first they all had. When the women testified, the apostles would not believe. When the apostles testified, Thomas would not believe.

6. We all know what happened. Our Lord graciously granted, etc., but He said : ' Blessed are they that have not seen and have believed.'

7. This is one lesson. Our Lord speaks to us. Thomas thought it hard he had not the evidence the rest had. *He was not content with what was sufficient.* This *the great lesson.* Doubtless sight is more than the witness of other men.

8. Let us take the Gospel of St. John. There are miracles more wonderful than in the other gospels, *i.e.* those addressed to the intellect, not the imagination, etc. ; and he testifies to the truth, and so do the Christians around him. John xxi. 24, ' This is that disciple who giveth testimony of these things, and hath written these things that we may know that his testimony is true.' The early Christians had no greater evidence than we have,

but they believed it more vigorously; hence they went through so much.

May 8

PATRONAGE OF ST. JOSEPH

1. INTROD.—'Yet a little time, and ye will not see me,' etc.

2. That time when Christ came to each apostle, was at the death of each. He says the time was short of this life—and though He was going they would go soon; and He only went before them to prepare a place.

3. Yet though their life was short, how long it seemed by being so full of suffering.

4. St. Paul's sufferings (though greater, perhaps): 2 Cor. xi. 24-28,[1] Acts xx. 22-23,[2] 1 Cor. iv. 11-13.[3]

---

[1] 'Of the Jews five times did I receive forty stripes save one. Thrice was I beaten with rods, once was I stoned, thrice I suffered shipwreck, a night and a day I was in the depth of the sea; In journeyings often, in perils of waters, in perils of robbers, in perils from my own nation, in perils from the Gentiles, in perils in the city, in perils in the wilderness, in perils in the sea, in perils from false brethren; In labour and painfulness, in much watchings, in hunger and thirst, in fastings often, in cold and nakedness. Besides these things that are without, my daily instance, the solicitude for all the churches.'

[2] 'And now, behold, being bound in spirit, I go to Jerusalem, not knowing the things that shall befall me there: Save that the Holy Ghost in every city witnesseth to me, saying that bonds and afflictions wait for me at Jerusalem.'

[3] 'Even unto this hour we both hunger, and thirst, and are naked, and are buffeted, and have no fixed abode; And we labour, working with our hands: we are reviled and we bless; we are persecuted and we suffer it: We are blasphemed and we intreat: we are made as the refuse of the world, the offscouring of all until now.'

5. And so of all Christians then. They were tried with long unsettlement and uncertainty—their lives in their hands ; persecution any day—inscription in the catacombs—' O wretched we,' etc.—' If in this life only.' [1]

6. And so of all the saints—confessors, ascetics, etc., etc.—they are all in trouble ; and when we think of them we think of pain, penance, etc.

7. This is what supported them, hope, viz. that Christ comes again, that their sufferings would end with this life ; that they would be rewarded by being with Him.

8. Hence heaven was their *patria*, their HOME—Family, Father, peace—all was trouble here.

9. There is but one saint who typifies to us the next world, and that is St. Joseph. He is the type of rest, repose, peace. He is the saint and patron of home, in death as well as in life.

10. Let us put ourselves under his protection.

August 7 (*Ninth Pentecost*)

[THE OMNIPOTENCE OF GOD AND MAN'S FREE-WILL]

1. God is almighty, but still this does not mean that He can do everything whatever, for if so He could do contradictions. There are some things, of course, which are impossible to Him because the very thought of them is an absurdity, *e.g.* He can never cease to be holy ; He can never wish to cease to be holy, etc., etc.

2. And so again, much more when He created,

---

[1] 'If in this life only we have hope in Christ, we are of all men most miserable.'—1 Cor. xv. 19.

He Himself, as it were, put obstacles in the way of
the exercise of His omnipotence—things which once
were possible ceased to be possible. He made a
sort of covenant with creation in creating. He
forthwith made Himself a minister to His creation,
which could not stand of itself.

3. And much more when He created rational
beings, who can exercise a will of their own, and do
right or wrong, He can't do what He would. We
say, ' Thy will be done.' It is difficult to conceive
how. When God had once created a being who
could do right and wrong, He suspended His own
prerogative of ' His will being done.'

4. Especially when He makes a covenant, for
then He is bound by its terms. And further, such
beings bring His attributes into operation and they
seem to contradict each other—as justice and love.

5. I come to this conclusion : that men who
rely on the boundless mercy of God do not understand how the matter stands. He has other attributes, and they act according to the case—' Let
me alone,'[1] power of intercession. God chose the
Jews, etc. They are an example of what I mean.
He willed their salvation. He did all things He
could [2] for them, and He cast them off. How awful
is this—His will was not done ! By creating beings
who could have a will of their own, He circum-
scribed His own power.

6. Now I am led to these thoughts by the epistle
and gospel of the day.

---

[1] ' Let me alone, that my wrath may be kindled against them.
. . . And Moses besought the Lord,' etc.—Exod. xxxii. 10-11.

[2] This ' could ' is a preacher's word ; it must not be theologi-
cally pressed. See Note 18, p. 343.

7. Go through the epistle[1] and gospel.[2] Isa. vi. 10, ' Blind the heart of this people, and make their ears heavy, and shut their eyes ; lest they see with their eyes, and hear with their ears, and understand with their heart, and be converted, and I heal them.' Matt. xiii. 14 [above passage quoted], John xii. 40 [same passage quoted], Acts xxviii. 26 [same quotation].

8. Our last [end]—our ' enemies may come about us,' etc. God forbid.

August 28 (*Twelfth Pentecost*)

[GOD OUR STAY IN ETERNITY]

1. The lawyer asks, ' What shall I do ? ' etc. Our Lord refers him to the duty of loving God.

2. Now that this is our plain *duty* is clear. It is the *condition* of heaven. But it is more than that— I wish you to see that it is the nature of things.

3. We all wish to live a long life. We are all fears and awe at death. Why ? Well, partly because it is the loss of life ; but more, because it is leaving what we know and going to what we do not know, and for judgment. This world our *home*—it is going into a strange country. This is the main reason.

4. Men (especially Protestants) talk vaguely of going to glory, etc. Now let us contemplate what it is, going into a strange country. What will be our happiness there ? Let us look at it in a common-sense way. What is to constitute our happiness ? What is to occupy us in eternity ? Why, even of *this* world men get tired ! You hear of old people

[1] 1 Cor. x. 6-13. [2] Luke xix. 41-47.

who are ready to die, not because they like death but because they are tired. Now if many men are tired of eighty years, supposing they were to live on till two hundred, would not they be *tired* then ? The world, too, would get more and more strange to them—solitary. Much more eternity.

5. Some men say, ' We shall see the wonders of the universe '—curiosity gratified. And they will take us a long time certainly, and memory will fail, so that we may begin again when we forget. But how soon we get tired of sight-seeing ! We long to get home.

6. Home, that is it ; what is our home ?

7. God and the love of God.

8. Thus *necessitate medii*.

Christmas Day

[THE ADVENT OF CHRIST FORETOLD]

1. INTROD.—There are many subjects in which we have nothing in common and cannot sympathise with each other. But if there is a day which puts us, high and low, rich and poor, on a level, it is this. Angels at Nativity, Resurrection, and Ascension, are above us even in their nature and speech.

2. Fall—the Evil One getting usurped possession of the earth.

3. But deliverer promised from the first, and even the time of His coming, though long after, determined.

4. Therefore expectation of freedom all through the East, and in the West.

5. No event thus known beforehand. God's providences in the natural world are generally sudden—a great man arises accidentally ; great discoveries — and wars, as *the present*.'[1] How sudden—and so end of the world.

6. But this contrasted to them. It was as well known beforehand as many of the calculations of science, like the eclipse we had a few days ago—all upon deep principles of law.

7. And so now that He is come, though the time of His second coming is not determined as the first, let us be sure that all is decreed, and goes upon fixed laws in its season, though His coming is put off again and again, and we are deceived. Thus in the physical, terrestrial world all is confusion at first sight—the earth rises and falls, water rushes in, the face of the land changes, but all on *law*.

8. So, whether the temporal power is established or falls—

9. Only let us be ready for His coming.

June, 1871 (*Trinity Sunday*)

[MYSTERIES]

1. INTROD.—Our happiness consists in loving God. And we cannot love Him without knowing about Him. And we cannot know about Him, ever so little, without seeing that He is beyond our understanding, *i.e.* mysterious. These are thoughts for to-day.

2. What do we mean when we speak of God ?

---

[1] The Franco-German War.

The Creator. Well, how could He make all things out of nothing ?

3. Or again, our Judge, who speaks in our *conscience*; and yet, how can He read our heart ?

4. Or again, Providence. Yet how can He, in spite of the laws of Nature, and the separate wills of ten thousand minds, turn everything to good for each of us ?

5. Union of justice and sanctity with mercy ; power with skill.

6. Thus to be religious at all, to know and believe anything of God, we must believe what we cannot understand, *i.e.* mysteries. It is as our Creator, Judge, Providence, having being, and upholding good that we love Him.

7. And so of revealed religion. The Holy Trinity, the Incarnation, why are these revealed ?—to give us reason for loving God.

8. Show how they lead us to love God.

9. But why need we love God ?—because we are to live after death. And then, where shall we find ourselves if we have not love of God ?

10. Those things here—(1) sensible comforts, (2) activity, (3) affections.—where are they then ?

July 2

(*At St. Peter's*)

[THE VISIBLE TEMPLE]

' Whether you eat, or drink, or whatsoever you do, do all to the glory of God,' 1 Cor. x. 31.

1. What do these words mean ? What do they enjoin upon us ?

o

2. We have our duty towards God, our neighbour, and ourselves. Now we may in a certain way fulfil these duties without doing them to God's glory.

3. *E.g.* we may do our duty to God from mere fear, or from habit, or from human respect; from expedience, *e.g.* going to Communion once a year, saying prayers, keeping from particular sins—being respectable—this right, but not enough. To our neighbour from pity, from benevolence, from family affections—this too, good, but not enough. And so to ourselves. We may be virtuous, and proud or self-conceited. That is, we may do things good, and in a certain sense be good in doing them, *yet not to the glory of God*, i.e. because *not from love*. This is one thing, then, that is meant by the text.

4. Then again, what is meant by doing *all things* ? We have only rare opportunities of doing our duty. How can we eat and drink to [the glory of God] ?

5. (1) Eating and drinking. (2) Use of the tongue —bad conversation. (3) Reading—curiosity. (4) Amusements in kind and in reason.[1] (5) Work— idleness, justice. (6) Sickness. (7) Punishments and penances.

6. Thus the whole day—'Pray without ceasing' —Matt. v. 16,[2] Phil. iv. 8.[3]

And so especially the worship of God. God has told us to pray. Now let us apply this to the

---

[1] Perhaps 'season.'

[2] ' So let your light shine before men, that they may see your good works, and glorify your Father who is in heaven.'

[3] ' For the rest, brethren, whatsoever things are true, whatsoever modest, whatsoever just, whatsoever holy, whatsoever lovely, whatsoever of good fame; if there be any virtue, if any praise of discipline, think on these things.'

service of God. To pray together, and publicly.
This implies, of course, rites of religion, and buildings to perform them in. How can these be done
to God's glory? Now, I can understand men
saying, 'No religious rites, no common worship; religion is private and personal.' But I cannot understand [them] saying, 'It is common and public, it
has rites, it has houses,' and not to bring those
houses under the commandment of glorifying God,
being edifying, etc.

7. Now how do we glorify God in religious houses
or churches? In making them *devotional*. No
matter what architecture, etc., *devotional* is the
end, towards God and towards men.

8. And costly ('of that which cost me nothing,'
etc.[1]) as a means of expressing devotion—Aggeus
i.,[2] Isa. lx. [13],[3] Apoc. xxi.[4] Hence David, 1 Par.
xvii.[5]—Ps. cxxxi. (*memento Domine*, David); 1 Par.
xxix.[6]—[his] zeal for the house of God; his singers,
his psalms—1 Par. xxv.[7] This made him *according
to His own heart* [1 Kings xiii. 14].

9. Now you know what this tends to. Why is it
that I come before you to-day? It is because I felt
a profound appreciation of the work in which your

[1] 'Neither will I offer burnt offerings unto the Lord my God
which cost me nothing'—2 Kings xxiv. 24.

[2] Where the people are reproved for neglecting to build the
Temple.

[3] 'The glory of Libanus shall come to thee . . . to beautify the
place of my sanctuary; and I will glorify the place of my feet.'

[4] Description of the New Jerusalem.

[5] David's purpose to build the Temple.

[6] David, by word and example, encourageth the princes to
contribute liberally to the building of the Temple.

[7] The number and divisions of the musicians.

priest was engaged, and a true sympathy in his
exertions. I recognised in him a zeal for the honour
of God's house such as that of David, whose spirit
was troubled that his God had no abode fit for Him.
I knew that for years and years his spirit chafed
within him that he could not perfect in this place
that idea of solemnity and beautifulness in the visible
temple which he had in his mind. Twenty years
and more, to my knowledge, has this idea occupied
his mind. Then, too, he honoured me by asking
me to take here some part in promoting his work,
which he has committed to me now. Then he did
a part—and now, by his persevering zeal, and the
munificence of pious men, he has been able to do
more; and he urges you, through me, to take part in,
and to complete his service of zeal and love. And
in the next place he calls [you] to a religious act in
a religious way. He appeals to you on a Sunday,
not on Monday, Tuesday, etc. He has taken the
legitimate ecclesiastical means of asking for your contributions, which is possible on a Sunday. He does not
take means of raising money which are not possible
on a Sunday; he does a sacred work on a sacred day.

[Further], his object has special claims from the
circumstances of this church. It is the mother
church of Birmingham. It is dedicated to St. Peter.
In subscribing to it you are testifying your loyalty
to the Holy See in its troubles. Lastly, on the feast
of the Visitation, when all Nature rejoices and Mary
sings the *Magnificat*—2 Cor. viii. 7.[1]

---

[1] 'That, as in all things you abound in faith, and word, and
knowledge, and all carefulness; moreover also in your charity
towards us, so in this grace also you may abound.'

July 30 (*Ninth Pentecost*)

THE JEWS—[CHRIST WEEPING OVER JERU-SALEM—LUKE XIX. 41-47]

1. Only one nation thus selected.
2. And that from its very root.
3. Two thousand years before our Lord, *i.e.* four thousand nearly from this time.
4. This people has had records, not traditions only.
5. It is a specimen of God's governance, in the midst of prevailing confusion, all over the earth.
6. Two cautions : (1) Children suffering for their parents.
7. (2) Tower of Siloam.
8. Mercies, rejection of mercies, punishment.

August 6 (*Tenth Pentecost*)
THE DIVINE JUDGMENTS

I said last Sunday, ' Jews suffering for the sins of fathers.' Is not this condemned by to-day's parable, in which Christians will be behaving like the Pharisee ?   *Answer.* — (1) Not by private decision.   (2) Not individually, but nationally.

1. I mentioned last week the subject of the Jews, but I could not continue without explaining clearly about judgments.   To continue, first there is judgment in the *next* world—yes, but in this also. In one sense *all* suffering is a judgment of sin—in one sense consequence of *Adam's* sin ; (1) individuals, (2) nations.

2. But it does not therefore follow that *we* can say what are judgments and what not.

3. This is what religious men are very apt to do by their private judgment. Irreligious men scout the idea [of divine judgments].

4. Some indeed force themselves upon us, because *all* feel this, *e.g.* (1) if a man were struck dead for lying, [or] (2) if he committed sacrilege against the Holy Sacrament, stealing, etc.

5. But (1) if in party matters, in which good men are on both sides, if in political, he uses his private judgment, he is wrong.

6. Yet how often this is done! a death, a misfortune is interpreted our own way.

7. Again, (2) national judgments. First, this does not show that the suffering nation is worse than others. Tower of Siloam—Pharisee and publican.

8. Nay, nor that the people of that time are worse, for they *may* be suffering for the sins of the fathers.

9. Thus we come again to the Jews. They may be in judicial blindness, but not by the fault of this generation.

10. They were taken without the merit of individuals into covenant, and now they are put out. And since no one can say, 'Jesus is the Lord but by the Holy Spirit,' therefore, as Protestants are blind but without their fault, so the Jews.

Rather thus :

INTROD.— The Pharisee judged the publican. Thus I am led to the subject I touched on last week. Instances : to say a man is wicked because unfortunate — Job's friends ; to say sudden death is a sign, etc. ; to take party or political views ; to say nations are special sinners who suffer—as France—Tower of Siloam.

Censoriousness is judging by our private opinion. But certainly there are judgments. What is on record ? What God says, either by revelation, or the voice of mankind, or by the Church. *E.g.* a case of lying followed by death—for *vox populi*, etc. ; a case of blasphemy or insulting the Blessed Sacrament. Then as to nations, there is only *one* case revealed, the Jews, and even in that case we do not judge individuals—(explain).

Charity thinketh not evil—quote 1 Cor. xiii.

August 13 (*Eleventh Pentecost*)

CONTINUING THE SUBJECT [OF DIVINE JUDGMENTS]

1. INTROD.[1]—We have in the Old Testament, but we have nowhere else, an unveiling of God's providence. It is not so now. The fortunes of the Church and of the Holy See are not commented on now unerringly. Then there were inspired prophets and inspired books : but there are none such in these times. Thus Scripture is once for all.

2. Interpretation of the history of the Israelites and the nations around, especially Israel—*always against their own will*, Ezek. xx. 32.[2] No nation on earth has so great a history as the Jews ; none has so great a future.

---

[1] Marginal note against Introduction: 'This should be at the end.'

[2] ' Neither shall the thought of your mind come to pass by, which you say, We will be as the Gentiles, and as the families of the earth, to worship stocks and stones.'

3. Worldly prosperity does not go with true religion now, as it did then. Then, in order to show *that there was a God*, He wrought in a special way —[also] *in order to show that He did work*; and it is our evidence of a Providence till the end of time.[1]

4. God has given us the greatest evidences in the fact of the Jewish people.

5. Three great visitations : in Egypt ; in Babylon, taken from their land ; and now in the world at large.

6. Moses' prophecy : ' Ye shall not be as the nations.' They were *so unwilling* to be a special people.

August 20 (*Twelfth Pentecost*)

[DIVINE JUDGMENTS CONTINUED]

1. INTROD.—Epistle and gospel are on formality of Jews. This brings me to the subject which I wish to continue.

2. Prophecy, if disobedient, idolatrous, to be scattered, Lev. xxvi., Deut. iv.

3. This fulfilled in the first captivity and dispersion—few returned, etc.

4. But return they did. And then a *second* and a worse dispersion to this day.

5. Now why ? For they boasted to *keep* the law ; no idolatry.

6. It is clear that they must have committed a grave fault ; and it was this—they kept the law only in the letter, not in the spirit.

[1] There is a note which was apparently intended for insertion in this paragraph, enumerating the different kinds of inspired prophetical writings—history, psalmody, ethics, predictions.

7. ' Neighbour ' in to-day's gospel, and so *external* purity, etc. ' I fast twice a week,' etc.

8. The prophets had warned them in vain. ' I will have mercy and not sacrifice.'

9. Consequently they understood no part of the true meaning of their Scriptures. As they made precepts formal, so they made prophecies of the Messiah carnal.

10. And it ended in their being *blind*, and rejecting the Saviour when He came.

11. This then the great sin—greater than any former—the crucifixion of our Lord.

12. ' His blood be upon us and on our children.' So unto this day.

13. This then why they are without homes, without honour, and without spiritual light—from that curse which they invoked upon themselves.

14. You will say that no one can really suffer for the sins of others. True, they will be judged according to their light. But the reason they have no more light is because their fathers sinned.

15. Let us beware, for we at least can ruin ourselves.

August 27 (*Thirteenth Pentecost*)

[DIVINE JUDGMENTS CONTINUED]

1. INTROD.—One out of ten lepers returned thanks, and he a Samaritan ; an election. Thus reprobate were the Jews.

2. In consequence they cast off their Saviour, and were in consequence cast off by God.

3. Now it will be observed they have from the first been wanderers more than other people—in Abraham's time, in Egypt, in the wilderness—but still unsettled. In *unsettled times* some stay necessary.

4. Hence *their Temple* as a pledge, 2 Sam. vii. 10.[1] A pledge of the *gathering together* of the people.

5. Hence it was so beautiful, etc.

6. While it remained, they remained. When it fell, they were scattered.

7. Hence in early times holy men believed and predicted that it never could be rebuilt.

8. Hence Julian attempted to rebuild. Who Julian was.

9. The more wonderful because it was the notion of the Fathers that Antichrist will rebuild Jerusalem.

10. What happened.

11. They never will be able to rebuild this temple till they get back into their land—never to get back till they become Christians—and then it will be a Christian and not a Jewish temple which they will build.

12. I end as I began when I spoke on this subject first. It is *a wonderful proof of the providence of God.* And He will not desert His Church or frustrate His word now, though perhaps not by miracle.

---

[1] ' And I will appoint a place for my people Israel, and I will plant them, and they shall dwell therein, and shall be disturbed no more.'

September 17 (*Sixteenth Pentecost*)

[DIVINE JUDGMENTS CONTINUED]

1. INTROD.—I have lately been speaking of the wonderful history of the Jews, which bears so much on the conviction which we have of the truth of Christianity. We read in to-day's gospel of the Jews, and so continually, and we know our Lord was a Jew, our Lady a Jewess, etc. Yet how little do we know about them, etc., etc.

2. *The Jewish history is the beginning of Christianity and of its evidences*. The mustard seed. Abraham the mustard seed, the father of the faithful. God has founded one church, and that from the beginning. Slow, *as geological formations*. As we cherish a plant—in *the hothouse*, etc.

3. It was the divine purpose that that seed, as existing in Abraham, should fill the earth. He meant gradually to train the people, his descendants, till at length the Christ or Messias should be born among them, and in His name they should [go] forth, etc.

4. He did not use them in order to cast them off. The gifts and callings, etc.[1] Jerusalem instead of Rome, etc.[2]

5. But when the time came, they would not— they thought God could not do without them. ' Stones—children of Abraham.' ' Many shall come,'

[1] ' As concerning the gospel, indeed, they are enemies for your sake ; but as touching the election, they are most dear for the sake of the fathers. *For the gifts and calling of God are without repentance.*'—Rom. xi. 28-29.

[2] If the Jews had not rejected Christ, Jerusalem would have remained the Holy City.

etc.   Parable of the great supper and the vineyard.
' Lo we turn to the Gentiles.'

6. This is a warning to all Christians.   It is a
warning to the Roman people who seem to have
cast off the Holy See, for it is not certain that the
Pope might not change St. Peter's see, and it is quite
certain that he might simply leave Rome as Jerusalem was left.

7. It is a warning to each of us.

September 24 (*Seventeenth Pentecost*)

[THE OLD AND NEW TESTAMENTS]

1. INTROD.—On the gospel.

2. ' The Lord said to my Lord.'[1]

3. Great truths put obscurely in the law.   Both
as regards prophecy and religion and morals.

4. The law of Moses and the Old Testament like
a bud, and the new law the open flower, *e.g.*—

5. The first commandment.

6. The thoughts of the heart—' with all thy
heart,' Matt. v. ; ' If thy eye is single.'

7. Impurity, Matt. v.—divorce and polygamy.

8. The second great commandment—parable of
the good Samaritan.

9. But something the same—*faith*, the *Church*, the
order of ministers, and rites.

10. But all these might be *dead* without love of
God, etc.

11. Let us beware lest we are outside Christians.

[1] ' The Lord said to my Lord, Sit on my right hand. . . . If
David then call him Lord, how is he his son ? '—Matt. **xxii.**
44-45.

March 31, 1872 (*Easter Day*)

[VICTORY OF GOOD OVER EVIL]

1. This day commemorates the victory of truth over falsehood, of good over evil, of Almighty God over Satan—quote Matt. xxviii. 1.

2. Not a recent event, the existence of evil—millions of ages ago, a revolt in heaven — rebel angels ; thus Satan the god of this world. And the conflict began first in heaven—'Michael and his angels.' Then the devil was cast out, and came down to the earth. Then it went on to the greater conflict with the Son of God.

3. Wonderful there should have been such a conflict and such a victory.

4. (1) No evil without His permission. This is one wonder.

5. (2) Then when permitted, He might have destroyed it by a word ; but He suffered it.

6. (3) He might have let it run its course, and die as a conflagration dies out.

7. (4) But He determined on a conflict and a victory.

8. (5) And a victory of apparent weakness over force.

9. This was His will, and since He chose this way, we believe it to be the best way.

10. This has been the character of the conflict ever since. There has been a conflict, and a victory of weakness over might. Martyrs.

11. Holy See.

12. Comfort of this time.

13. We do not know what is coming, but we do know that we shall conquer.

April 7 (*Low Sunday*)

[FAITH CONQUERING THE WORLD]

1. Faith is inculcated on us both by the epistle and gospel of this day.

2. What is faith ? Why it is that secret inward sense in our conscience and our heart that God speaks to us, accompanied by a sense of the duty to obey Him [1]—a sort of voice or command bidding us to believe, telling us to yield ourselves to Him.

3. Thus, if we hear any one scoff at religion, speak against God, or against our Lord, or the Blessed Virgin, the saints or truths of the Gospel, or at the Church, we are spontaneously shocked and turn away. And if unhappily we listen or read, a feeling of remorse and distress and sorrow comes upon us.

4. Faith not opposed to reason, but anticipates it. It is a *short* cut.

5. It is (1) evidently the beginning of religion. And (2) it was a new thing when our Lord came (except among the Jews). (3) It 'overcame the world.'

6. It overcame the world. St. John prophesied when he said it should 'overcome.' How would Christianity have progressed without it ?

7. It overcame the world—by contrast, 'When the Son of man cometh,' etc.[2]

---

[1] See Note 19, p. 343.

[2] '. . . shall he find, think you, faith upon earth ? '—Luke xviii. 8.

8. We need not take this to mean there will be *no* faith, but observe a contrast.

9. We do not know when this time will be, but we understand from what we see that a time *will* come. The unbelief now is dreadful, and should remind us of that time.

10. Let us pray that when He comes we may be found watching.

11. The trial came on the apostles suddenly, their faith failed.

April 14 (*Second Easter*)

[FAITH FAILING]

1. INTROD.—The good Pastor hardly made Himself known to His disciples than He went to heaven. *He went away before men believed in Him.*

2. This was His will—'Not to all the people.' Enumerate how few—the most five hundred brethren at once—but then, as it seems, 'some doubted.'

3. For it was His will that ' the just should live by faith,' Hab. ii. 4—and then thrice in St. Paul.[1]

4. Accordingly elsewhere He says, ' We live by faith, not by sight ' [2]—so Abraham's faith. So our Lord's miracles. And He said, Mark xi. 22-23, ' Have faith in God. Amen I say to you, That whosoever shall say to this mountain, Be thou removed, and cast into the sea ; and shall not stagger in his heart, but believe that whatsoever he saith shall be done unto him ; it shall be done.'

---

[1] Rom. i. 17, Gal. iii. 11, Heb. x. 38.   [2] 2 Cor. v. 7.

5. Thus the FOUNDATION of the Church is faith, Matt. xvi. 13-18, and when faith goes the Church goes. The angels : ' Ye men of Galilee . . . so also will he come again.' [1]

6. *The Church cannot go till faith goes* ; and as the Church will last as long as the world, therefore when faith dies out the world will come to an end.

7. I repeat few had faith when our Lord went, and few will have faith when He comes again. The foundation of the Church.

8. Hence the words, Luke—' Shall He find faith on earth ? '

9. All this makes us look to the future, especially when there is a failure of faith.

10. The prophecies distinctly declare a failing of faith.

11. On listening to prophecies in circulation [2]— not to be trusted.

12. Of course I am not denying that holy people, nuns, etc., sometimes prophesy, but Scripture is surer, 2 Peter.[3] Of course it requires an interpreter, but still there is something to guide us in the literal text.

13. The awful future—' of that day and hour knoweth no one '—but it is profitable to read the words of Scripture, though we but partially understand them.

---

[1] ' Ye men of Galilee, why stand you looking up to heaven ? this Jesus who is taken up from you into heaven, shall so come as you have seen him going into heaven.'—Acts i. 11.

[2] On the number of these prophecies and their character, see Poulain, *The Graces of Interior Prayer*, p. 346 [English translation].

[3] The reference may be to 2 Peter iii. 9, ' The Lord delayeth not his promise,' etc.

April 21 (*Third Easter*)

[THE SECOND COMING]

1. INTROD.—' *Modicum*,' etc. ' A little while ' [1]
—the disciples were perplexed.

2. Our Lord spoke as if He were to come again
soon. And certainly many of His disciples thought
He would. They thought not exactly that He
would end the world, but that He would come to end
the present state of it, to judge the wicked and
introduce a holier world. Nay, at one time even
the apostles.

3. But no one knows when, not even the angels.

4. It seems to have been our Lord's wish that His
coming should always appear near.

5. He gave indeed signs of His coming, but every
age of the world has those signs in a measure.

6. The signs were the falling away and the coming
of some great enemy of the Truth called Antichrist,
who should bind together all the powers of the
world ; that as there was war between the good
and bad angels in heaven, so between the servants
of Christ and Antichrist on earth.

7. This then is our state. In every age things
are so like the last day as to remind us that perhaps
it is coming ; but still not so like that we know.

8. Every age is a semblance, a type in part of
what then at last will be in fulness.

---

[1] ' A little while, and now you shall not see me ; and again a
little while, and you shall see me.'—John xvi. 16 (opening words
of the gospel of the Sunday).

P

(Same as last ; another scheme.)

1. ' *Modicum.*'

2. So they would explain the angels' words, ' *Viri Galilaei.*' [1]

3. And the mass of the disciples did think our Lord would come back soon.

4. Our Lord said ' no,' ' but of that day,' etc.— ' like a thief in the night,' etc.—2 Peter iii. [10],[2] 2 Thess. ii. 3.[3]

5. Here, then, signs mentioned—viz. *discessio* [a revolt] and Antichrist.

6. Before the end a great spiritual war between Antichrist and the remnant of believers in the world.

7. You may say, ' Then the time of Christ's coming *is* known.'

8. No, for this reason—every time is such as to be *like*, and to remind us of the last day.

9. True, always [cause for] fear—the world always seems ending.

10. It is the great mercy of God, and the power [of prayer that delays the end].

11. However, at length the time will come.

[Some alterations or additions were made in secs. 7-9, which it has been found impossible to embody in the text given above. Their *placing* must be left to the ingenuity of the reader.]

Sec. 7. (*a*) ' In spite of this, in every age almost, Christians have thought the end coming.' (*b*)

---

[1] See footnote 1, p. 224.

[2] ' But the day of the Lord shall come like a thief . . .'

[3] ' Let no man deceive you : . . . for unless there come a revolt (*discessio*) first, and the man of sin be revealed,' etc.

' Moreover, though its fulness at the end, always in the world ; many Antichrists.' (c) ' But still it is our duty ever to look out for Him.'

This last, viz. (c), is followed by—' 8. Hence He has made the end *always* seem near.'

Another addition to or substitution for sec. 8 is, ' At this time things very [?] like the end.'

Added in pencil as a substitution or addition to sec. 9 : ' It will also keep us from being over frightened now about present signs.'

April 28 (*Fourth Easter*)

[PROPHECY]

1. INTROD.—I have said that as our Lord went away suddenly, so will He come again. Next, that there will be a great token of His coming, viz. a falling away. Thirdly, that it will still be sudden, because that falling away is in almost every age, or, at least, again and again.

2. Now some passages in Scripture about the falling away : 1 Tim. iv. [1],[1] 2 Tim. iii. [1-5], *ib.* iv.[2] [3],[3] 2 Peter iii. [3-4].[4]

3. About the suddenness, Matt. xxiv. 27, ' For as lightning cometh out of the east, and appeareth

---

[1] ' Now the Spirit manifestly saith, that in the last times some shall depart from the faith, giving heed to spirits of error, and doctrines of devils.'

[2] ' Know also this, that in the last days shall come dangerous times. Men shall be lovers of themselves . . . having an appearance indeed of godliness, but denying the power thereof.'

[3] ' For there shall be a time when they will not endure sound doctrine,' etc.

[4] ' In the last days there shall come deceitful scoffers, walking after their own lusts, saying, Where is the promise of his coming ? '

even unto the west, so shall the coming of the Son of man be.'

4. Infallible word, commented on by theologians through ages : ' Blessed are those who hear,' etc.

5. Of course at all times there is a spirit of prophecy in the Church, and there are holy men and women, though there is no proof of this [in the stories now abroad].

6. It seems to me a great pity that Catholics leave Scripture prophecy, which is the infallible word, for rumours and stories about prophecies without foundation, *e.g.* at this very time.

7. Orval coming up again [1] (vide *Rambler*, vol. iv. p. 73).

8. Shifting according to circumstances—instance of 1748.

9. But still the word of God stands sure and cannot be superseded. If they are true, they co-operate with Scripture and do not oppose it.

10. Now this great contrast between these so-called prophecies and Scripture, the one prophecy good, the other evil.

11. Those who are always looking for good, are always disappointed ; but it is our comfort and glory to know that the Church always triumphs, though it seems always failing.

12. Hence two lessons : (1) The bad state of things is to remind us of His coming and its suddenness. (2) We are encouraged under it by the feeling it is our *special portion* to be in trouble, 2 Cor. iv. 8-9.[2]

---

[1] See Poulain, *The Grace of Interior Prayer*, p. 345 [English translation].

[2] ' In all things we suffer tribulation, but are not distressed ; we are straightened, but not destitute ; We suffer persecution, but are not forsaken ; we are cast down, but we perish not. . . .'

13. Three lessons : (1) To remind and warn. (2) To calm us, because in every age. (3) To give us faith and hope, from the sight of the Church's continual victory.

May 5 (Fifth Easter)

[HOLY SCRIPTURE]

1. We are so ignorant, and the world so confused, that there is a natural desire to know the future (trust in superstitions, fortune-tellers, etc., etc.). A future must come, and we know nothing about it, and desire to know it.

2. Fortune-tellers about ourselves and public affairs—almanacs ; and so Catholics have their prophets.

3. All those reports such as Catholics are apt to be beguiled with, have two tokens of error. They do not appeal to or carry on Scripture prophecy ; next, they are different from Scripture prophecy, as I said last week.

4. Now, though there was no direct comfort and instruction to be gained from Scripture prophecy, it would be a duty to keep it in view, because it *is* in Scripture—because it is the inspired word of God.

5. And this great evil arises from neglecting it, because Protestants take it up and interpret it wrongly ; they interpret it against *us*—*our* Scripture becomes a weapon in their hands because we have relinquished it to them.

6. But great *edification* does come from reading Scripture prophecy ; and a blessing is promised on those who read. Very little is told us about the

future ; nothing to gratify our curiosity, but with it real edification.

7. The Apocalypse brings before us the conflict between Christ and the world.

8. And so of other Scriptures—the Gospel the best spiritual book—St. Paul's epistles, the Psalms.

9. Pius VI.'s declaration.[1] This why so many French and Italians have become infidels.

10. To know Christ is to know Scripture—an anchor.

May 12 (*After Ascension*)

[THE WONDERFUL SPREAD OF CHRISTIANITY]

1. INTROD.—On the wonderful beginning and spread of Christianity.

2. (Describe it.) Twelve men, etc., etc.

3. So they went on gaining ground for centuries, till at length, etc.

4. Then how great their greatness ! Think of the Pope, etc., etc.

5. Yet which was the more wonderful of the two ? Why it is not wonderful that a temporal power should have temporal strength.

6. Another most remarkable thing is that while it was gaining ground, it all along thought that it was failing, and the end was coming.

7. They did *not* think so in the time of its great prosperity, when it really *was* failing.

8. (Now this presentiment of failure is to show

[1] Letter to Martini, Archbishop of Florence, ' on his translation of the Bible into Italian, showing the benefit which the faithful may reap from their having the Holy Scriptures in the Vulgar Tongue.'

the strength of the Almighty. We have this grace
in earthly vessels.)

9. It arises from the prophecies. We know evil
in this world, not good, is promised us.

10. Again, it is a type to bring before us the last
age when it will fail (God so contrives the events
of this world that, etc.), and when Christ will come
from heaven at the last moment to save.

11. (Horsley's letter.[1])

12. Passages from Malvenda about Rome.

13. The wisdom of God is stronger, etc.

June 9 (*Third Pentecost*)

[THE FALL OF MAN]

1. INTROD.—The ninety-nine are the angels, the
one is man.

2. Man is one because perhaps there are indefinitely more angels than men ; and next, because
Adam was one head, the head of our race. We all
sinned in Adam, but each angel who fell sinned in
himself.

3. The account of Adam's fall.

4. Now, to understand how great it was, we must
consider Adam's high gifts. It was a miracle almost,
a violation of his nature and state, that he fell, for
he had so many gifts.

5. Had he been like us we could understand it ;
but he was not like us. But on his falling he *lost*
those gifts, and became what men are now, and that
we can understand.

---

[1] See *Discussions and Arguments*, pp. 107-8 where the letter
is quoted.

6. He came under God's anger—he was prone to sin ; he was under captivity of the devil. The whole face of the world external was changed, as winter instead of summer—that *world*, I may say, deprived of angels, of God's countenance, and full of the devil ; even innocent things became infected and means of temptation.

7. He lost those gifts, and therefore, when he had offspring, he transmitted to them that nature which he had ; but he could not transmit those gifts which he had forfeited.

8. Such, then, is our state as children of Adam. We are what he was after sinning—in precisely the same state—and that state is called ' original sin.' *We have not* the advantage which Adam had.

9. Now, if a man says this is mysterious, hardly consistent with justice, I answer : (1) The whole of revelation must be mysterious, we do not know enough to defend it, because it is part of a whole system.

10. (2) God is not bound to give us high gifts such as He gave Adam. It is sufficient that He gives us such grace that it is our fault if we do not go right.

11. (3) But, again, Christ came to set all right.

June 16 (*Fourth Pentecost*)

[THE WORLD, THE FLESH, AND THE DEVIL]

1. INTROD.—The whole creation travaileth.

2. All creatures must be imperfect and tend to corruption if left to themselves. All creation *which we see*—the visible world.

3. The visible world requires a support to its laws ; they cannot support themselves.

4. And still clearer as regards separate beings. All things *in fluxu et transitu.*

5. Brute animal passion—but without sin—but no brute passion but exists in man.

6. Such excesses the gift of reason is to hinder and subdue ; and therefore sin in not doing so.

7. But the conflict so strong that it requires the grace of God.

8. Now we see the state to which original sin, the sin of Adam, has reduced us. It has rendered us like the brutes, because it has deprived us of grace, yet left us in sin.

9. This stripped human nature is called in Scripture *the flesh*—(Cain's fratricide, the flood, destruction of Sodom, state of things when our Lord came)—

10. And is our second giant enemy. Our first enemy is the devil.

11. Now trace the effects of the flesh—the growth of evil in individuals, in bodies ; the power of example—encouraging each other, appealing to each other ; false maxims—affecting to *teach.*

12. This *the world*, a creation of the flesh—our third great enemy.

13. Thus fallen man has to fight against three great enemies.

14. Let us *never forget* we are servants and soldiers of Christ, Eph. vi. 11-17.[1]

[1] ' Put you on the armour of God, that you may be able to stand against the deceits of the devil. For our wrestling is not against flesh and blood, but against principalities and powers, against the rulers of the world of this darkness, against the spirits of wickedness in the high places. Therefore take unto you the

June 23 (Fifth Pentecost)

[THE WORLD REJECTING GOD]

1. All men like to be independent and have their own way, and in many things they can profitably be so and get on more to their advantage than when they are under rule, but—

2. In one thing they cannot—in religion and duty.

3. And for this reason : because we are made up of two principles which war against each other. One or other must be the master.

4. Satan knew this, both man's desire to be independent and the impossibility of it. He knew that man must either be God's servant or his own, and that he, man, did not know this. So he tempted him with, 'Ye shall be as gods,' and waited securely for his consequent falling under his own power.

5. Therefore man, rejecting his true Lord, admitted a usurper. This brings in atheism, *i.e.* idolatry with immorality. And therefore he always tends to get worse and worse, and unless God interfered he would become unbearable.

6. But God has always pleaded with man (' My spirit shall not always,' etc., and ' The Spirit intercedes '), and thus reserved a remnant. This remnant has pleaded for the world and saved it. It is the salt of the earth.

armour of God, that you may be able to resist in the evil day, and to stand in all things perfect. Stand therefore, having your loins girt about with truth, and having on the breastplate of justice; And your feet shod with the preparation of the gospel of peace; In all things taking the shield of faith, wherewith you may be able to extinguish all the fiery darts of the most wicked one. And take unto you the helmet of salvation, and the sword of the Spirit (which is the word of God).'

7. The deluge—till only eight persons. Earth filled with violence. ' They ate and drank,' etc.

8. Sodom. ' If ten persons.'

9. When our Lord came. Rom. i.

10. Ever since, it has been the elect few who have saved the world and the Church.

11. When at length ' He shall not find faith on the earth,' He ' cometh.'

12. On what in this age takes the place of professed idolatry, and is really atheism.

August 4 (Eleventh Pentecost)

[MIRACLES—I]

1. INTROD.—The gospel miracle ; other miracles.

2. People say, Why are not miracles now ? (1) in complaint ; (2) in unbelief. We know there are *not such* nor *so many* as once.

3. But let us consider why miracles were necessary in the beginning—the then state of the world. Even if the great powers of the world had been inspired to enforce Christianity, how would that prove it *true* ?

4. Mere men as the preachers, so *weak*, they would need something to give them *authority* and *weight*.

5. (1) The world had to be startled and awed, which weak preachers could not do ;

6. (2) Secondly, to be convinced, which worldly, powerful preachers could not do.

7. A miracle when *real* is what man cannot do.

8. It was just suited to the case. Common sense tells us it is just what *would* convince us.

9. Why not now then ? It was necessary, especially in the beginning.

10. And hence it is still accorded by God in converting the heathen—St. Gregory Thaumaturgus, St. Martin, St. Augustine, St. Patrick, St. Boniface, St. Francis Xavier.

11. But though we have not miracles as in the beginning, (1) dealings of God with the human soul are like miracles.

12. And (2) so are providences and answers to prayer. (Not miracles now, because want of faith. *Vide* the gospel).

August 11 (*Twelfth Pentecost*)

[MIRACLES—II]

1. INTROD.—Why we do not see miracles.

2. We believe that miracles *are* wrought now, though they are few.

3. I have spoken of miracles wrought by apostles of countries.

4. And so of saints. If I am asked why miracles scarce, I answer, Saints are scarce. We cannot conceive common men doing miracles.

5. You will ask, *Why* are saints scarce now ? It has ever been that times vary. There are sometimes bursts of supernatural power and greatness.

6. So the Psalms, xliii.,[1] lxxiii.,[2] lxxxviii. (finis),[3] and Isaias li.[4]

---

[1] *Deus auribus nostris.* In which the Church commemorates former favours and present afflictions.

[2] *Ut quid Deus.* A prayer of the Church under grievous persecutions.

[3] ' Be mindful, O Lord, of the reproach of thy servants,' etc.

[4] An exhortation to trust in Christ. He shall protect the children of His Church.

7. But when there *are* saints there are great miracles.   St. Philip.

8. But you will say, If there are few saints on earth, yet there are many in heaven ; why do they not do miracles from heaven, as St. Philip used to do, as we read in the accounts appended to his life ?

9. Because we have not *faith*—not *individuals* merely, but the population.   (Enlarge on this.)

10. *Vide* Luke xix. 26, Matt. xxi. 27, Mark ix. 23, Mark vi. 5.

11. Because men say, ' Unless we see signs and wonders,' etc., in a haughty way.

12. Miracles now come as *a reward* to faith, in those who do not look out for them.   Not denied then.

August 18 (*Thirteenth Pentecost*)

[CHRIST'S PRESENCE IN THE WORLD]

1. INTROD.—We have read, Sunday after Sunday, as to-day, of our Lord's miracles ; but did we see Him, I do not think that [the miracles] would most strike and subdue us.

2. Not His works, *but Himself.*

3. But here I explain something.   Strange to say, it was His will that, seen by casual spectators, He should seem like another man, Isa. liii. 3 [1]; and hence John i. 5, 10,[2] and Mark vi. 3.[3]   And the Samaritan

---

[1] ' His look was as it were hidden and despised, whereupon we esteemed him not.'

[2] ' The light shined in the darkness ; and the darkness did not comprehend it.'   *Ib.* 10, ' He was in the world, and the world was made by him, and the world knew him not.'

[3] ' Is not this the carpenter, the son of Mary, the brother of James, and Joseph, and Jude, and Simon ? are not also his sisters here with us ?   And they were scandalised in regard of him.'

woman, John iv. And this specially so in the case
of bad men, Luke xxiii. 11,[1] John xix. 9.[2]

4. When we had seen Him two or three times, if
we were not utterly dead to truth ·we should find
that He had made a deep impression on us, on
looking back, though we did not perceive it at the
time, Luke xxiv. (Emmaus).

5. Next, supposing we could stay and gaze on
Him, then what would first strike us would be His
awful infinite repose, the absence of all excitement,
etc., etc. All that is told us of Him, all His words and
works, brings out this—and doubtless His aspect.

6. Next, if we could still look on, if we could see
His eyes, two things would strike us; first, His
seeing us through and through. Hence He is often
said to 'look.' Mark iii. 5, 'And looking round
about on them with anger'; *ib.* viii. 33, 'Who, turning about and seeing his disciples, threatened Peter,'
etc.; *ib.* xi. 11, 'And he entered into Jerusalem, and
having viewed all things round about.'

7. Secondly, compassion. Mark x. 21, 'And
Jesus looking on him loved him'; Luke xxii. 61,
'And the Lord turning, looked on Peter : and Peter
remembered the word of the Lord.'

8. And then when He began to speak ! the tones
of His voice ! John vii. 46, 'The ministers answered,
Never did man speak like this man'; Matt. vii. 28,
'And it came to pass, when Jesus had fully ended
these words, the people were in admiration at his
doctrine : For he was teaching them as one having
power.'

[1] 'And Herod and his army set him at nought, and mocked him.'
[2] 'And Pilate said to Jesus, Whence art thou ?'

9. Hence He *draws* men. Matt. ix. 9, 'And He saw a man sitting in the custom house, named Matthew : and he said to him, Follow me. And he rose up, and followed him.' Virtue going out of Him. Mark v. 30, 'And immediately, Jesus knowing in himself the virtue that had proceeded from him, turning to the multitude, said, Who hath touched me ? ' *ib.* vi. 56, 'And whithersoever he entered, into towns, or into villages, or cities, they laid the sick in the streets, and besought him that they might touch the hem of his garment : and as many as touched him were made whole.'

10. All this, even though He did no miracle.

11. This is what we must look for in heaven.

12. And yearn for it[1] in the Blessed Sacrament.

August 25 (*Fourteenth Pentecost*)

[THE 'TWO MASTERS']

1. INTROD.—Two masters. *Why* cannot we serve two masters ? Most men wish to serve God and the world.

2. What is it to have a master ? what is meant by it ?

3. Not merely an employer ; this not enough.

4. A master is one who has some hold over us. In old times slaves, but now it is by compact. If I promise, if I take wages, I willingly take a master. As children are naturally subject to parents, so, by free will, servants to masters. They may *change*, but while they have a master they are *bound*.

---

[1] These last words are barely, if at all, legible.

5. Now on *serving* a master. Consider St. Paul, Eph. vi. 5-6.[1]

6. And if so of all masters, so especially of the good—idea of a *household*.

7. Now we see what in religion is meant by God being our master. (1) He has created and *bought* us. (2) We have made an everlasting contract with Him. (3) It is not a contract in this or that— as *employers*—but we are of His household and family. (4) We are one of His, and must study His interests. (5) He is a good master.

8. *Hence,* if our Lord is our master, we can have no other master, and we must be full of zeal and love.

9. He has given Himself *wholly* to *us.*

10. The other—*Mammon!* So not only we can't have two ; we must have *one.*

11. Now let us ask ourselves : *Is* in fact God our master ? Do not we follow our own will, taking one day one master, another another.

12. There would not be all this variety of religions, and this infidelity in the world, if men really made God their master. They would soon agree together. On men of no party. Apoc. iii.—Laodiceans.[2]

September 1 (*Fifteenth Pentecost*)
[MIRACLES]

1. Introd.—Miracle on the widow's son at Naim.

2. Open, public—so on Lazarus, John xii. Matt.

[1] ' Servants, be obedient to them that are your lords according to the flesh, with fear and trembling, in the simplicity of your hearts, as to Christ ; Not serving to the eye, as it were pleasing men ; but as servants of Christ, doing the will of God from your heart.'

[2] It is not clear where these words were intended to come.

ix. [6], ' that you may know.' [1]   So Acts iii. [2]; so Elias, 3 Kings xviii. [3]

3. But many others our Lord *forbids* the proclaiming. Thus He takes the blind men into a *house*, or charges them, etc., Matt. ix. 27 ff. [4]   And again, still more remarkably Jairus's daughter, Mark v. 43, [5] Luke viii. 56. [6]

4. Now this will tell us how to answer the question about miracles now. There are miracles now, but not such miracles as in the beginning—not public ones. They were in order to establish the religion —but now the religion established.

5. Then they might be wrought by bad men—by Judas—Matt. vii. 22. But now they are marks of sanctity of the persons or the things by which they are wrought.

6. Hence (1) the workers do not *proclaim* them.

7. (2) Not so marked, by running into [*i.e.* not easy to be distinguished from] providences.

8. (3) Not so discernible—to one, and not to another.

---

[1] ' But that you may know that the Son of man hath power on earth to forgive sins, (then said he to the man sick of the palsy,) Arise,' etc.

[2] The miracle upon the lame man.

[3] Elias cometh before Achab. He convinceth the false prophets by bringing fire from heaven ; he obtaineth rain by his prayer.

[4] ' And as Jesus passed from thence, there followed him two blind men, crying out and saying, Have mercy on us, O Son of David. And when he was come to the house, the blind men came to him.'

[5] ' And he charged them strictly that no man should know it.'

[6] ' Whom he charged to tell no man what was done.'

Q

9. (4) No *necessity* to believe them, for *the Church does not propose them*.

10. (5) Not to be urged on unbelievers.

11. As I have said before, the miracles of the Catholic Church are those which are personal to ourselves. (1) Goodness of God to us in the course of life. (2) His grace given to our souls.

September 8 (*Sixteenth Pentecost*)

['THE RICHES OF HIS GLORY']

1. INTROD.—The epistle [Ephesians iii. 13-21].

2. Do you understand St. Paul's words, 'The riches of his glory,' etc. ?

3. We have here a glimpse of what heaven is. 'Eye hath not seen,' etc.

4. It was the support of St. Paul against the world.

5. The world has *its* 'depth' and 'height,' etc. Illustrate deep science, high power, glory, etc.

6. It is this which makes the world the false prophet ; it preaches and seduces us with false maxims.

7. It is grievous to say, but it must be said, that almost all we read, the periodical press, is in this respect a false prophet.

8. The devil said he had ' all the kingdoms of the earth.' Things good under bondage of evil.

9. Therefore God gave us the Church—as the true Prophet to bring the glories of heaven before us.

10. All sacraments, etc., with this object.

11. So Scripture a *revelation* of the next world—especially our *Lord's person*.

12. And so the saints and their history—a whole family round our Lord.

13. This is the reason why we are allowed to think so much of our Lady ; why she is *given* us to employ our thoughts. Protestants say we make too much of her. Now which is best, to think too much of *her*, or of the *world* ?

September 22 (Eighteenth Pentecost)

[DISEASE A TYPE OF SIN]

1. INTROD.—The paralytic in the gospel.

2. The cures to typify the spiritual disorders and diseases of mankind. This *one* reason of the special character of our Lord's miracles.

3. And it is well to consider the *variety* of bodily diseases with this view. They are horrible, but we may be sure that the various spiritual maladies are far more horrible.

4. And the *least* sin, for its quality is so bad—in this it goes beyond bodily diseases, for bodily infirmities admit of degrees much more. And it goes beyond the analogy of disease in these respects : (1) because universal to the race ; (2) because so intense.

5. But the case of sin may be likened to the analogy of offences against the senses, as to which the least imperfection is *destructive* ; *e.g.* the sweetest nosegay spoiled by one bad scent of one dead leaf. One drop of bitter in the most pleasant drink. And so of hearing, one discordant note. And so in the sciences—in astronomy the slightest motion

[vibration in an observatory]—or in the mirror or glass the slightest dimness ; and in chemistry, poisons ; and in medicine, etc.

6. The whole creation marred. Then why did God allow it ? I answer—

7. That is a question not for the present time. You don't inquire *how* a fire arose before you have extinguished it.

8. Next, our Lord came to *destroy* sin. This the characteristic over all other religions ('not the righteous,' [1] 'repent ye,' [2] the lost sheep); they [other religions] acknowledge sin, but they cannot cure it.

9. He takes away the guilt, and the power [of sin].

10. This by His death and passion.

11. This the fundamental doctrine—texts.

October 13 (*Twenty-first Pentecost*)

[FORGIVENESS OF INJURIES]

1. INTROD.—To-day's gospel [the king taking an account of his servants].

2. Parallel passages ; Luke xvii. 3-4.[3]

3. So far easy, for it is scarcely supposable that

---

[1] ' I am not come to call the righteous, but sinners to repentance.'—Mark ii. 17.

[2] ' Jesus preached : Repent ye, and believe the gospel.'—Mark i. 15.

[3] ' Take heed to yourselves : If thy brother sin against thee, reprove him ; and if he do penance, forgive him. And if he sin against thee seven times in a day, and seven times in a day be converted to thee, saying, I repent ; forgive him.'

one should have so little generosity as to refuse forgiveness to one who confessed himself wrong and asked to be forgiven.

4. But when he does not ask to be forgiven ; if he persists in opposition and injury, and goes on doing harm, and takes a wrong course. Yet this commanded too. The Lord's Prayer—Matt. vi. 14-15,[1] Mark xi. 25-26,[2] Rom. xii. [18-20].[3]

5. Or again, supposing he does not do so, asks to make it up, still there may be, you may say, such difficulties as these : I may wish to keep at a distance, for :

6. (1) *E.g.* I cannot trust him; he is a dangerous man.

7. (2) He is likely to do me spiritual harm.

8. (3) The sight of him is a temptation, an irritation to me ; we shall be best friends at a distance.

9. (4) I shall be a hypocrite if I make it up, for I don't like his doings.

10. (5) I ought to protest against him.

11. ANSWER.—'If you *in your hearts forgive* not

---

[1] ' And if you will forgive men their offences, your heavenly Father will forgive you also your offences : But if you will not forgive men, neither will your Father forgive you your offences.'

[2] 'And when you shall stand to pray, forgive, if you have ought against any man : that your Father also who is in heaven may forgive you your sins. But if you will not forgive, neither will your Father that is in heaven forgive you your sins.'

[3] 'If it be possible, as much as is in you, having peace with all men. Not revenging yourselves, my dearly beloved, but give place unto wrath : for it is written, Revenge to me ; I will repay. But if thy enemy be hungry, give him to eat; if he thirst, give him to drink : for doing this thou shalt heap coals of fire upon his head.'

every one his brother ' [Matt. xviii. 35]. You must
love him. Col. iii. 12-13 [1]; Matt. v. 44-47.[2]

12. OBJECTION.—' But I do not like him.' How
can I love him ? *This* is a fundamental difficulty.

13. ANSWER.—Can you pray that you may meet
him and love him in heaven ? You and he are both
far from what you should be ; and each has to
change. Look on the *best* part of his character—
learn sympathy with him. Think how he suffers.
Purgatory useful for this—to bring you and him
nearer to each other.

October 20 (*Twenty-second Pentecost*)

[FINAL PERSEVERANCE]

1. INTROD.—Epistle for the day, perseverance in
grace.

2. Two things plain : (1) perseverance necessary,
Matt. xxiv. 13,[3] Ezech. xxxiii. 18.[4]

---

[1] ' Put ye on therefore, as the elect of God, holy and beloved,
the bowels of mercy, benignity, humility, modesty, patience ;
Bearing with one another, and forgiving one another, if any
have a complaint against one another : even as the Lord has
forgiven you, so do you also.'

[2] ' Love your enemies. do good to them that hate you, and
pray for them that persecute and calumniate you ; That you
may be the children of your Father who is in heaven, who maketh
his sun to rise upon the good and bad, and raineth upon the
just and the unjust. For if you love them that love you, what
reward shall you have ? do not even the publicans this ? And
if you salute your brethren only, what do you more ? do not
also the heathens this ?

[3] ' He that shall persevere to the end shall be saved.'

[4] ' For when the just shall depart from his justice, and commit
iniquities, he shall die in them.'

3. (2) Not in our power, but a special gift of God. We cannot merit it.

4. Now what is merit ? (Explain.) By ourselves not only not perseverance, but nothing can we merit.

5. Because (1) by ourselves we can do nothing pleasing to God, because of our sinfulness ; and (2) because how can anything we do be worthy of *heaven* ? what proportion ? Luke xvii. 7-10.[1]

6. (1) Therefore the grace of God, and (2) His promise ; thus we can be said, first, to please God, and secondly, to merit.

7. And these two by the merits of our Lord and Saviour.

8. But there are two things we cannot merit— the first grace and the last.

9. As to the first grace, it is plainly God's free bounty which has made us Christians.

10. As to the last, it is God's free bounty, in spite of the accumulation of merits. No extent of merit is sufficient to gain perseverance—the just may fall, however holy, etc. Think of Solomon ; think of Judas. It is a special gift to die in grace.

11. Two conclusions. First let us continually pray that God would give us this special gift of dying in grace.

---

[1] 'But which of you, having a servant ploughing or feeding cattle, will say to him, when he is come from the field, Immediately go sit down to meat ? And will not rather say to him, Make ready my supper, and gird thyself, and serve me, whilst I eat and drink ; and afterwards thou shalt eat and drink ? Doth he thank that servant for doing the things which he commanded him ? I think not. So you also, when you shall have done all these things that are commanded you, say, We are unprofitable servants : we have done that which we ought to do.'

12. This may comfort us when we lose our friends, that God may in His mercy have taken them then, when they were in grace.

January 12, 1873 (*Sunday in Epiphany*)

[MANIFESTATION OF THE KINGDOM OF CHRIST]

1. INTROD.—The Magi.

2. They were a prophecy and anticipation of what was coming.

3. We know the kingdoms of this world became the kingdom of Christ.

4. Two things wonderful : (1) that such a conquest should be made ; (2) that it should be prophesied.

5. That kingdom is passed by, three hundred years ago. We have, however, the *remains*— cathedrals, ruins of abbeys—the usages of society, etc.

6. So that we are known as the ' old religion.' And what is old comes from our Lord, and what is new came from men.

7. This, then, is the wonderful manifestation of past times.

8. But now it is wellnigh past—while it lasted it was comparatively easy to believe when there was only *one* religion.

9. But now Satan, who has his instruments in every age, says : ' There are so many religions, none is true ; they are all false.'

10. Those who live will find a *wave* of infidelity overspread the land. What they are to do.

11. There is another *manifestation* [1] : ' Come and
see '—whereas men keep you from coming and seeing.
' A witness in court '—we say, ' Let us actually
see him.' But no—here it is ' so many religions,
etc., Catholicism is going down,' or ' Catholics are a
fallen race,' etc., etc., instead of above, ' Come and
see.' Reading the Gospels. John ix., Luke xvii.
By ' religious men ' is meant those who have
experiences.

January 27 (*Third Epiphany*)

[MEN OF GOOD WILL]

1. INTROD.—The centurion in the gospel of the
day. Account in St. Matthew, in St. Luke.

2. He was a heathen, etc. This is how our Lord
began the Church, when as yet there was none, and
addressed Himself to those who were well inclined,
and gained them.

3. This is what is meant by men of good will in
the angels' song.

4. Instances : Nicodemus, John viii. ; Gamaliel
in Acts v. ; Luke ix. [49], ' who followeth not us ' [2] ;
Syrophoenician [woman], Matt. xv., Mark vii.

5. And so now. We must not repel them or treat
them harshly, or laugh at them, etc.

6. They illustrate the secret work of grace—from
grace to grace.

---

[1] The other *manifestation* seems to be the Church with her
notes. The claims of this witness to be interrogated are put off
with ' There are so many religions,' etc.

[2] ' And John, answering, said, Master, we saw a certain man
casting out devils in thy name ; and we forbade him, because he
followeth not with us.'

7. Tests of being *bonae voluntatis* [of good will]—
not justice, sense of fairness, and benevolence, though
these are praiseworthy—and we must be grateful to
such men.

8. But (1) humility from sense of sin. ' Lord, I
am not worthy.' ' Even the dogs,' etc.

9. (2) Sense of duty. ' I am a man under
authority.'

10. (3) Devotion. ' He has built us a synagogue,'
Luke vii.

11. Let us beware lest those who have less advan-
tages than we have outstrip us. ' Many shall
come from the east and the west,' etc.

March 2 (First Lent)

[GOD OUR STAY IN ETERNITY]

1. INTROD.—We must draw near to God.

2. This means to contemplate, to recognise, to
fear, to love. Now let us see the necessity of this.

3. Here we are tempted to make the world our
God, because we see it, and do not see God.

4. But consider what our state is when we are
dead ; our senses then are all gone.

5. Consider this : we have five senses, and we
know what a deprivation the loss of any one—
sight or hearing or touch or feeling—any one.

6. But in death they all go together. See what
we are reduced to. It is true we cannot have any
bodily pain—and that is what people are apt to say,
' All his pain is over.'

7. True, but is there no pain of the mind ? Do

we know how acute pain of the mind is ?—surely we know it even in this life.

8. Let us consider our being suddenly cut off from all intercourse except with ourselves—a truly solitary confinement ; worse, for that here is only loss of hearing, *i.e.* conversation.

9. Supposing in addition it comes on us that we should not be thus, except for our own fault !

10. Now it is clear that we should have no remedy unless God visited us and gave us light.

11. The light of glory, the light of heaven, the only thing.

12. But suppose we have no desire for it, no love of it.   Suppose we look back in fond *regret* to this world.

13. Therefore the love of God is the *only* way in which we can be happy.

June 22 (Third Pentecost)

[THE LOST SHEEP THE TYPE OF FALLEN MAN]

1. INTROD.—Gospel, one sheep in wilderness, man ; the ninety-nine, angels.

2. Contrast between angels and man. They so great, we so low.

3. Yet Psalm viii. 4-5, ' What is man,' etc.[1] ; ' out of weakness were made strong ' [2] ; ' when I am weak, then I am strong ' [3] ; ' these things the angels desire,' etc.[4] ; ' joy among the angels of God.' [5]

[1] ' What is man, that thou art mindful of him ? or the son of man, that thou visitest him ?   Thou hast made him little less than the angels,' etc.

[2] Heb. xi. 34.   [3] 2 Cor. xii. 10.

[4] ' Which things the angels desire to look into.'—1 Peter i. 12.

[5] ' . . . upon one sinner doing penance.'—Luke xv. 10.

4. For, see the difference. Even angels fell; and even for angels no restitution. You would think they were more convertible—they had no powers to return.

5. Could, then, any being return, if not angels ?

6. Man not only in the image of God, but of the beasts of the field.

7. Incarnation.

8. All things possible with God.

9. Hence a great multitude.

10. Hence *saints*.

11. Woe is us, if *elect*, yet such as we are.

January 4, 1874

[THE NEW YEAR]

1. Difference of feelings of young and old towards a new year.

2. The young with hope and expectation; the mature with anxiety.

3. The young look forward first for a change— each year brings changes. And to them they are changes, as they think, for the better; they are older, stronger, more their own masters, etc.

4. And secondly, the future is unknown, and excites their curiosity and expectation.

5. It is different with them who have some experience of life. They look (1) on *change* as no great good; they get attached to things as they are, etc.

6. But (secondly) the ignorance of the future, so far from being good, is painful—in truth it is one

of our four wounds. Ignorance of all things, especially of the future—of what a day may bring forth—of suffering, bereavement, etc.

7. Thus, like railway train, bowling away into the darkness.

8. Ignorance what sufferings and bereavements are in store—of death—of the day of death. We *walk over our own dying day*, year by year, little thinking.

9. It may be a work-day, or holiday, or a 'many happy returns' [day].

10. All things make us serious. *This we know,* that death is certain ; and then the time comes when there will be *no* change—for time is change—and no ignorance.

June 28 (*Fifth Pentecost*)

[THE JEWISH AND THE CHRISTIAN CHURCH]

1. 'Unless your justice [exceed that of the scribes and Pharisees, you shall not enter into the kingdom of heaven,' Matt. v. 20].

2. The Jews, then, God's people, and their Church God's Church. It was the Ark. The world lay in wickedness, and in the wrath of God, except that holy Church which God founded by Moses. The Pharisees its rulers.

3. It was salvation, for 'salvation of the Jews.' So now.

4. It taught God's law. 'Moses' seat.' So now.

5. Indefectible, never to end. You will say it ended. No, it changed into the Christian Church.

6. But though Jewish Church could not fall away,

its members could. And *so now*. Even its rulers
could fall away, though they taught what was right
—Moses' seat ; and so could the body of its people,
and *so it did*. They relied *on their privileges*, and
were cast off. St. John the Baptist said, ' Flee
from the wrath to come,' to Pharisees coming to
His baptism. And so Christians may [fall away].
This is a warning to us, and St. Paul so makes
it, Rom. ii.

7. Therefore whatever is said to or about the
Jews is a warning to us.

8. Thus what is said about the Samaritans.
(Who were the Samaritans ?) Many are singled out
as better than the Jews. (1) The good Samaritan ; (2) the grateful Samaritan.[1] They are like
Protestants. So Protestants may be better than
we in spite of ' salvation from the Jews.'

9. Nay, heathen were better than the Jews, *e.g.*
centurion—' Many shall come,' etc., Matt. viii. 11-
12 [2] ; Tyre, Sidon, Sodom [3] [Matt. xi. 21-23].

10. Thus at present countries on the Continent—
they may be cast off as the Jews were. Protestants
in England may be better.

11. But we must look to ourselves. Many are
called. *Strive* and *seek* [Luke xiii. 24].

12. All those who are in earnest, though they
know their imperfections, must not fear.

---

[1] The leper who returned to give thanks.

[2] ' Many shall come from the east and the west, and shall sit
down with Abraham, and Isaac, and Jacob, in the kingdom of
heaven. But the children of the kingdom shall be cast out.'

[3] See p. 47 (footnote).

August 2 (Tenth Pentecost)

[REVELATION—WORD OF GOD (I)]

1. INTROD.—I have been reading from Scripture, viz. an epistle and gospel. Why ?

2. What is meant by Scripture, Scriptures ? Writings, *the Word of God*, or *revelation*—through *different* ages.

3. Why has God given us a ' Word ' ? Because we are so ignorant.

4. Two Testaments. First with one nation (Old), then with people of *all* nations (New).

5. The Bible, the Book.

6. By the by, why are Catholics said to *burn* the Bible ? They never do, or have (unless they committed an act of sin) ; but what they *burned* was not the Bible but a Protestant translation. (Also without comment.)

7. The Church *comments* and *explains*. Now as to the Old Testament, or the Word of God to the Jews,

8. Law and prophets,

9. Till our Lord came.

August 9 (Eleventh Pentecost)

REVELATION—WORD OF GOD [II]

1. INTROD.—Recapitulation. Scripture — Scriptures—two Testaments—Bible—teaching, and therefore inspiration.

2. When I say ' inspired '—not in science or art, etc.

3. Difference of Old and New—Old imperfect, and through so many ages ; New perfect, and once for all in one age.

4. Here I shall speak of the New. The Apostles —inspired—our Lord God. Heb. i. 1-2.[1]

5. OBJECTION.—Why not their words [inspired], if their writings ? Why not their speeches ? Why not their conversation ? Of course it was. All they said about RELIGION was. They might not know about the earth going round the sun, etc.

6. But it might be objected, on the other hand, that such sayings were not recollected. But some might be.

7. This is what Catholics called ' tradition,' and in which we differ from Protestants. Meaning of the word ' tradition.' *Vide* epistle for this Sunday.[2]

8. Things we know by tradition : (1) that Scripture is the inspired Word of God ; (2) what books the Bible consists of—for these Protestants need tradition ; (3) the Mass, etc.

9. And so natural. Every school, every set of workmen, go by tradition—' common law ' is tradition.

10. Hence we say there are two parts of the Word of God, written and unwritten.

11. But still, surely tradition *may* go wrong. Yes, and Scripture may be wrongly interpreted.

---

[1] ' God, who at sundry times and in divers manners spoke in times past to the fathers by the prophets. Last of all in these days has spoken to us by his Son, whom he hath appointed heir of all things, by whom also he made the world.'

[2] 1 Cor. xv. 1-10. ' For I delivered [*tradidi*] unto you first of all which I also received.'

12. Therefore *the Church* decides, as being infallible.

13. Hence there may be mistaken reports of miracles, prophecies, etc., but we must see what the Church says about them.

March 28, 1875 (*Easter Day*)

[THE SEEN AND THE UNSEEN WORLDS]

1. INTROD.—This is the greatest day of the year, because it is the day on which our Lord rose from the dead. He said while He died on the Cross, '*Consummatum est*'—'It is finished,' and in the Resurrection we behold the fruit of His 'finishing.'

2. (1) The miracle itself—and this special, because without corruption ; others [who were miraculously raised to life] died again. (2) Next it is a *reverse* after a sorrowful week. (3) It was a conquest of the foe. (4) It was the exaltation of our nature.

3. But further, it gives us a great lesson, never to despair. There are two worlds, and nothing which we see in this world images to us what is going on in the next.

4. This world runs by laws. All things go on as at the beginning of the Creation. The sun rises and sets ; and so human affairs. They thought by killing Him to have stamped out religion.

5. And so now—the political world, commercial, scientific ; telescopes, calculations, ships, etc., etc.—but another world going on *too*. This world a *veil*.

6. The mass of men only see this world. Each

R

man enters in this world with hopes for a career,
etc., etc. Not wrong in minding this world, but in
not minding the next. Their view of life.

7. The flood ; ' marrying and giving in marriage '
—*but* another world *too*.

8. We walk by faith, not by sight.

9. Therefore acts of faith, hope and charity.

10. Therefore attending Mass, in which the whole
mystery of redemption, atonement, resurrection,
etc., [is set forth].

11. Let us thank God for giving us eyes, and
pray Him to give others eyes too, for He died for all.

Perhaps no laws in heaven, but every act from
God's personality ; and each perfect in itself, so that
we could not reason from one to the other.[1]

June 6 (Third Pentecost)

THE SACRED HEART

1. INTROD.—Many devotions in Holy Church.
This is one which has spread of late years, more, I
may say, than any other. To-day is the special
feast of it ; and [this] leads me to explain in what
it consists.

2. Our Lord is One. He is the one God. He
took on Him a manhood, a body and soul; that body
from Mary. Still, He was one, not two—one, as
each of us is one.

3. We too, in our way, are each of us one, though
we are two—soul and body—and the body has parts ;

---

[1] This paragraph is placed at the end. It was written on an
empty space, and it is not clear where it was meant to be.

[nevertheless] each of us is *one*. This is what is meant by speaking of our Lord's [oneness] as we speak of our own.

4. And though each of us is thus composite, we can love each other as one, though of so many parts. And in like manner, though our Lord is God and man, with a soul [and body], we can contemplate Him as one, and worship, love Him as one.

5. Further, if I said I loved the face, or the smile, or liked to take the hand of my father or mother, it would be because I loved them. And so, when I speak of the separate portions of our Lord's human frame, I really am worshipping Him. So in the Blessed Sacrament we do not conceive of His Body and Blood as separate from Him.

6. Devotions at various times [and ages]—the Wounds, the Blood, the Face—and in like manner the Heart. *We worship* [*each*] *as Him,* as that One Person who is God and man ; we worship [*Him*] by the memento, the pledge of His Heart.

7. Why ? The Heart a *symbol*—so the Wounds and the Blood. [In contrast with these] a symbol is sometimes that which [only] expresses and reminds —thus water, oil, wine, bread.

8. What is the Heart the symbol of ?—of His love, His affection for us, so that He suffered for us—the agony in the garden.

9. Moreover, of His love in the Holy Eucharist.

10. The Heart was the seat, first, of His love for us ; secondly, of His many griefs and sorrows.

[*The following were appended, apparently as alternatives :*]

7. Of two things especially to remind us now, when the world is so strong—His power and His love. He will overcome by love.

8. The Heart is the emblem of His love—in worshipping It we worship Him.

Christmas Day

[CHRISTMAS JOY]

1. Almighty God condescends to be represented in human language as hoping, fearing, suffering disappointment, repenting, feeling anger, etc. But there are two human feelings and affections which may be predicated of Him, not in the way of figure, but *proprie*—joy and love ; of course I mean as being perfectly free from human passion.

2. Of the two great festive seasons of Easter and Pentecost [on the one hand], and Christmas [on the other], Easter, with the fifty days of Pentecost, is the season of love, Christmas of joy.

3. I need hardly say so—our churches, our altars are dressed up as token of our joy—and our houses, according to our opportunity—and we meet together for social enjoyment, and to provide festive meals and entertainments of various kinds for the poor and for children. And all this, of course, is right, and is the proper token of our faith and hope, of our Christian joy. It is, I say, the *season* of joy, and therefore it is fitting that we should exhibit these signs of our being full of joy.

4. But a warning needs to be given. It is quite

possible, rather, alas! it is not uncommon, for men to stop at, to get no further than the outward signs. Nay, I may say that it is quite plain in a country like this; in a place like this we may—nay, we do—content ourselves with rejoicings which are temporal, earthly, visible, without going at all to what is the real reason, after all, for those external signs. All around us men are doing so, and thus we are led to do as they do.

5. Therefore most necessary to recollect that there are two sorts of joy, earthly or outward, heavenly or inward, and that we may easily place the former in the place of the latter.

6. We shall understand best what the true joy is by what is told us in Scripture of the first Christmas. If that joy really consisted in anything external, joy could not have been there. (1) Go through the journey to Bethlehem—winter—slow journey—lagging behind—no room in the inn, as the inn was *full*, doubtless the stable also—caravanserai—the stable, etc. State of the stable—not like our stables, neat and clean. This is what the shepherds found. They themselves had a hard time of it, watching their flock by night, but they came to a worse place; not so cold, but less like a home. Yet, I say, they rejoiced. Contrast of Herod in his palace close by. (2) The angels sang 'Glory to God in the highest; and on earth peace to men of good will'; and the angel said to the shepherds, 'Behold, I bring you tidings of great joy,' and the shepherds returned 'rejoicing': and Mary [in] the *Magnificat* at an earlier time shows her thoughts. Yet what were the outward circumstances?

7. Paragraph in newspaper : ' Somehow Christmas festivities fall flat when one has grown up.' The
shepherds, etc., rejoiced even in [the midst of] their
own outward discomfort and hardships ; but men
of the world cannot lastingly rejoice even in the
midst of their good things. Oh how this shames
our delicacy, our desire of comfort, etc. ! Of course
we may thankfully take what God gives us ;
but at least, while we rejoice in these gifts, let us
not forget to let our inward spiritual rejoicing keep
pace with our external.

8. Let us recollect the apostle's words. [*Perhaps
the preacher quoted here from the epistle read at the
first mass of Christmas* : ' The grace of God our
Saviour hath appeared to all men, instructing us
that, denying ungodliness and worldly desires, we
should live soberly, and justly, and godly, in this
world ; looking for the blessed hope, and coming of
the glory of the great God and our Saviour Jesus
Christ.'—Titus ii. 11-13.]

December 26 (*St. Stephen*)

[THE MARTYRS]

1. INTROD.—The first martyr—what meant by a
martyr — witness for the truth. Christ the first
martyr,[1] but He *more* than a martyr.

2. There is one God, but He was forgotten by all
the earth (except the Jews).

---

[1] ' Thou sayest that I am a king. For this was I born, and for
this came I into the world, that I should give *testimony to the
truth*.'—John xviii. 37.

3. If one God, only one religion. But every nation had its own god or gods, and they never thought of interfering with each other.

4. God suffered this for a long while (Acts xiv. 16 [1]), but at length, etc.

5. Hence preachers and evangelists, apostles— but men did not like to be interfered with. It was a new thing ; hence persecutions, and the preachers became martyrs.

6. In Jerusalem they first suffered, because they came in collision with the prejudices of the Jews— such St. Stephen—then a wider range—the apostles all martyrs.

7. The *Te Deum* calls them an army—(enlarge upon this). Contrast to Mahometans—nay, to Protestantism, which spreads, not indeed by persecution, but by the patronage, etc., of the State. What can be more wonderful than an army conquering by being beaten ?

8. The most horrible deaths ; stoning is bad enough, but it [was] only one way—St. Andrew, St. Bartholomew, St. Peter, St. James, St. Paul, St. John (oil)—the young, the old, the weak, the strong, men and women.

9. FIRST REFLECTION.—*Thus* are *we* Christians. What, under God, do we not owe to them ?

10. SECOND REFLECTION.—How *comfortable our* lives are ! The thought of the martyrs should support those too who are in pain, etc., and those who see their friends in pain.

11. All this should humble us.

---

[1] ' Who in times past suffered all nations to walk in their own ways.'

January 9, 1876

[LIFE A PILGRIMAGE]

1. Life a journey or pilgrimage, Gen. xlvii. 9, (Jacob),[1] Luke xiii. 33,[2] John xi. 9.[3] This is a thought befitting the beginning of the year.

2. In a journey we have a start and a goal. So life. Again, in a journey, obstacles—rivers, mountains, etc. So in life, temptations.

3. Now journeys have different lengths—so different lives have different lengths ; one man dies old, another young—each life is *long enough* to reach the goal. Each length according to capabilities—one can go three miles an hour, another four, etc.

4. The length of each is determined by the length of light. No one has to travel in the dark, John ix. 4[4] and xi. 9-10[5]—as one man's journey might be near the pole, another's far south—different times of year.

5. If we linger or deviate on a journey, the light goes.

6. Have *we* not lingered or gone out of the road ? Double loss of time if we have to get *back* ; and then how to find the way ?

[1] ' The days of my pilgrimage are a hundred and thirty years : few and evil, and they have not come up to the days of the pilgrimage of my fathers.'

[2] ' Nevertheless I must walk to-day and to-morrow.'

[3] ' Are there not twelve hours in the day ? If a man walk in the day, he stumbleth not.'

[4] ' I must work the works of him that sent me, whilst it is day : the night cometh, when no man can work.'

[5] ' If a man walk in the day, he stumbleth not, because he seeth the light of this world. But if he walk in the night, he stumbleth, because the light is not in him.'

7. We shall have to run.

8. Perhaps a carriage—increase of grace.

9. Now let us think of the past year and the year to come.

February 20 (*Sexagesima*)

[CHRIST OUR FELLOW-SUFFERER]

1. INTROD.—We have to labour and suffer, as I said last week,[1] but we have this support and consolation, that Christ labours and suffers with us. This a great subject.

2. Adam fell. God never puts on us more than we can do ; He gives grace sufficient.

3. But it is much more than this. He might have forgiven and restored us *without* Christ's death, but He has done so in a more excellent way.

4. The Prince of Wales going into a labour prison, putting on dress of convicts, having his hair cut, all for the sake of converting convicts. So—

5. Christ has sought us—but more, for He has wrought and suffered for and instead of us.

6. Still more ; not only He has taken *ours*, but has given us His—the vine and branches—one body, He the head, Rom. xii. [5][2]; 'Why persecutest thou me ? ' [Acts ix. 4].

7. We are all [that] He is—sons of God—full of grace—heirs of heaven.

8. Is not this sufficient to sweeten labour ?

---

[1] There are no notes of the sermon here alluded to.

[2] 'So we, being many, are one body in Christ.'

February 27 *(Quinquagesima)*

[COMMUNION WITH GOD]

1. God the Creator of all—all things *depend* on Him.

2. But the happiness of intellectual beings is not only [in] dependence [upon], but in *union* with Him.

3. This union shows itself in communion—that is, a fellowship—intercourse of thought, or a spiritual conversation.

4. The fall of Adam has placed a huge obstacle, as a wall or a mountain, between us and God, and Christ has broken it down. He has opened the kingdom of heaven to all who believe. This is why He took flesh and came on earth.

5. Now this communion requires love and grace on the part of God, and faith and prayer on the part of man.

6. In His part God is not wanting. His love is as expansive, as diffusing, as powerfully and constantly overflowing as the sea, or as the wind, or as the flame, and whereas their expansion is for evil, that of the Divine Attributes is for good.

7. Now we have instances of this communion between God and man in Scripture clearly defined.

8. Enoch ' walked with God '—and Noe. What is meant by ' walking with God ' is plain ; men who are companions on a journey *talk* while they *walk*. The two journeying to Emmaus ; our Lord joined them—this was communion.

9. Another image is that of *friend*. Abraham is

friend of God, 2 Paralip. xx. 7,[1] Isa. xli. 8,[2] James ii. 23.[3] Friends are in possession of each other's confidence ; and Gen. xviii. [17], ' Shall I hide from Abraham what I am about to do ? '—and [Abraham's] intercession for the cities.

10. And so Moses—Num. xvi. 18 and Ex. xxxiii. 11.

11. What was, then, the privilege of the few, for the Jews were ' servants ' in Judaism, is the right of all Christians. *Vide* Luke xxii. [4], 'friends,' and John xv. 15, when our Lord speaks of ' omnia quaecunque,' etc.

12. CONCLUSION.—(1) Those who make friends of the *world* cannot have this Divine friendship ; (2) Those who *have* that Divine friendship have a disgust of worldly friends. ' Jesus Christ the same yesterday, and to-day, and for ever.'

First Lent [1876]

[SIN]

1. INTROD.—This is a time when the Church calls upon us to put off sin—both the *reatus* [guilt] and punishment of it—and the indwelling power.

2. That there is such a thing as sin—something distinct from everything else—I shall take for granted ; it is an offence against God : ' against Thee only have I sinned.'

3. It is different from a mistake, intellectual,

---

[1] ' Didst not thou our God kill all the inhabitants of this land . . . and gavest it to the seed of Abraham *thy friend* for ever ? '

[2] ' . . . the seed of Abraham my friend.'

[3] ' And the scripture [Gen. xv. 6] was fulfilled, saying, Abraham believed God : . . . and he was called the Friend of God.'

social, or practical ; different from an offence against beautifulness, etc.

4. I shall take this for granted. And the question is about its *gravity*—is it of little consequence or great ?—*this* is my point.

5. Now here I shall dwell on one consideration, viz. of what Almighty God thinks of it, by what He has done in consequence of it.

6. The GOSPEL. What is meant by Gospel, and why ?

7. It is the coming of God in our flesh, thus to humiliate Himself—to suffer, to preach, etc., etc. Can it be a light thing to bring about this ? This is indubitable if Christianity is true—there cannot be two opinions.

8. Nay, He had to suffer—to be tortured—to be crucified. Texts.

9. His terror : it was more then than the outward appearance, John xii. [27],[1] Luke xxii.,[2] Heb. v. [7].[3]

10. Now what is to be said to those *who ignore all this* ?

March 12 (*Second Lent*)

[HELL]

On future punishment—on hell.

First, we are not fair judges of the malignity of sin.

[1] ' Now is my soul troubled ; and what shall I say ? Father, save me from this hour : but for this cause I came unto this hour.'

[2] The agony at sweat of blood.

[3] ' Who in the days of his flesh, with a strong cry and tears offering up prayers to him that was able to save him,' etc.

1. Because like men who have ever lived in a mine, and never seen the light of day.

2. Because skill in any art (and so in holiness) raises the standard.

3. Because culprits make bad judges.

Secondly, God is a consuming fire ; sanctity burns what is not holy.

Thirdly, consider Scripture. St. John Bapt., ' burn up the chaff '—Matt. xxv., Mark ix., fire— St. Luke, Dives and Lazarus—St. Paul, St. Peter, St. John, St. Jude.

March 19 (*Third Lent*)

[PUNISHMENT OF SIN]

1. Recapitulation—God ' a consuming fire ' [Deut. iv. 24] ; the nature of things ; His nature cannot alter ; He cannot alter it ; He cannot make sin a blessedness, or make it other than antagonist to Him.

2. An atmosphere—we cannot live in water, or except in air—a sinful soul cannot breathe the atmosphere of the spiritual world ; that atmosphere is fire to it.

3. While in this world punishment is sometimes delayed ; but even here it commonly comes as heathens witnessed, (thus old men suffer for their youth). But [if not here] certainly afterwards— a ' fiery indignation ' [Heb. x. 27], etc.

4. Not only deliberate sinners, but even God's own children ; and this is what I wish to bring

before you, especially this evening. This is the doctrine of purgatory.

5. Such is the divine law—even after repentance and reconciliation after a firm faith ; yet those whom God loves, who die in grace, nevertheless suffer for the sins which they did before their conversion and after it.

6. Matt. v., ' last farthing.'

7. 1 Cor. iii., ' by fire.'

8. (1) Delaying repentance. ' I will repent by and bye '—but purgatory.

9. (2) Every sin has its punishment.

10. (3) Joy that there is a purgatory.

11. (4) The willing plunge. The content of purgatory—next to the content of paradise.

March 26 (*Fourth Lent*)

HOW TO ESCAPE PURGATORY

1. The first thing to do is to be in constant union here with our Lord and Saviour ; that is, in a state of grace.

2. This we are able to do through the sacraments and our own care—that care is to avoid mortal sin. Venial sin no one [can avoid] but by special privilege ; but it is our own fault if we fall into mortal.

3. If we are always in and out of grace (1) shall we persevere ? (2) at least we shall not save ourselves from purgatory.

4. Next, if we are in grace and reunited to Christ, our penitential works tell—1 Cor. xi., ' judged ' ;

(1) prayers—' Knock, and it shall be opened ' ; (2) alms ; (3) fastings.

5. Thirdly, indulgences. Still depending on a state of grace.

6. Fourthly, but better than all, contrition.

7. Two kinds of contrition. With love or with fear ; for God or for self.

8. Anyhow there must be hatred, grief, resolve.

9. But contrition with love does everything ; it saves without the sacraments when they can't be had.

10. St. Vincent Ferrer and his penitent (*Bail*, t. 5).

April 16 (*Easter Day*)

[GIFTS OF THE RESURRECTION]

1. INTROD.—This day is the foundation of all our hopes for eternity. Recollect that our souls will never die ; the body dies, but not the soul ever ; always in being. The body dies—rises ; but there is no break of continuing being as regards the soul.

2. What condition are our souls in to *encounter* immortality ? Who is there who, if he can bring himself to think steadily, would like to live for ever with no better outfit for eternity than he has ? Who would like to go out of this world to judgment with no clearer conscience than he has ?

3. In this tremendous difficulty our Lord came to be our Saviour. The Son of God came, etc., etc. He died. He took upon Him all our miseries, and made Himself a sacrifice.

4. And he has gained us great gifts by which to reverse our state. Salvation consists in five. We

have virtues which God cannot have, *e.g.* faith
and hope, but these [five] gifts are much more ;
[they make us] 'partakers of the divine nature'
[2 Pet.i.4]. Five—GRACE and TRUTH, John i.16-17[1];
LIGHT and LIFE, *ib.* 4, 9,[2] and *ib.* xiv. 6, 'the way,'
etc.[3]; PEACE or JOY, *ib.* xiv. 27.[4]   So in apostolic
greetings in the Epistles.   All five Divine Attributes
—'partakers of the divine nature.'

5. The first is grace or holiness (instead of un-
holiness).

6. The second truth (instead of ignorance), witness
to the truth—faith—hearing.

7. The third is light—*seeing, knowledge,* everything
clear—as eyes correspond to ears.   John viii. 12 [5];
ib. xii. 35, 36.[6]

8. Fourth, life, John x. 10,[7] 28,[8] *ib.* iv. 14,[9]
ib. v. 24.[10]

9. Fifth, peace or joy, John xiv.,[11] *ib.* xx. twice [12];

[1] ' And of his fulness we have all received, grace for grace. . . .
The law was given by Moses ; grace and truth came by Jesus
Christ.'

[2] ' In him was life; and the life was the light of men. . . . The
true Light, which enlighteneth every man.'

[3] ' I am the way, and the truth, and the life.'

[4] ' Peace I leave with you, my peace I give you. . . . Let not
your heart be troubled.'

[5] ' I am the light of the world.'

[6] ' Walk while you have light, that the darkness overtake you
not. . . . Whilst you have the light, believe in the light.'

[7] ' I am come that they may have life, and have it more
abundantly.'

[8] ' I give them [my sheep] life everlasting.'

[9] ' The water that I will give him shall become a fountain of
water springing up to life everlasting.'

[10] ' He who heareth my word . . . hath life everlasting.'

[11] V. *supra.*

[12] The salutation ' Peace be to you,' after the Resurrection.

joy, *ib*. xv. 11,[1] 1 John i. 4.[2] All five in John xvii. [Christ's prayer for His disciples].

10. Oh how different is all this from the ideas and language of the world !

11. Let us recollect, to realise it in ourselves is the only true way of keeping the Resurrection.

November 19 (*Twenty-fourth Pentecost —Sixth Epiphany*)

[THE FIRST AND SECOND ADVENTS]

1. The mustard seed.

2. The Church between the two comings of Christ.

3. Those comings both awful, Mal. iii. and Mal. xxiv. 29, etc.

4. [But] this difference—the first expected ; the latter sudden—Mark xiii.—the ten virgins.

5. The first—Jacob's prophecy [the time fixed, *i.e. when* the sceptre shall have departed from Judah] —Daniel's 70 weeks=490 years.

6. The second [sudden] like the Flood and [the destruction of] Sodom—Luke xvii. 26-30.

7. Hence ' watch and pray,' Mark xiii.

8. And so St. Paul—a first duty to *wait*, 1 Thess. i. 10 [' to wait for his son from heaven '], Rom. xii., and Heb. x.

9. But it may be said, What difference between this and waiting for the death of each ?

---

[1] ' These things I have spoken to you, that my joy may be in you, and your joy may be filled.'

[2] ' These things we write to you, that you may rejoice, and your joy may be full.'

S

10. Against building and planting—progress.

11. Making this structure and polity of visible society a god to be worshipped, though the individual dies.

12. No, all we see will come to nought, however great and beautiful, Isa. ii. *finis.*

December 3 (*First Advent*)

[THE SECOND ADVENT]

1. The gospel this day a portion of our Lord's prophecy [of the destruction of Jerusalem and the second coming], rising out of the apostle's admiration of the beauty of the Temple.

2. It seemed to them too beautiful to be destroyed.

3. This is the way with men ; they wonder at their own great works ; they look up to the great works of their fellows ; and when they are able to trace out the beauty of God's creation, that too they make an idol, and bow down before their own work, loving the map [which they have made] of it, and say they have discovered it to be too beautiful to be broken.

4. It is well for man, an *homuncio*, thus to think, for he can do a great thing but once ; but God destroys His own works, however beautiful, because He could from His infinite resources create many worlds each more beautiful [than] those that were before it.

5. And His own works He regards not, if they have not that note of *sanctity* which He breathed on them in the beginning.

6. Therefore when the Jews, His own people, came to nought, if He did not spare the work of His own hands, much less [was He likely to spare] Herod's work.

7. Babylon and Nabuchodonosor.

8. Now in this [the present] state of society it is pride, not open sensuality [which is conspicuous]; *i.e.* think of the greatness of an army, of a popular assembly, of some queen's ball. But whenever the world looks imposing and likely to last, *that* is the most likely time that it will be brought to an end, or at least [is the likely time] of some great judgment.

December 10 (*Second Advent*)

THE IMMACULATE CONCEPTION

1. The great feast of this church [of the Birmingham Oratory], being the mystery to which it is dedicated.

2. Describe Adam's state [before he fell], and original sin. He became a child of wrath—enemy of God—and the dwelling-place of the evil spirit—[*Lex orandi lex credendi* : this last point illustrated by the] exorcisms at baptism.

3. Now, could this be the state of the Blessed Virgin ?

4. [It could not be.] How is this proved ? By *meditating* on the Incarnation. (Explain)—deeper and deeper knowledge the saints have in gazing on the Beatific Vision—and in this life the more we meditate on divine truths the more we find.

5. She is [the] Mother of God. He not merely

inhabited a man, etc. Doctrine of the Incarnation.

6. Therefore immaculate in [her] conception.

7. Hence the Holy Fathers, etc., and so on to our times, till Pius IX. has made it an article of faith.

8. It does not, cannot interfere with the supreme glory of her Son, but subserves it.

December 17 (*Third Advent*)

[SIGNS OF THE SECOND ADVENT]

1. Sign of our Lord's coming, though we don't know the day, viz. an apostasy or revolt—ὁ ἄνομος [the lawless one, 2 Thess. ii. 8]; Antichrist [cf.] ἡ ἀνομία, Matt. xxiv. 12.

2. Give circumstances of St. Paul saying so— belief that our Lord was *then* to come when St. Paul wrote.

3. Our Lord says, Matt. xxiv. [9, ' Then shall they deliver you up to be afflicted, and shall put you to death : and you shall be hated by all nations for my name's sake ']—contrast of prosperity, *ib.* 38, [' For as in the days before the flood they were eating and drinking . . . so also shall the coming of the Son of man be '], and persecution, the greatest persecution, as holy men have anticipated.

4. But why will they not persevere, as [the] first Christians [did] ? Want of faith (*vide* verse 12). We can do all things by faith if we have faith ; but false reason cuts at the root (*vide* verse 24, false prophets).

5. Sophistry and false reason—even the elect.

6. This all is opening on us—like the last age.

7. But as sun shining through clouds, or as a dying man kept alive by prayer, always going and never gone, so (for the chance of more conversion and more elect), the world ever dying.

8. Alas! the next generation—young people, I fear for you! [1]

9. Let us at this time of year pray that as Christ on His first coming came with preparation, so we may be prepared for His second coming.

December 24 (*Fourth Advent*)

[THE FIRST ADVENT]

1. 'A thousand years as one day.' Quote 2 Pet. iii. 7-8.[2]

2. Illustrated in preparation for Christianity. Abraham two thousand years before His coming.

3. He was told, ' In thee [shall all the kindred of the earth be blessed,' Gen. xii. 3], but his faith tried by the delay.

4. Mount Moriah the illustration of that faith which was against sight, for Isaac was the child of promise.

---

[1] Father John Pollen, S.J., remembers the great impression made on him by this sermon, and especially by the pity expressed for the rising generation. He heard it as a boy at the Oratory School.

[2] ' But the heavens and earth, which are now, by the same word are kept in store, reserved unto fire against the day of judgment and perdition of the ungodly men. But of this one thing be not ignorant, my beloved, that one day with the Lord is as a thousand years, and a thousand years as one day.'

5. This a type of all holy men ; instances in Heb. xi. 13.[1]

6. Not only did not our Lord come, but all events seemed to look the other way.

7. Prophets said again and again, *Persevere in faith* ; but what chance was there when the people rebelled and apostatised, and there were captivities, etc., and at last deportation of the whole people to Babylon ?

8. Elias and the seven thousand—a remnant.

9. Solomon, ' There hath not failed [so much as one word of all the good things that he promised by his servant Moses '], 3 Kings viii. [56] ; Isaias to Hezekiah, Isaias xxxvii. 32 [2] ; Habacuc iii. 18.[3]

10. At length Herod king ; a heathen—but man's extremity God's opportunity. Christ at length came.

11. Apply this to these times—and personally to individuals.

[A line along the margin shows that § 8 was to be inserted in § 7, presumably after ' apostatised.']

December 31

[THE PAST NOT DEAD]

1. We are accustomed to keep the beginning of the year, but not the ending ; we congratulate each

---

[1] ' All these died according to faith, not having received the promises, but beholding them afar off.'

[2] ' For out of Jerusalem shall go forth a remnant, and salvation from Mount Sion.'

[3] ' But I will rejoice in the Lord ; and I will joy in God, my Jesus.'

other on the new year, but we let the old year go its way. Why is this ?

2. It is, first, because the old year, whether it was a happy year or unhappy, suggests thoughts of pain. If unhappy, that is painful ; if happy, it is [painful] because it is gone.

3. Also, because the past year is dead, and whatever is dead naturally inflicts pain upon us. And therefore we turn to the *new* year with hope.

4. But is it really dead ? No ; in one sense it is awfully alive. All things live to God—the past as well as the present. No ; *to us only* the past year is dead, and to us also one day it is to [be] alive again. On the last day the books will be opened, chronicling all events. Quote Apocalypse xx. 12.[1]

5. Think of the number of events—*e.g.* in the newspapers—yet they are nothing to the sum-total.

6. Every soul has its history ; every soul is immortal and independent.

7. What are the events of the year but a history in millions of souls of the unceasing warfare between good and evil. We talk of battles in the world, etc., but what are they ?

8. How many have gone right ? how many wrong ? how many turning-points for life ? how many have died good and bad, young and old ?

Photographs ; light from distant stars not yet arrived here. How much we need God's protection ; the future quite dark.

---

[1] ' And I saw the dead, great and small, standing in the presence of the throne ; and the books were opened : and another book was opened, which is the book of life : and the dead were judged by those things which were written in the books, according to their works.'

May 13, 1877 (*After Ascension*)

[PARTICULAR PROVIDENCE]

1. INTROD.—[The Ascension] the end of the miraculous series of events which our Lord's life comprises. From birth to Ascension, as is said in the Creed,

2. Till He shall come to judge.

3. The world goes on by fixed laws, and they are such as in themselves are good, and subserve and proclaim His General Providence. All these contrivances and final causes, etc. But nothing personal in this—a cold system. He does not speak. No encouragement to us to speak to Him—Acts xiv. 17 [1] and xvii. 26-27.[2]

4. But He has been more merciful than this—*the hairs of our head numbered. Particular Providence* everywhere and always. How was He to show this particular providence ? By suspending the laws [of Nature] by miracles.

5. This He did. But that particular providence He has mercifully brought [out] in a distinct form, first in the Mosaic, and then in the Gospel economy. He has suspended His laws.

[1] St. Paul's address to the Iconians : ' Nevertheless he left not himself without testimony, doing good from heaven, giving rains and fruitful seasons, filling our hearts with food and gladness.'

[2] St. Paul's address to the Athenians : ' And hath made of one all mankind to dwell upon the whole face of the earth, determining appointed times, and the limits of their habitation. That they should seek God, if haply they may feel after him, or find him.'

6. Especially when, after suffering, He ascended to heaven.

7. He promises us heaven. He has gone first to prepare a place for us individually there.

8. *Patria*—Heb. xi. [13], pilgrims [1]; Eph. ii. [19].[2]

9. *Sursum corda*—Col. iii. 1.[3]

10. We think of meeting our *friends* in heaven; we do not think of Him who is the best of all friends.

11. Don't say we don't know Him; Gospels, especially Gospel of St. John, bring Him close to us.

12. *Sursum corda*—Col. iii. 1. Pray without ceasing, after pattern of Luke xxiv. 52,[4] Acts i. 14.[5]

May 27 (*Trinity Sunday*)

[THE HOLY TRINITY]

On this day we close our celebration of the merciful truths of the Gospel by a solemn commemoration of the Holy Trinity,

1. Lest we should forget who and what God is.

2. He has so humbled Himself, *e.g.* our Lord's human life, also the Holy Ghost—*a gift* poured out—received—quenched—[*al.*] extinguished—grieved.

3. Therefore the Church appoints this feast, that

---

[1] 'All these died according to faith, not having received the promises, but beholding them afar off, and saluting them, and confessing that they are *pilgrims* and strangers on the earth.'

[2] 'You are no more strangers and foreigners.'

[3] 'Therefore if you be risen with Christ, seek the things that are above, where Christ is sitting at the right hand of God.'

[4] 'And they adoring went back into Jerusalem with great joy.'

[5] 'All these were persevering with one mind in prayer.'

we may have that holy fear, and awe, and wonder at Him which becomes His greatness, while we believe in Him and love Him.

4. State the doctrine—that there is a Divine Trinity or Triad, a Divine Three in heaven. Each is God in the fulness of Divine Attributes, yet there is only One God, as the Creed says—this is the beginning and end of the Holy Truth—we cannot say more or less.

5. Three devotional sentiments towards it—faith, fear, love—all three feelings together.

6. Faith—that there should be a mystery, congruous. He might not have told us, but if not, still we might be sure there was one. Unitarians—*Credo quia impossibile.* I would not believe in a God who had no mysteries.

7. Awe, as I have said [secs. 1-3].

8. Love ; the mystery no difficulty, for *each part* of it is clear ; the most ignorant can confess God the Father—then [God] the Son, etc.[1] Though how all three [propositions] are true together, and why the second does not contradict the first, etc., the wisest cannot know. And in heaven we shall know all.

9. The Mystery brings before us the peace, as well as the love which [we] shall have in heaven.

June 24 (*Fifth Pentecost*)

[ANGER]

1. INTROD.—Epistle [1 Pet. iii. 8-10], Gospel [Matt. v. 20-24].

[1] See p. 158, footnote.

2. The anger thus spoken of by our Lord[1] is a sin against *charity* ; it is something more than indignation, for it is a *personal* feeling, the consequence of some slight or injury to oneself.

3. And more than want of self-command. Passion or irritableness, which is parallel to concupiscence, a sin against self. Passion or irritableness leads a *child* to beat the ground. To shout, to abuse, to strike is a relief. All this is sinful, but not [*in se*] against charity ; one may really love the person who provokes us.

4. Yet, though it [anger] is not this common affection, in spite of the phenomena being the same, it is a common sin, and far worse than an affection.

5. It shows itself in this, that it does not go off or evaporate ; it remains as spite, resentment, a grudge, a desire of revenge—and who will say this is not common ?—in a feeling of repulsion, alienation, hatred.

6. *How* wrong it is we shall see by the contrast of the *Christian* feeling, as darkness is understood by light—how beautiful the generosity, the nobleness of returning good for evil ! Joseph and his brethren ; David with Saul.

7. I have said it is a personal feeling ; but there is a kind of hatred, which is only partially personal, or only at first, but when the keen personal feeling is gone, leaves a habit of hatred and repulsion—a dull negative feeling. This too is against charity.

8. It may be said, indeed, How can I help it ? I

---

[1] 'Whosoever is angry with his brother, shall be in danger of the judgment.'

don't like the man, as I don't like a certain taste or sound, etc.

9. On the other hand, you must feel towards all men as those you can bear to meet in heaven.

10. This one effect of purgatory, to burn away in every one of us that in which we differ from each other.

August 5

[THE END OF MAN]

1. Why are we placed here on earth ? This is a question which comes often to children, and is the beginning of their responsibility.

2. Too often the question ceases to be asked by the young soul; but it drowns the thought in the levity of the small world of children around it.

3. But I repeat it, my brethren, think of it now— *Why* are you here in this world ? Were you put here merely to eat, drink, sleep, etc., for a certain [number] of years, to marry, to grow old, to die ? Were you put here merely to get on in life, to make a fortune and a name, to gain power, influence, to be in a position to gratify ambition, etc.? You know you have a higher end than this.

4. Now consider what the real reason is. You were put here to prepare yourself for a higher and eternal state; and for this all the riches, power, name —all the cleverness, sharpness and knowledge you may have or acquire, nay, I will say, all the industry, all the affectionateness, all the good-heartedness you have by nature (though these qualities are entirely good)—will not avail at all.

5. You are come to make the raw material of your souls into (as I may say) a vessel of honour for the Lord's house above.

6. Consider the instance of various trades on earth, and you will understand—bread, pottery, moulding, and the fine arts—a building, a statue.

7. So there is the raw material of your soul—it is called in Scripture the flesh ; it is human nature in the rude condition to which Adam's sin has reduced it. Take the instance of the brute animals—you will in a measure understand what human nature is—the passions, etc.

8. On bringing the soul into shape—the small trials of every day.

9. How different good old men are from what they were when young. So, on the other hand, you can't help moulding yourself. Woe to you if you mould the wrong way.

June 9, 1878 (*Pentecost*)

[THE COMING OF THE HOLY GHOST]

1. INTROD.—The Holy Ghost, whose feast is to-day, is God. But God is the object of every day's devotion, not of festivals. Saints, our Lord's Humanity, have festivals. What is to-day ? (This is so large a subject that I fear I shall hardly say all I wish this morning.)

2. God is in Himself all good, and not only all good, but one characteristic of that goodness is the attribute of communicating that goodness to all His creatures. He gives Himself to them in order

that they may in their measure partake of that perfect[ion] which is He.

He is not only the Giver but the gift, and this day we thus view Him as the gift ; for, considered [as] the great and heavenly gift of all good, He is the Holy Ghost ; therefore this day is the solemn commemoration of that mercy of God by which He has given Himself to us. The gift—(keep to that—say if we have peace, etc., etc.)—and this a feast of St. Philip, etc. ; *vide* sermon on Whitsunday, p. 146.

3. But further. God the Holy Ghost is not [only] the great gift, but the promised gift. His goodness is especially shown in His giving us Himself in spite of difficulty and resistance. This is a world of sin and evil, created good by Him in the beginning, and therefore His goodness is specially shown in reparation, and in the triumph of His goodness over evil at the end of a long contest occasioned by sin. And here is another aspect of this day—it commemorates the end of a great and long course of providence, the accomplishment of promise and prophecy. It was not only a gift, but a promised gift. Hence our Lord speaks of it as ' the promise of the Father.'

4. A long process involving in it the mission of the eternal Son to mankind ; the world had to be made fit in the fulness of time—meanwhile the chosen people, etc.

5. Promises and prophets—a long expectation.

6. And when our Lord had come, then, not for a long time, but still for a time, for forty days, the suspense continued.

7. The apostles in expectation, ' Lord, wilt thou at this time,' etc.

8. At last Whitsunday came ; wind and fire ; Malachias iii., ' Fire upon earth '—Holy Ghost by fire.

July 21 *and* 28 (*Sixth and Seventh Pentecost*)

ON THE NEW CREATION

I

1. We find from St. Paul that *its* life [*i.e.* the life of the New Creation] is gratitude for our Lord's sufferings for us, 2 Cor. v.; Gal. ii., sin.

2. Gratitude implies (and requires) (1) sense of sin ; (2) faith.

3. Leads to (3) hope ; (4) hope implies fear.

4. And gratitude is a kind of love.

II

But love is charity, such as is necessary to fulfil the command for ' eternal life,' ' Thou shalt love the Lord thy God with,' etc.,

Involves

1. Gratitude.

2. Likeness to God. Like loves like, *i.e.* love of appreciation.

3. The love of friendship—' Abraham the *friend* ' ; John xv., ' friends '—which involves a mutual consciousness of love—John xxi., ' Lord, thou knowest,' etc.

4. Companionship—' Walk before me ' ; ' Walk with me '—journey to Emmaus.

5. *Dilectio*—preference.

(Twentieth Pentecost)

[FAITH AND THANKSGIVING]

' Unless you see signs and wonders, you believe not,' John iv. 48.

1. INTROD.—This gospel opens a subject too long to treat well to-day, especially as this day has subjects of its own, one of which I cannot pass over.

2. How is it that our Lord seems to accuse the nobleman of unbelief ?

3. He certainly does in some sense, but in what sense ?

4. His disbelief was not as if he did not believe our Lord's power ; he did not try our Lord's power to get *evidence* (see the narrative), but he was (naturally indeed) so earnestly set upon his one desire, his son's recovery, that he did not show resignation. He urged our Lord to make haste.

5. Contrast Martha and Mary—' Lord, he whom thou lovest is sick ' [John xi. 3]. And the event showed how fully they might trust—for [though] He did not make haste, still he who was even dead was raised again.

6. Ephesians v. 19-20[1]; Phil. iv. 3[2]; 1 Thess. v. 18[3] ; 2 Cor. vi. 10.[4]

[1] ' Speaking to yourselves in psalms and spiritual canticles, singing and making melody in your hearts to the Lord ; Giving thanks for all things in the name of our Lord Jesus Christ to the Father.'

[2] ' In everything, by prayer and supplication, with thanksgiving, let your petitions be made known to God.'

[3] ' In all things giving thanks ; for this is the will of God in Christ Jesus concerning you all.'

[4] ' As sorrowful, yet always rejoicing.'

7. I am led to these remarks by the thanksgivings to be made in this day's service for the answer to the prayers we have been offering by direction of his Lordship for a blessing on this year's harvest and the trade and manufactures of this country.

8. The distressed father in the gospel asked for a miracle ; we do not, but our cases are the same— whether by miracle as he, or by providence as to us, both he and we prayed to God for an object. We have both severally received what we ask for.

9. His distress and ours.

10. He showed his gratitude, and so, I trust, shall we.

11. He was admonished—(go through his case).

August 28, 1849 [1]

THE CREED—DE DEO—I

1. INTROD.—On the *articles* not embracing the whole truth—a number of others, but we believe whatever the Church teaches ; if you are in difficulty this the great rule—(enlarge—come to be taught, no use coming else). Why called the Apostles' [Creed] ?

2. By ' God ' we mean one who is all-perfect— this is the only idea of God ; therefore the heathen gods are called ' not-gods.' [2] They do not answer the idea.

3. (Not pleasant to inquire into the proofs ; it is

[1] The rest of the volume consists of *Catechetical Instructions.*
[2] Jer. ii. 11; *ib.* v. 7,

T

an irreverence, therefore pass over it lightly.[1]) We
are obliged to believe it, for else, was this world
for ever ? If not, who created it ? and who created
its Creator, etc. ? Thus it is simplest, we cannot
help believing in a God, nay, believing the most
incomprehensible attribute, viz. that He had no
beginning.

4. God must be all-perfect, for (1) He has made
the world, and therefore must be more perfect
than that which He made. He has given to it of
His fulness, therefore is there wisdom, power,
beauty, etc., in the world (think of the human soul)
—then He much more so. This thought alone gives
us an indefinitely high notion of God, considering
the extent and wonders of creation.

5. Next, think that He created from nothing.

6. Go through His attributes.

7. The one singled out is ' Almighty,' and for two
reasons : (1) Because we are to consider, not the
time *before* creation, but creation and after ; (2)
because it is the *Creed*, which has reference to God's
omnipotence.

8. ' Creator of heaven and earth ' ; (1) Creating
from nothing ; (2) number of attributes discovered
from the material world ; if there be beauty, He
is beautiful ; if Spirit, He Spirit, etc.

9. Creator of angels, men, things inanimate.

10. Proof of all this from above : (1) Two most

---

[1] He would also have felt it superfluous in 1849 'to inquire
into proofs.' 'Whatever my anxiety may be about the future
generation, I trust I need at present have none in insisting,
before a congregation, however mixed, on the mysteries or
difficulties which attach to the doctrine of God's existence,' etc.
—*Discourses to Mixed Congregations*, p. 265.

incomprehensible [mysteries] from the nature of
the case—eternity *a parte ante* [*i.e.* before creation],
and creation from nothing, and if these, what shall
we not give to Him ? (2) Idea in human mind, in
conscience, and hence His moral attributes holy,
just, ever vigilant, all-seeing. (3) The visible world
and all the senses. (4) The variety of attributes
which the world and the soul shows—wisdom, greatness, and minuteness, grace and beauty, comeliness, goodness. (5) Providence—therefore all good.
Providence as shown in general [and] in our own life.

11. Doctrine of the Holy Trinity.

[*September* 4]

DE DEO—II

1. Recapitulation—from the conscience and our
personal history we have all the great doctrines about
God which so much concern us, and which would
suffice for our believing in Him, *though there was no
external world*, viz. holiness, justice, omnipresence,
ever-watchfulness, mercy, and future retribution.

2. About the argument from the external world,
and why it is dangerous at this day[1]; *because it
tells us nothing about sin*; it [the world] was made
before sin.

3. The attributes the external world adds—infinite power, wisdom, skill, etc.

4. Additions : (1) From the nature of the case
one perfection implies another. (2) Eternity *a
parte ante*, creation from nothing, etc., from the
nature of the case.

[1] See Note 20, pp. 343-4.

5. How is this faith, if it is gained thus by reasoning ?—(explain—how reason goes a certain way to draw a conclusion)—that is not faith—(explain the process)—*desire of the truth*.

6. How faith is a completion through grace ; this grace may be given to those who know not revelation ; but if revelation comes in their way it will lead them to it.

7. This is why Catholics hold apostasy so wretched a thing—it is not the mere change of opinion, but a going against grace.

September 11

DE ANGELIS—III

1. Angels the first work of God.

2. Different from the human race, as created all at once ; not from a pair—myriads—almost an infinite number like the stars ; nine ranks, yet there may be *more* unknown.

3. Immaterial—their appearing in human form— Raphael in [book of] Tobias.

4. Incorruptible ; immortal in their nature.

5. Their knowledge ; perfect from the first, not learning by *discursus*, first one thing, then another ; knowing a thing wholly at once. They do not know the future—nor men's hearts, except from divine revelation. God alone knows these—(bad angels tempt by objecting evil or exciting the thoughts).

6. Created in grace. And first, What is *grace* ?— something beyond *nature*. Nothing can love God

really and know Him, and attain to heaven, without a gift beyond itself.

7. The fall of the angels—*pride*—as sin of thought, for it was *all* the sin they *could* fall into, being spiritual natures. Pride is relying on oneself for happiness, not on God's grace ; envy would follow, viz. against men. Their *naturalia remanserunt integra*—they lost (1) supernatural beatitude, intuitive vision of God [1] ; (2) justice and grace ; (3) their intellect darkened, and their will confirmed in evil.

8. They range the earth and dwell in the air.

9. They do not properly possess the mind of the possessed except indirectly, by raising fantasies, etc. Of sinners and unbaptized, the *soul* is not possessed but ruled ; hence even innocent persons are sometimes possessed.

10. Good angels were confirmed in grace.

11. Guardian angels for the faithful, and perhaps for the *infideles et reprobati.*

September 25

DE MUNDO VISIBILI ET BRUTIS—IV

1. On the visible world, as described in Genesis ; created by degrees.

2. Created good—in what sense ?—relatively good. A better world conceivable ; all creatures, as such, imperfect—grace perfects. He has not given His grace to all [creatures].

3. This seen especially in the phenomena of brute animals ; how far they are like men—in struc-

---

[1] *I.e.* in prospect.

ture and make—remarkably like—one idea *physically*—for man is an animal and something [besides]. On the brute animals in contrast with men. They have not souls.[1]

4. First : They do not know they exist ; they cannot *reflect* ; they are like our minds in dreams or vacant vision or hearing ; they don't anticipate death ; they may see other brutes killed, but don't fear ; no burying bodies—no despair of life, or suicide.

5. Second : Sensations—nothing more ; they hear sounds, but do not know what is meant by them ; they cannot speak.

6. Third : They act upon their sensations in a mechanical way, as by smell, etc.

7. Four : [They] eat and drink, etc., for the sake of eating and drinking, etc.—not in excess—still because mechanical.

8. Five : No abstract ideas—of justice, truth, etc.—no idea of duty.

9. Six : No governing power in their affections.

10. Seven : No perfectibility.

Hence they cannot sin, though they have impulses, etc., which in man are sin. Man is apt to argue that a thing is not sinful if it is natural, whereas it may be sinful *in him*, who has means to prevent it.[2]

October 2

DE GRATIA ET GRATIA AMISSA—V

1. INTROD.—After brute animals we come to man.

---

[1] He is using the word soul in the popular sense.

[2] Cp. *Discourses to Mixed Congregations*, p. 149.

2. Man a compound being—how soul and body can be together a mystery,[1] and what follows, though strange, not so much so [*i.e.* not so mysterious]—compounded of body which aims at sensible good, and soul which aims at spiritual. Hence *grace given* that there might not be war.

3. This the state of Adam—original justice, grace —moreover, absence from death and the *vestigia mortis.*

4. Adam sinned ; he could not have had a lighter trial. What was his punishment ?   A stripping of this grace, etc.

5. Enlarge on this as humbling man, [viz.] as a mere creation of God he is very imperfect—*Pulvis es,* etc. [' Dust thou art, and to dust thou shalt return ']—[but now] he is not [as] in that state he would have been in had he not had grace. [Parable of] good Samaritan [the wounded man being typical of our race after the Fall]—evil of souls, four wounds—of body, death, and disease. As living things gasp and die under an exhausted receiver, though air is not part of their nature.

6. This state of man after the Fall—it is called original sin—and since Adam's sin is imputed, it shows itself in the above privations.

7. No one but has grace enough to save him —sufficient grace—but we cannot add up correctly many times running.[2] Things needed not be yet are—efficacious grace.

8. Process of grace ; actual grace, drawing a man on, one grace improving [improved upon ?]

---

[1] Cp. *Parochial and Plain Sermons,* vol. iv. p. 283.
[2] See *Discourses to Mixed Congregations,* pp. 128-9.

leads, *de congruo,* to another—so to contrition with desire of the Sacrament, which justifies, viz. habitual grace.

9. Children, habitual grace—but still actual grace is needed besides.

10. Grace of perseverance.

11. Our Lady without original sin.

12. The effect of this to humble us—creatures imperfect.

October 9

DE REDEMPTIONE—VI

1. Sin leads to the doctrine about Christ : ' And in Jesus Christ, His only Son, our Lord . . . born of the Virgin Mary,' *i.e.* God coming in the flesh.

2. Consider the *cumulus* of sin—all the sins of every individual through centuries, and to the end of the world. The offence to God, how great !— infinite—though the malice finite.

3. God might have condemned all men—He might have pardoned all—and that without any satisfaction ; but He determined to take a punishment *equal* to what their sins deserved. Now man could not pay this, and therefore Christ came, who was God.

4. God passed over the angels who fell. He looked lovingly upon man, His youngest creation, and, as great doctors teach,[1] He would have become

---

[1] Though by no means generally: see *Sermons to Mixed Congregations,* p. 321 note.

incarnate even if man had not fallen, though He then would not have suffered, viz. to show the *glory* of His Attributes in a created nature.

5. Christ's coming prophesied of through so many ages. Holy men looking out for Him.

6. Why His coming delayed—to show God's free decrees.

7. Jesus—(explain the word): (1) Saviour, Phil. ii. [9-10],[1] Acts iii. [6],[2]—the own name of a person always conveys tenderness and familiarity. (Saviour.) (2) Joshua His type—all saints have delighted in it [viz. the name Jesus].

8. Christ—Prophet, Priest, and King.

October 16

DE TRINITATE—VII

1. INTROD.—The mention of the Redeemer leads us to a great mystery.

2. It is to be expected that there are mysteries ; we cannot tell [beforehand] what—and those which *are* are sure to surprise us, and we say : ' I expected some, but not this, for this is so strange.' [3]

---

[1] ' For which cause God also hath exalted him, and hath given him a name which is above all names : that in the name of Jesus every knee should bow,' etc.

[2] ' In the name of Jesus Christ of Nazareth arise and walk.'

[3] ' I consider that this mysteriousness is, as far as it proves anything, a recommendation of the doctrine. I do not say that it *is* true *because* it is mysterious ; but that if it *be* true, it cannot help being mysterious. It would be strange, indeed, as has often been urged in argument, if any doctrine concerning God's infinite and eternal Nature were not mysterious. It would even be an

3. A mystery is but a mark of infinity. *Vide* published discourse.[1]

4. We may be sure that every apparent *explanation* is a mistake, a heresy. We must begin by confessing it unintelligible.

5. Mystery of Trinity, briefly put.

6. On the analogy of the elements—published discourse.

October 23

DE FILIO DEI—VIII

1. INTROD.—On the divinity of our Lord.

2. God from God, Light from Light ; analogies— the word, the sun, and

3. Passages of Scripture—Proverbs ; wisdom— Isaias ix., John i., Phil. ii., Col. i., Heb. i.

4. Mistakes of Protestants.[2]

October 30

DE DOMINIO SEU REGNO CHRISTI—IX

1. INTROD.—Our Lord in the first place God ; but also, He has *redeemed* us with a *price*.

objection to any professed doctrine concerning His Nature, if it were not mysterious.'—*Parochial Sermons*, vol. vi., ' Faith without Demonstration.'

[1] ' The outward exhibition of infinitude is mystery ; and the mysteries of nature and grace are nothing else than the mode in which His infinitude encounters us and is brought home to our minds,' etc.—*Discourses to Mixed Congregations*, p. 309.

[2] *Ib.* pp. 346 ff.

2. Hence contrasted to this world, which is the (usurped) kingdom of Satan—god of this world.

3. Contrast the two, the mediatorial kingdom of Christ [and the kingdom of Satan] as in the Two Standards, beginning with John xvii.

4. An empire—(explain what an empire is)— Psalms ii., xliv., lxxi., lxxxvii., Isaias xliv., liv., lx., Apoc. xix.

5. (Contrast the two as in the Two Standards.) Prophecies—lamb and lion, Isaias xi. 6,[1] Isaias ii. 2.[2]

6. Spreading by meekness—unlike any other empire : strong in weakness.

7. Exemplified at this moment. State of the Pope.

8. Yet wars, etc.[3] Yes, but the *strength* is not through war, etc. Explain therefore ' gathering of every kind ' in but not of [the world].

9. Contrast the kingdom of Christ and Satan as in the Two Standards.

November 6

DE NATIVITATE CHRISTI EX VIRGINE—X

1. INTROD.—' Conceived by the Holy Ghost, born of the Virgin Mary.'

2. Predestination of the Blessed Virgin, even before the foresight of the Fall.

---

[1] ' The wolf shall dwell with the lamb, and the leopard shall lie down with the kid ; the calf and the lion and the sheep shall lie down together ; and a little child shall lead them.'

[2] ' And in the last days the mountain of the house of the Lord shall be prepared on the top of the mountains,' etc.

[3] Probably in reference to the crusades, and perhaps to the military defence of the Papal states.

3. Gen. iii. [15][1]—*inimicitias* [enmities]; *ipsa* [she].

4. Parallel of Eve and Mary—this idea of a woman kept up through Scripture in types, though the relationship to the Shiloh [Gen. xlix. 10] is not always preserved—(1) Sara, Ishmael scoffing [at]; (2) Mary, Moses' sister ; (3) the canticle of canticles.

5. Isaias vii. [14].[2]

6. When our Lord came, perhaps no need of further notice ; yet (for our Lady did not come forward at once into public view—*e.g.* in Catacombs) in prophecy, Apoc. xii., [she is prominent] to the end of time.

7. Particulars. Christ might have been born in the ordinary way, but other way more fitting— Immaculate Conception. [Her question to the angel], ' How shall this be ? ' [Her] vow of virginity —first who did so [*i.e.* made this vow]—why married ; a true marriage.

8. Conceived of the Holy Ghost — all works belong to the Three Persons [of the Blessed Trinity] —but as wisdom is attributed to the Son, etc.

9. Christ had *all* grace from first—did not grow in grace.

10. [Our Lady suffered] no pain in child-bearing ; Eve *é contra* ; hence in representations of our Lady [before the manger] she is made kneeling, etc.

11. Ever virgin.

12. Mother of God—this to secure the doctrine of the Incarnation. *Vide* published Sermon.[3]

[1] ' I will put enmities between thee and the woman, and thy seed and her seed ; she shall crush thy head,' etc.

[2] ' Behold, a virgin shall conceive,' etc.

[3] ' The Glories of Mary,' etc., in *Discourses to Mixed Congregations.*

PASSUS ET CRUCIFIXUS—XI

1. INTROD.—*Sub Pontio Pilato.*

2. This is introduced to mark the fulfilment of prophecy, which fixed the time.

3. Forty weeks—four empires—Genesis xlix.—fortunes of Judah—Herod—the Romans.

4. Hence the crucifixion instead of stoning. Thus other prophecies fulfilled.

5. On the ' fulness of time '—one (Roman) empire —universal peace — Greek philosophy — [heathen] religions worn out.

6. Another reason for ' Pontius Pilate,' viz. to prove the historical reality of our Lord's coming against Docetae, etc. Nay, in last century Dupuis with his three hundred years sooner.

7. On the contrary, God *was* man ; God suffered, died, was buried, etc. ; but not as God, but as man —in His human nature.

8. Still it was His will who is Highest to make Himself lowest. Indeed, it is in all its parts the most awful of mysteries—death of the cross : (1) what hanging now is, yet indefinitely worse—the ignominy of the position ; as we fix noxious birds up ; (2) nakedness ; (3) contempt and mockery— His disciples leaving Him ; (4) no part of the body without its suffering ; (5) His delicate make more susceptible of pain.

9. Pains of His soul—the bloody sweat—no support from God or from sense of innocence ; feeling of guilt ; feeling of responsibility.

10. Yet the cross our triumph—sanctified by Him

who hung on it ; predicted under the [figure of] brazen serpent. It is now a means of grace.

November 20

MORTUUS, SEPULTUS—XII

1. INTROD.—' Dead and buried ; He descended into hell.'

2. *Dead.* He died for our sins—but also because He came subject to the laws of our fallen nature ; man, though not naturally immortal, was not to die. ' Dust thou art,' etc.—even our Blessed Lady, Enoch, Elias, and so Christ.

3. Hypostatic union preserved even in blood, which after the Resurrection was all gathered up.

4. Buried. This mentioned to show He was dead.

5. Hell eternal prison ; purgatory ; Limbo Patrum.

6. He went there, not as the others, but to triumph and take them out.

7. And so on the third day He rose again.

8. Even the instruments of the Passion a triumph ; the cross—its meaning changed : He sanctified it. History of its finding.

9. The goodness of God not only in saving us, but in condescending to our weakness in religion ; difficult to form *spiritual* ideas of God—the populace and [the] philosophers. Hence He has deigned [firstly] to take a body, [and secondly], with [it] a [personal] history.[1] And this is perpetuated in the

---

[1] 'While, then, Natural Religion was not without provision for all the deepest and truest religious feelings, yet presenting no *tangible history* of the Deity, no points of His personal character (if we may so speak without irreverence), it wanted that most

two great devotions of the Blessed Sacrament and
of our Lady.

November 27

RESURREXIT ET ASCENDIT—XIII

1. INTROD.—These articles are also mysteries in
the Rosary. You should be familiar with the narrative of them in Scripture—(read it).

2. Our Lord remained forty days on earth—why
forty ? the flood ['was forty days upon the earth,'
Gen. vii. 17]; [the Israelites] forty years in the
wilderness; Moses (forty days) on the mountain;
Elias ['walked in the strength of that food forty
days and forty nights unto the mount of God,' 3
Kings xix. 8]; our Lord [fasting forty days] in the
desert; hours of His death [forty hours in the
tomb].

3. His state [after the Resurrection]—wonderful;
He came and He went. His dwelling, perhaps though
[*some word has been omitted*] on a terrestrial paradise
where [were] the bodies of the saints who were raised
with Him—especially [also] Enoch and Elias, who for
their delay claimed the sight of Him.

4. What He taught—the constitution of the
Church, the orders of the Hierarchy, the matter and
form of the Sacraments.

5. At length He ascended at midday; He was
taken down from the cross and buried in the evening

efficient incentive to all action, a starting or rallying point,—an
object on which the affections could be placed, and the energies
concentrated.'—*Oxford University Sermons*, p. 23. The italics
are our own.

—rose again in the morning. This was not a proper place for His glorified body ; He ascended of His own power as God and as man. [See] *Catechismus Romanus.*

6. ' *Sitteth* on the *right* hand '—(explain).

7. There He sits as our one Mediator and Intercessor—quote Rom. viii. 34,[1] Heb. vii. [24-25].[2] In what His intercession consists—in presenting His human nature.

8. Difference between [His and the] Blessed Virgin's intercession ; He is God ; she is powerful through prayer ; hence we do not say to Him, *Ora pro nobis.*

9. Also He ascended to fix our minds on heaven in love ; to exercise our faith in One who is absent ; to give ground for our hope.

10. Conclusion of foregoing.

December 4

INDE VENTURUS EST, ETC.—XIV

1. INTROD.—[' Thence He shall come to judge the living and the dead.']

2. Particular judgment—some think the soul is not taken up to Christ literally, for it [*i.e.* this] is introducing the wicked into heaven, but only intellectually.

---

[1] ' Christ Jesus that died, yea, that is risen also again, who is at the right hand of God, who also maketh intercession for us.'

[2] ' But this, for that he continueth for ever, hath an everlasting priesthood. Whereby he is also able to save for ever them that come to God by him, always living to make intercession for us.'

3. The soul of the just goes to purgatory, unless a Saint; of the sinner to hell.

4. General judgment at the end of the world: it will come suddenly.

5. Signs previous, though unheeded then.

6. Preaching of Gospel all over the earth; now this has in great measure been done.

7. Apostasy—love of many waxing cold—1 Tim. iv. [1],[1] 2 Tim. iii. [1-2].[2]

8. Antichrist, 2 Thess. ii. [3].[3]

9. Fire burning up all things, and becoming the purgatory of the living just—[general] resurrection.

10. The judgment—reasons for it; first, to show the full consequences of good and evil in individuals; to clear the just; to bring shame to the wicked. Wisdom iv.

11. Secondly, to justify God—Ps. lxxii. 16-17,[4] Ps. xlix.[5]

12. Matt. xxv. [32],[6] division of good and bad, as if the separation had *already* been made.

13. No venial sins, only mortal sins [judged] at last judgment.

---

[1] 'Now the Spirit manifestly saith, that in the last times some shall depart from the faith, giving heed to spirits of error,' etc.

[2] 'Know also this, that in the last days shall come dangerous times. Men shall be lovers of themselves,' etc.

[3] 'And then that wicked one shall be revealed,' etc.

[4] 'I studied that I might know this thing. It is a labour in my sight; until I go into the sanctuary of God, and understand concerning their last ends.'

[5] 'Gather ye together his saints to him . . . and the heavens shall declare his justice.'

[6] 'And all nations shall be gathered together before him: and he shall separate them one from another, as the shepherd separateth the sheep from the goats.'

U

14. Necessity of confessing sins now, that we may not have to confess them then.

December 11

ET IN SPIRITUM SANCTUM—XV

On the condescension of the Holy Ghost. Creation implies ministration, and is the beginning of mysteries. It passes the line, and other mysteries are but its continuation.

December 18

SANCTAM ECCLESIAM CATHOLICAM—XVI

On the Church as means of grace—the seven sacraments, etc. On the principle of communication of merits.

January 4, 1850

REMISSIONEM PECCATORUM—XVII

1. Forgiveness of sin the proclamation of the Gospel—and a new idea. It was *reminding* men of what was necessary for them, which in the world they forget. Mortal sin, how great an evil ! hence to forgive as great an act as to create or raise the dead.

2. The great boon—because not everywhere. Grace everywhere, not forgiveness, though in order to forgiveness : forgiveness on contrition.

3. Forgiveness through Christ (first of all created

natures) when on earth, through the Church; first through baptism, next through penance (no sin the Church cannot remit). These two [Baptism and Penance] the *Sacramenta mortuorum.*

January 8

CARNIS RESURRECTIONEM—XVIII

1. On mysteries without number all through revealed religion—[our] ignorance *how* things are. The Creed begins with mystery, with mystery it ends. Resurrection of the body.

2. Matter, it would seem, could not be made spiritual (ancient philosophers) [1]—apparently the means of temptation; cause of ignorance, of death, etc.; retards the soul.

3. Heathen philosophers of old time called the body a prison, etc., as if the soul was pure ; they made much of the soul ; hence to say the body was to be raised, to them a shocking doctrine, Acts xvii.

4. And again, they thought sins of the flesh no

[1] 'Among the wise men of the heathen, as I have said, it was usual to speak slightingly and contemptuously of the mortal body; they knew no better. They thought it scarcely a part of their real selves, and fancied they should be in a better condition without it. Nay, they considered it to be the cause of their sinning; as if the soul of man were pure, and the material body were gross, and defiled the soul. *We* have been taught the truth, viz. that sin is a disease of *our minds*, of ourselves ; and that the whole of us, not body alone, but soul and body, is naturally corrupt, and that Christ has redeemed and cleansed whatever we are, sinful soul and body. Accordingly *their* chief hope in death was the notion that they should be rid of the body.'—*Parochial Sermons*, vol. i. p. 276, 'The Resurrection of the Body.'

harm, *because* the flesh; it disgusted them to [be told] the body should rise again, for it implied the need of self-discipline and mortification—the body being worth something.

5. But in truth all, soul as well as body, imperfect —all creation imperfect; the grace which can make the soul perfect makes the body [perfect] too.

6. Christianity, then, raises the body—Incarnation —Mary—relics of martyrs.

7. Every one will rise with his own body—the same body—

8. With all their members perfect, and all defects removed;

9. Yet so far the same that the martyrs will have their scars.

10. Immortal.

11. Four properties [of the risen body]—impassibility, brightness (not the same to all), agility, subtility.

12. Reflection upon glorified bodies.

January 11

VITAM ÆTERNAM—XIX

1. INTROD.—The Creed begins with God, it ends with ourselves; the last articles have reference to us.

2. Eternal life. Life means more than existence, for the lost live.

3. It means blessedness or beatitude; and this is called life, because there is no word which can fitly describe it; so we must use such words as occur.

4. By blessedness is meant our greatest good, and this from the nature of man can be nothing temporal, but must be something eternal. If a man thought his happiness to end, or were not sure, he would not be happy.

5. It consists in seeing God ; not only seeing His glory, or a likeness of Him, but Himself. Since it is His nature or essence which will be seen, no likeness will do, for no likeness is there of His essence.

6. It is seen by means of the *lumen gloriae*, which raises the soul above itself—' In Thy light shall we see light.' It is by an immediate union to God, and our intellect is raised above itself in order to it.

7. This light of glory raises the soul above itself. It [the soul] is what it is, but it is bathed and flooded with a heavenly light ; it puts on a divine form, so that men are called gods. A red-hot iron, etc.

8. Such is essential blessedness—consisting in the possession of God. The soul ever sees God present, wherever it is—the rapturous nature of this privilege. We (most men) know so little of intellectual joys here, that few illustrations can be given. Most intense, yet continuous. (Happiness in itself—happiness of convalescence—happiness of tears ; soothing, etc.—happiness of coming before the Blessed Sacrament—not happiness merely of success, etc., as on earth, *i.e.* of having gained, at possessing—saints' raptures.)

9. So much so that the soul could dispense with everything else—the blessed would not want friends from the earth. Each could well bear to lose the memory of everything else for God.

10. But God has added these additions : all the blessed will see each other, and rejoice in each other's glory,

11. And the honour of each other.

12. The glories of the heavenly palace.

13. Let this thought comfort us in the troubles of this life, and the prospect of purgatory.

January 3, 1858 (*Octave of St. John*)

[CHRISTIAN KNOWLEDGE]

1. Christian knowledge is made up of four parts —of the Creed, John iii. 11, of the doctrine of the Sacraments, Acts i. 3, of the Ten Commandments, Matt. xxii. 37, and of prayer, Luke xi. 1.   And these four make up the teaching which is called the Catechism.

2. We are accustomed to think the Catechism belongs to children only, and think it does not concern grown men and women—Catechumens— but this is not so.   The Council of Trent appointed a *Catechismus ad Parochos.*

3. This is shown in the very name catechism, from κατηχεῖν, to ring in the ears again and again.

4. There is great danger of our knowing only part of what God has revealed, and danger of our forgetting what we know.   Therefore it is necessary, again and again.

5. Feeling all this deeply, I have resolved, *opitulante Deo*, to begin a set of strictly catechetical lectures in the Mass on Sundays, viz. *the four parts above mentioned.*

6. I know how careful our Fathers are in bringing before you the truths of revelation. I know how you have profited by their teaching. But there is the danger that some or other of the truths should be omitted unless there is some system of catechising, catechetical instruction, at least from time to time. You may hear one thing three or four times and *another not even once*. You may know a great deal on some subjects, more than Catholics ordinarily do, and not enough on others.

7. St. Paul said he had taught *all the* counsel of God. It is as necessary to know all our duty as to practise it all; and we cannot practise it all without knowing it. What we should aim at is knowing all and doing all.

8. In this consists *perfection*. Perfection does not lie in heroic deeds, or in great fervour, or in anything extraordinary—many, even good men, are unequal—but in consistency. This is what old Catholics have when good, in opposition to converts, and therefore this congregation needs it especially.

9. And so Christian knowledge is not the knowing about saints or about devotions and the like, though all this is excellent, but in knowing the four things above.

10. On the Catechism as an instrument of converting Protestants.

January 10

[THE CREED]

1. The Creed begins with the word from which the name creed is taken, *credo*, I believe. Observe

it is ' I believe,' not ' I conjecture,' ' I am of opinion,' ' I know,' but ' I believe.'

2. There are many things which we ' conjecture,' ' expect,' ' reckon,' or ' guess,' *e.g.* the future generally, the weather, the state of trade, our own prospects, health, fortune, etc., and we have surmises and suspicions about who are our friends, who our enemies, and we put no great confidence in such guesses, because we find we are often wrong. This is not what we mean when in the Creed we say ' I believe.'

3. There are many things we have opinions about, and strong opinions, and with very little doubt or fear, *e.g.* what we have learned by long experience of life. Experience is all in all to many men—to the farmer, to the physician, to the navigator, the politician, and to all men—hence it is that we trust the old ; they may not be always right, but still their experience gives them a right to speak. Opinions may be trusted, but yet they are not infallibly certain, because sometimes men change their opinions. This, then, is not what is meant by ' I believe.'

4. There are many things we know, *e.g.* by our senses, by common sense, by reason. Thus we know what we see with our eyes—all that is round about us, the world, the sky, the earth, etc. And by common sense and reason that two and two make four, all the points of moral conduct, the difference of virtue and vice, conscience, etc. ; [in such matters] there is no doubt or fear, but certainty. But this is not ' I believe.'

5. What, then, is ' I believe ' ? It is at first sight

as uncertain, doubtful, as any of them, a conjecture, but really more certain than [mere] knowledge. To believe is to accept as true what we are told. What more weak, for people are continually taken in ? Why then strong ? Because it is God's word— (enlarge on this : ' Let God be true, and every man a liar ' [1])—through the Church.

6. It comes from a divine grace.

7. Exhortation to believe against appearances, and to pray for faith.

January 17

[REVELATION—I]

1. Last week I spoke of faith as being acceptance of the word of God as declared by the Church, and since God is not seen, it is by grace ; hence Eph. ii. 8, ' For by grace you are saved through faith, and that not of yourselves, for it is the gift of God ' ; and Heb. xi. 6, ' But without faith it is impossible to please God. For he that cometh to God must believe that he is, and is a rewarder to them that seek him.'

2. Now it may be objected that these two—God and recompense—can be known by nature without grace—see Romans vii. I answer (1) With great difficulty and many obstacles from passion, etc. (2) They are not enough—St. Peter in Acts iv. 10-12 [2] ;

---

[1] Rom. iii. 4.

[2] ' Be it known to you all . . . that by the name of our Lord Jesus Christ . . . even by him this man standeth before you whole. . . . There is no other name under heaven given to men, whereby we must be saved.'

our Lord Himself, John xvii. 3 [1] ; or John iii. 16 [2] ; the Baptist, John iii. 36 [3] ; St. John the evangelist, John i. 10-12 [4] ; St. Paul, Acts xvi. 31 [5] ; grace, 1 Cor. xii. 3.[6]

3. Now these truths [spoken of in the texts just referred to] are not known by nature, but by God's word—(illustrate). By natural reason we know many wonderful things—the sciences—all those wonderful things of this day—inventions, historical researches, antiquities dug up from the earth, knowledge of the stars, etc., etc.—but not *all* the knowledge of men could bring us one step nearer to the knowledge of those things which concern our salvation. These are *only* known by revelation, or by the express word of God.

4. This is what is called revelation, because the veil taken off, or, in other words, by the express word of God.

5. The word of God—(explain)—two kinds ; Scripture and Tradition.

6. This why faith is necessary. And even what we could know by nature (God and recompense), we must receive on faith.

[1] 'Now this is eternal life, that they may know thee the only true God, and Jesus Christ, whom thou hast sent.'

[2] 'God so loved the world, as to give his only begotten Son, that whosoever believeth in him may not perish, but may have life everlasting.'

[3] 'He that believeth in the Son hath life everlasting : but he that believeth not the Son shall not see life.'

[4] 'He was in the world, and the world knew him not. . . . But as many as received him, he gave them power to be made the sons of God, to them that believe in his name.'

[5] 'But they [Paul and Silas] said, Believe in the Lord Jesus, and thou shalt be saved, and thy house.'

[6] 'No one can say the Lord Jesus, but by the Holy Ghost.'

7. EXHORTATION.—' Let God be true, and every man a liar.' One man thinks one thing difficult, another another.

January 24

[REVELATION—II]

1. I used last week the word revelation in connection with faith.   And now I am going to explain more exactly what it is, and why it is necessary.

2. Revelation is necessary, faith is necessary, on account of our ignorance, which is one of the four wounds of human nature.

3. Now does it not seem wonderful—but so it is—that we may know so much of so many things, but so little of the things of God ?   Contrast human knowledge and religious ignorance—so many different opinions.

4. Hence, if we are to know anything of God, it must be quite in a different way, viz. by His expressing—speaking to us, or by His word—the word of God—and His word is revelation.   For revelation means taking a veil away.   (Illustrate Isa. xxvi., 2 Cor. iii.—veil over their heads ; veil on Moses' face.)   *Still* a veil, as in Blessed Sacrament—mysteries.   Still, whatever we know of unseen things is by the revealing word of God.   Hence by faith, not by sight, hearing by the word of God.

5. Faith, then, receives the revealing word of God through the Church.

6. Now what does the word of God say ? through what and when does it speak ?—through the Church, in two ways—written Scripture, unwritten tradition

7. Enter into Scripture and tradition ; (1) parts of Scripture ; (2) parts of tradition.

8. All things we receive by faith : not only Scripture, or only tradition, but both, for there is not a word of Scripture, whether of prophet, evangelist, etc., nor of tradition, which is not the voice or word of the Church—Heb. i. 1.

9. Embrace whatever God reveals as soon as you know that it is revealed.

January 31

[FAITH]

1. I have now explained what is meant by the word of God, by revelation, and by faith, and why they are necessary.

2. There is great correspondence between things of the body and of the soul. We cannot see without light ; and even with light we need eyes, and in the dark we grope our way. Now by nature our souls are in darkness, ignorance, etc. Thus you see how it is there is need of God's word, revelation, and faith.

3. And here you see the reason of a solemn declaration, ' Without which there is no one can be saved.' We are going a journey, etc.

4. Our Lord's words, John iii. 18.[1]

5. And still more if they refuse light, John iii. 19.[2]

6. This is one great reason why the light of faith is necessary, because we are so ignorant.

---

[1] 'He that believeth in him is not judged. But he that doth not believe is already judged : because he believeth not in the name of the only begotten Son of God.'

[2] 'And this is the judgment : because the light is come into the world, and men loved darkness rather than the light : for their works were evil.'

7. Now you will say, ' Is ignorance the fault of men in general ? if so, how ? if not, why are they punished with the loss of salvation ? '

8. No one is punished except for his own fault. No one is punished except for rejecting light. God gives light all over the earth—enough to make men advance forward.

9. Explain : from one grace to another, from one step to another—*prayer*.

10. And thus those who are in a great deal of ignorance may be saved if they are doing their best, and their ignorance invincible.

11. Heathen, heretics (material), may have divine faith.

12. Who these are is secret. All we know is about ourselves. Application to ourselves.

February 7

[APOSTLES' CREED—I]

1. Now I have explained what is meant by the word of God, by revelation, by faith. Now after the preliminaries we come to the Creed. You must not mind my saying the same thing over and over again —κατήχησις.

2. The Creed, then, since it is received by faith, must be revealed doctrine ; so it is.

3. Next it is called Apostles'. Why ? force of the word—because nothing can be of faith, nothing is revealed, except what comes from His apostles. No revelation since—once for all—as sacrifice, etc.

4. Not the whole of the apostles' doctrine, but a certain portion.

5. Why not the whole ?   Because it is impossible ;
the Church alone can tell us the whole ; it is [*an
illegible word here*].   We do not for certain know
till the Church tells, *e.g.* Immaculate Conception.

6. Are we not bound to believe the whole ? Yes,
with implicit faith—(explain).

7. But what is put down in the Creed is definite
and simple, *e.g.* first into three, then into twelve.

8. So much, because fundamental ; for teaching.

9. Because easy of memory.

10. Because intelligible for strangers who ask
about it as a mark of unity.

11. So the cross—Jesus.   Simple and intelligible.
' Christian is my name, Catholic my surname.'

February 21

[CREED—II]

1. I said last that the Creed did not contain all
that we had to believe, but certain portions, and
this is put into our hands for various reasons.

2. First, as a badge of what our religion is :
' Christian is my name, Catholic my surname.'   The
sign of the cross—so the Creed.

3. Next, as what is fundamental—which ' infants
in grace know,' ' other foundation,' etc.   ' No one
can say Jesus is the Lord,' etc.   *Disciplina arcani.*

4. Thirdly, as being easy of memory, being only
a few clauses, a few words in each.

5. Three chief parts—twelve articles—(go through
them).

6. As to the twelve articles, there was a belief

that each apostle gave an article—thence called
Apostles' Creed ; but not so, but, as I said last time,
because it contains apostolic doctrine.

7. And hence there were originally lesser varia-
tions in the Creed in various parts of the Church,
in various countries. Rites and ceremonies vary,
and though the faith never varies, the expression
of it may. We have an instance of this in the
Creed of the Mass. (Exemplify.)

8. Each Church, then, had its own Creed, the
same except in few words, or a few articles put in
or out. The Creed which has remained and which
we use as the Apostles' Creed is the Creed always
used in Rome. Saying it at the Confessional of St.
Peter.

9. Another thing to be said about the Apostles'
Creed : the Nicene has additions because of *heresies*
—*Consubstantial*, etc. ; the Apostles' Creed that of
the Church of Rome, where heresy never was.

10. But lest the Creed should grow too large, the
Council of Ephesus determined that it should not
be added to, though heresies arose ; hence Theotokos
not introduced.

February 28

[FIRST ARTICLE OF THE CREED]

1. I have been many weeks engaged in explaining
what the Creed is, what is the need of it, and similar
questions. Now then at length we proceed to consider what it contains.

2. The first article begins, ' I believe in God,' or, as
in the Nicene, ' I believe in one God.'

3. Explain what we mean by God, viz. the one being of beings, self-dependent, etc., all-powerful, could create infinite worlds, each more beautiful than the one before, with all other infinite attributes ; yet what we know of Him is infinitely less than what we do not know.

4. Here, then, you see the Creed opens in mystery, and what is remarkable, though it is a point of faith, it is also a point of reason. Hence the heathen philosopher asked one, two, four, eight, etc., days to determine about God. Then in the Mass— *tremunt potestates*—the name of God not pronounced by the Jews. It is what every child understands, who prays to God, as far as the highest intellect.

5. Here you see what is meant by saying that faith is against reason, viz. above, because reason itself comes to truths which it cannot comprehend.

6. There is no article in the whole Catholic faith more mysterious than this, which is the elementary one—nay, which is the belief of nature, too, without grace, which Protestants hold.

March 7

[CREED, FIRST ARTICLE CONTINUED]

1. On the awful and incomprehensible nature of Almighty God. The sun a poor type of it, which we cannot gaze on.

2. Hence the Jews never named the name of God. Hence in the Mass it is said *tremunt potestates.*

3. Hence the Seraphim. Moses at the burning bush ; Apoc. i. 13, 17.

4. This will lead us to show how difficult it is

to speak of Him without contradictions. He is full of mystery.

5. Enumerate the mysteries contained in it. (1) No beginning ; (2) eternity by Himself ; (3) then a Creator after an eternity ; (4) out of nothing ; (5) ever working though ever at rest ; (6) everywhere as fully as if in one place, yet without parts ; (7) prescience ; (8) knowledge of our hearts ; (9) infinitely merciful and just ; (10) all-powerful yet blasphemed, etc. ; (11) all-loving and good, yet allowing sin ; (12) infinite, yet personal.

6. This prepares us for those mysteries which are of faith—the Holy Trinity.

7. As attributes in the divine nature which are all separate, yet all one, so there is a greater and higher mystery still, viz. three persons.

8. The Father, the Son, the Holy Ghost, each entirely the one selfsame God, as if the others were not.

9. Still more mysterious, because we have nothing like it on earth.

10. We should glory, not stumble, at mysteries. All religions profess to believe in, to meditate on, Almighty God, but,

11. How few do so, else the whole world would become Catholic. The world generally, though they say they believe in God, as little believes as it believes in Catholicism.

This also gave matter for a lecture for March 21 : thus—

1. The world full of mystery.

2. Much more the Maker of the World.

3. Much more the God not of reason merely, but of revelation . . . Holy Trinity.

x

May 8, 1859 (*Sunday afternoon lectures*)

INTROD.—I cannot determine what I shall lecture on till I know who will come, for the speaker speaks according to the hearers ; to speak for speaking' sake is mere human eloquence, and not practical, and this St. Philip opposed especially. His Fathers only converse, not preach.

However, so much is certain, that all hearers come to learn ; learning implies knowledge as its object. There are two kinds of knowledge, natural and supernatural. I shall be sure to lecture on either natural or supernatural knowledge. One word more, and that for the sake of spiritual profit, not mere curiosity.

May 15

[FAITH—I]

1. INTROD.—I said that there were two kinds of religious knowledge.

2. And each is gained in its own way. Natural by sight and reason, supernatural by faith.

3. Reason of distinction, because we *cannot* learn what is *above* nature *except* by faith. On natural religion by sight and reason.

4. Natural religion is from God, sight and reason are from God. They are good as far as they go. They do for this world, but they never can get us to heaven.

5. Now the great bulk of mankind live merely by sight and reason ; their religion is natural religion.

6. (Here we have the comments of fact upon the ' narrow way.')

7. Describe how men live by sense and reason, natural good feeling, good sense, honesty, uprightness, manliness. If asked their opinion of any thing, act, or opinion or event, they will judge merely by their common sense ; then they go on to *supernatural* religion, and they still judge by reason, and so differ from each other.

8. And they will agree in some points with the others, not in others, hence *private judgment*.

9. Now I appeal to any one, if this is not the religion of most people. They would profess they only go by reason. The bulk of men live and die without faith. The notion of going by simple faith does not enter into their mind.

10. Nay, though they profess to go by Scripture, yet when there is anything they don't like, they explain it away.

11. Contrast faith and *everything* by faith.

12. Hence faith the foundation.

May 22

[FAITH—II]

1. INTROD.—I shall make this a recapitulation of the last. It is that the great majority of revealed religion is faith, whilst other religions, the religions of man, go by reason and conscience only.

2. It must be so, for faith is the correlative of revelation, faith in God's words and promises.

3. Natural men may be good fathers, gentle, simple, etc., and good soldiers, good citizens, great and good statesmen, good kings.

4. Now first, the religion of nature, or of good

persons, who are not Catholics. Contrasted with faith, they are benevolent, *e.g.*, but not simply because God tells them, but because their disposition carries them that way ; they don't think of getting a reward. Now contrast Tobias—faith in God's word.

5. Great patriot and soldier—Nehemias iv. 9, v. 19, xiii. 14.

6. Even though they are religious men, their belief is only a matter of opinion. Thus Protestants, saying that they may hold what they please ; they are amazed when you say that you are *certain* ; thus they have not the first principle of *faith*.

7. Now every one who lives with no higher religion than this comes short of eternal life. We may as well fly up to the sky as expect by these natural powers and exercises to get to heaven, because faith is away.

8. Now all acceptable religion is *because God has revealed this or that.* We are all apt to reason, and there is nothing wrong in reason, so that we do not oppose faith ; but the great thing is to make an act of faith, whatever we do ; to say, I believe this or that or the other on God's word—even in those things which we might know by nature,

9. Though not denying that those who are not Catholics may have this divine faith ; but it is only as they have it that they have any chance of salvation.

Or rather thus :

1. INTROD.—Importance of making act of faith. There are two things in religion—doctrines to be accepted and commands to be obeyed ; doctrines

may be taken by *reason*, commands by conscience. We must take both not by reason or conscience, but by FAITH.

2. Because faith must be the foundation of everything, and unless we begin with it, nothing is acceptable.

3. *God has spoken*—Rom. x. 17 ; 1 Thess. ii. 13. There are many things which we know by nature. God has said these over again, these and many new things in Revelation, but in order that they should be acceptable, we must accept on faith even those things which we know by nature. Whether reason is for, or scruples at doctrines, we must take them on faith.

4. *E.g.* the being of a God, immortality of the soul, future judgment, etc.

5. And thus we learn to take others also on faith, as the word of God. God has spoken.

6. INSTANCES.—Tobias, not rich, a benevolent man, but with faith.

7. Job, rich, abundant alms, etc.

8. Nehemias, a statesman, patriot, commander.

9. Esau, the instance of a man without faith, contrasted with Jacob, who had.

10. OBJECTION.—Protestants often good and religious, and seem really to live by faith.

11. *Distinguo.* Do they really go by faith, not by private judgment ? Do they really believe God has spoken this or that definite doctrine or command, or do they believe doctrines merely so far as reason teaches them, and commands as far as conscience ?

12. But if so, very well, invincible ignorance (draw out).

May 29

[FAITH—III]

1. I have said, nothing without faith as its foundation—Heb. xi. 6,[1] Eph. ii. 8[2]; faith implies an external message—Rom. x. 14,[3] 1 Thess. ii. 13.[4]

2. Yet, as I said, it is impossible to go into the world without seeing that the idea of taking one's doctrine from an external authority does not enter into their minds. It is always ' I think.' This is what is meant by private judgment—though Scripture, yet they put their own sense on Scripture ; they take these books, reject those, etc.

3. This is a most fearful consideration, considering we are saved by faith. And observe, it is quite independent of the question of what *is* the true doctrine, what *is* the true Church. You see most men do not GO THE RIGHT WAY. It is a previous question. They don't go the way of faith. From this it is plain, to go no further, that none but Catholics are in the right way, because *they alone* go by faith.

4. Now in this awful prospect the question arises, Does no one else go by faith ? Does no Protestant go by faith ?

---

[1] ' But without faith it is impossible to please God.'

[2] ' For by grace you are saved through faith.'

[3] ' How then shall they call on him in whom they have not believed ? or how shall they believe him of whom they have not heard ? and how shall they hear without a preacher ? '

[4] ' When you received of us the word of the hearing of God, you received it not as the word of men,' etc.

5. We can only answer by what we see. Well, they *profess* not to go by faith. If they *do* go by faith, at least they do not know it. Alas, it does seem as if we must say that the majority do not go by faith.

6. Do any ? I trust they do. I trust there is a remnant all over the world who *do* go by faith, and who so far are in the way of salvation, or rather, towards salvation. And in explanation how this is, I shall clear my meaning up more fully.

7. But first I shall answer an objection, viz. If they go by faith, why do they not join the Catholic Church, in which alone God speaks ? It is said, ' My sheep hear My voice.' I answer, they are out of the hearing of the Catholic Church, and therefore are in what is called invincible ignorance.

8. Now I will describe the state of such persons all the world over. Our Lord died for all, grace is given to all. Most men seem to profit nothing at all by it, but there are those who profit, *e.g.*

9. Conscience—there are two ways of regarding conscience ; *one* as a mere sort of sense of propriety, a taste teaching us to do this or that, the other as the echo of God's voice. Now all depends on this distinction—the first way is not of faith, and the second is of faith.

10. Characteristics of the first way—connected with pride. The proud will call the other kind superstitious. A person makes himself his own centre. He says, I shall hold just what seems to me, what my moral sense tells me, etc. The other considers it the voice of God, obeys it as such, a call to look out for more light.

11. Development of the idea of God, of faith in God, and of the feeling of the necessity of God's speaking in order to their salvation.

12. Hence to the evidences—the visible things of God, etc., etc.—history, providences, experiences.

13. A person may be a heathen—Mahometan, etc., etc.—and yet have this real faith in God, and so far he is on the way towards salvation. Their ignorance is involuntary and invincible, *i.e.* not their fault.

14. On being led on. Thus heathens, like the wise men, led into truth—the Ethiopians to Judaism; Abimelech's dream; Pharaoh's dreams. Job iv., spirit [1]; Job a just man. Magi, Ethiopians, the εὐσεβεῖς in the Acts. Means which the Almighty used before the coming of Christ.

N.B.—As just men existed before Christ came, why not at a distance from the Church ? for what the former is of time, so just men among the *heathen* is of space.

15. And thus St. Thomas said, ' An angel will speak from heaven rather than a soul fail.' On Christ's sheep hearing His voice ; thus it is a test whether persons come on towards the Church when they know about it ; invincible ignorance the only excuse. On the difference between death over-taking the shilly-shallying, who are not seeking, and on the earnest inquirer in invincible ignorance dying before he is a Catholic.

16. Case of Dr. A—— in his dreamy state, before death learning the truth.

---

[1] ' And when a spirit passed before me,' etc.

N.B.—Principles in the above.

1. It is part of the same mystery why death comes before inquirers are led into the truth, now as of old, for both depend on the parallel mystery why (1) our Lord did not come from the beginning of the world ; (2) why the Gospel is not preached all over the earth.   There is [*i.e.* would have been] nothing stranger in the Ethiopian dying before Philip came to him, than in a Jew of Solomon's day dying before the Gospel was preached ; neither had baptism.

2. What is faith before the revealed dogma is known, is superstition after, for God has now superseded the natural ways of seeking Him.

3. ' My sheep hear Me.'   Therefore it is only when there is invincible ignorance that this can be—being led on into the Church is the test.

July 3

[FAITH—IV]

1. INTROD.—What I have been saying is this, that even heathen (all men) to enter upon the road that leads to heaven, must live by faith ; by faith even as to those things which they know by reason.

2. And this is so, because God would take us out of ourselves and make us depend on Him—not make ourselves our own centre ; we must make God our centre.

3. Analogy of Nature—solar system, monarchy in society, etc.   Yet this difference, that in this world there are many ranks, etc., intermediate between the centre and ourselves, but as to religion, we every one depend on one centre alone—God.

4. The wishing to have ourselves our own centre is pride, the sin of Satan. (Enlarge on it.)

5. Instances of faith, inquiry, doubt, a want of faith. (1) Inquiry—the child Samuel. (2) Nobleman in 4 Kings vii., who would not believe Eliseus ; unbelief of St. Thomas. (3) Zachary ; doubt, and Nicodemus. (4) Our Lady's and St. Paul's faith. A fifth state, weak faith of Gideon : ' Lord, I believe.'[1]

August 14

ON LOVE

1. INTROD.—(1) On Love as not external to the Church (*i.e.* state of grace) as faith and hope may be. (2) As not in those who fall from grace, while faith and hope remain. As not the love of concupiscence or hope, nor gratitude, its object being the beauty of God.

Now I shall show how love comes after faith, through a distinct grace. Younger sons in Scripture—Jacob, not Esau—*vide* St. Francis de Sales.

---

[1] This section might be rewritten thus :—Instances of (1) inquiry—the child Samuel ['Speak Lord,' etc.]; (2) want of faith—the nobleman who would not believe Eliseus, 4 Kings vii. [' If the Lord should make flood-gates in heaven, can that possibly be which thou sayest '], and the unbelief of St. Thomas; (3) doubt—Zachary [Luke i. 18], and Nicodemus [John iii.]; (4) faith—our Lady's and St. Paul's faith. A fifth state, weak faith, as in the case of Gideon [Judges vi. 36-40], and the father of the boy possessed by the dumb spirit—' Lord I do believe; help my unbelief ' [Mark ix. 24].

2. On love. Remains of love in nature, as shown by the drawings of the heart, by people seeking comfort in religion, in trouble ; and this left in order that grace may work *with* nature, not against nature, *when* it works. Also as a sort of claim of God upon us, as if He marked us as His property.

On love being produced from faith through meditation.

3. By nature [man] has far more to do with other attributes of God—fear, etc., etc. For instance, I have said that conscience is the means of faith, but it teaches justice principally, which is the object of fear, not of love. Again, though there is great goodness in God's providence, yet in action the marks of particular providence not so obvious.

4. But it is the objects of Christian faith which cause love. Go through them minutely. At first sight original sin might be a doctrine which drives us from God. *O felix culpa*, atonement—much more still particular election. Then Mass and the Holy Eucharist, etc. Faith, you see, is *the* thing, or the *only* thing necessary as a means of love.

5. Faith leads to love *through* meditation. The things of faith, *e.g.* the whole doctrine of election is hard, but when once embraced it has its reward in its powers of kindling love.

Doctrine of election : (1) This little globe out of the whole world ; (2) not angels but men chosen ; (3) Old Testament elections, the younger for the older ; (4) we chosen out of the world to be Catholics.

6. And though this in the first place gratitude, not pure love, yet, since all God's dealings to us are so admirable and glorious, love is kindled at the same time.

7. All this is summed up, especially in the Gospels, so that as the Bible is the instrument of hope, so is the Gospels of love.

June 3, 1860

CONFIRMATION

I conceive that St. Thomas means that the *dona Spiritus Sancti* have the same relation to the motions of grace towards the supernatural end of man which moral virtue has to the motions of reason towards the natural end. They *dispose* the mind that it may be well moved by the Holy Ghost, as the virtues perfect the appetite that it may be well moved by reason. Also that he means by wisdom and understanding two speculative gifts, the latter apprehension, the former judgment, speculative apprehension or understanding being what Doyle's Catechism calls knowledge (comprehension) of mysteries, and speculative understanding or wisdom, the perfect appreciation (comprehension, grasp) of all subjects of religion, though Doyle calls it a gift of directing our whole lives and actions to God's honour.

By knowledge and counsel, two practical gifts— knowledge being a *judicium*, viz. an insight into duty generally, though Doyle says, ' a gift by which we know, etc., the will of God '; and counsel being an *apprehensio*, or what Doyle calls ' a gift by which we discover the grounds of the duty,' etc.

I should say, by which we take in all things correctly as they are.

Wisdom—the estimation of all things rightly with reference to *our end*.

Understanding—knowledge, mysteries.

Knowledge—knowledge of *means* for our spiritual welfare.

Council—or prudence, judging of things rightly.

Piety or godliness—directs *appetitus in alterum.*

Fortitude—against fear of world, etc.

Fear—against concupiscence.

NOTES

NOTE 1.

P. 1. 'Purity and Love,' etc., was written out in full, and published under the same title in *Discourses to Mixed Congregations*. The contrast between St. Peter and St. John on the Lake of Galilee is thus expanded :—'When they were in the boat and the Lord spoke to them from the shore, and they knew not that it was Jesus, first that disciple whom Jesus loved said to Peter : "It is the Lord," for "the pure of heart shall see God" : then at once Simon Peter in the impetuosity of his love, girt his tunic about him, and cast himself into the sea, to reach Him the quicker. St. John beholds, and St. Peter acts.'—*Discourses to Mixed Congregations,* p. 73.

NOTE 2.

P. 5. 'Human Respect.'—The description of Magdalene at the feast is drawn out in full in the sermon 'Purity and Love.' 'She who had come into the room, as if for a festive purpose, to go about an act of penance. It was a formal banquet . . . she came, as if to honour that feast, as women were wont to honour such festive doings, with her sweet odours and cool unguents, for the forehead and hair of the guests. And he, the proud Pharisee, suffered her to come . . . he thought only of the necessities of his banquet, and he let her come to do her part, such as it was, careless what her life was, so that she did that part well, and confined herself to it.' —*Discourses to Mixed Congregations,* p. 81.

NOTE 3.

P. 13. 'On the Fitness of Our Lady's Assumption.'—Most of the ideas found here are developed in the Discourse 'On the Fitness

of the Glories of Mary' (*Discourses to Mixed Congregations*, p. 360)
and 'The Glories of Mary for the Sake of Her Son' (*ib.* p. 342)
—*e.g.* 'He said, "Ought not Christ to suffer these things . . . ?"
He appealed to the fitness and congruity which existed between
this surprising event and other truths which had been revealed
concerning the Divine purpose of saving the world. And so, too,
St. Paul, in speaking of the same wonderful appointment of God :
"It *became* Him," he says, "for whom are all things, and through
whom are all things, who had brought many sons unto glory, to
consummate the Author of their salvation by suffering." Elsewhere, speaking of prophesying, or the exposition of what is latent
in Divine Truth, he bids his brethren exercise the gift, "according
to the *analogy* or rule of faith" ; that is, so that the doctrine
preached may correspond and fit into what is already received.
Thus you see that it is a great evidence of truth, in the case of
revealed teaching, that it is so consistent, that it so hangs together
that one thing springs out of another, that each part requires and
is required by the rest.'—*Discourses to Mixed Congregations*,
p. 360.

NOTE 4.

P. 15. 'On Want of Faith.'—Most of the ideas in these sermon
notes were expanded into the sermon ' Faith and Private Judgment.'
—*Discourses to Mixed Congregations*, p. 193.

NOTE 5.

P. 19. 'Faith and Doubt.'—This sermon was published under
the same title in *Discourses to Mixed Congregations.* This is how
some of the points in the Notes are expanded in the sermon.

Section 3. 'Persons converted to Protestantism,' etc.—'You
sometimes hear of Catholics falling away, who will tell you it
arose from reading the Scriptures. . . . No ; Scripture did not
make them disbelieve (impossible !) : they disbelieved *when* they
opened the Bible ; they opened it in an unbelieving spirit.'—*Ib.*
p. 127.

Section 5. 'It imagines Confession,' etc.—' I really do think it
is the world's judgment, that one principal part of a confessor's
work is the putting down such misgivings in his penitents.'—*Ib.*
p. 222.

Section 6. 'Doubt does not destroy intellectual conviction.'—
'Men may be convinced . . . and yet, after all, avow that they
cannot believe, they do not know why, but they cannot . . . their
reason is convinced, and their doubts are moral ones, arising in
their root from a fault of the will.[1] . . . It requires no act of
faith to assent to the truth that two and two make four: we cannot
help assenting to it ; and hence there is no merit in assenting to
it ; but there is merit in believing that the Church is from God ;
for though there are abundant reasons to prove it to us, yet we
can, without an absurdity, quarrel with the conclusion ; we may
complain,' etc.—*Ib.* pp. 224-5.[2]

NOTE 6.

P. 21. 'The Maternity of Mary.'—These notes were developed
into the sermon ' The Glories of Mary for the Sake of her Son.'—
Discourses to Mixed Congregations, p. 342.

Section 3. 'To erect her as a Turris Davidica,' etc.—' A mother
without a home in the Church, without dignity, without gifts,
would have been, as far as the defence of the Incarnation goes, no
mother at all. She would not have remained in the memory, or
imagination of men.'—*Ib.* p. 350.

Section 5. 'The third ground.'—The Church and Satan agreed
together in this, that Son and Mother went together, and the
experience of three centuries has confirmed their testimony,' etc.—
Ib. p. 348.

NOTE 7.

P. 25. Resignation of the souls in purgatory.—'How different is
the feeling with which the loving soul, on its separation from the
body, approaches the judgment-seat of its Redeemer ! It knows
how great a debt of punishment remains upon it, though it has
for many years been reconciled to Him ; it knows that purgatory

[1] Often from weakness of the will, which in matters of practical conduct makes a man scrupulous, unable to brush aside futile difficulties,
and the like—victims, as they would be called, of idle fears.

[2] In the evidences for religion ' non excluditur omnis dubitandi possi-
bilitas, sed solum dubitandi prudenter, et ideo mens sub voluntatis
motione relinquitur, ut deliberata formidine deposita, firmiter adhaereat
ei quod videt non posse nisi irrationabiliter in dubium revocari.'

lies before it, and that the best it can reasonably hope for is to be sent there. But to see His face, though for a moment! to hear His voice, to hear Him speak, though it be to punish! O Saviour of men, it says, I come to Thee, though it be in order to be at once remanded from Thee ; I come to Thee who art my Life and my All ; I come to Thee on the thought of whom I have lived all my life long. To Thee I gave myself when first I had to take a part in the world ; I sought Thee for my chief good early, for early didst Thou teach me, that good elsewhere there was none. Whom have I in heaven but Thee ? whom have I desired on earth, whom have I had on earth, but Thee ? whom shall I have amid the sharp flame but Thee ? Yea, though I be now descending thither, into "a land desert, pathless and without water," I will fear no ill, for Thou art with me. I have seen Thee this day face to face, and it sufficeth : I have seen Thee, and that glance of Thine is sufficient for a century of sorrow, in the nether prison. I will live on that look of Thine, though I see Thee not, till I see Thee again, never to part from Thee. That eye of Thine shall be sunshine and comfort to my weary, longing soul ; that voice of Thine shall be everlasting music to my ears. Nothing can harm me, nothing shall discompose me ; I will bear the appointed years, till the end comes, bravely and sweetly,' etc.—*Discourses to Mixed Congregations,* p. 81.

NOTE 8.

P. 47, Section 5. ' Even in caves (which are most alien to Christianity).'—' Only a heavenly light can give purity to nocturnal and subterraneous worship. Caves were at that time appropriated to the worship of infernal gods. It was but natural that these wild religions should be connected with magic and its kindred arts ; magic had at all times led to cruelty and licentiousness.'— *Development,* p. 215.

NOTE 9.

P. 109. ' *O commutationem.*'—' O commutationem ! Joannes tibi pro Jesu traditur, servus pro Domino, discipulus pro Magistro, filius Zebedaei pro Filio Dei, homo purus pro Deo vero.'—St. Bernard, quoted in 5th lection for Feast of Seven Dolours

Y

Note 10.

P. 78, 'Say, hast thou track'd,' etc.—From the poem entitled 'Taormini' from *Verses on Various Occasions*, p. 135, which runs as follows :—

TAORMINI

'And Jacob went on his way, and the Angels of God met him.'

> Say, hast thou track'd a traveller's round,
>   Nor visions met thee there,
> Thou couldst but marvel to have found
>   This blighted world so fair ?
>
> And feel an awe within thee rise,
>   That sinful man should see
> Glories far worthier Seraph's eyes
>   Than to be shared by thee ?
>
> Store them in heart ! thou shalt not faint
>   'Mid coming pains and fears,
> As the third heaven once nerved a Saint
>   For fourteen trial-years.

Magnisi.   *April* 26, 1833.

The reader who wishes to enter into the thought of this poem should turn to the sermon 'St. Michael—The Powers of Nature' (*Parochial and Plain Sermons*, vol. ii. pp. 358 ff.) See also *Apologia*, p. 28.

Note 11.

P. 139, Section 8. 'Joshua.'—'There is this peculiarity in Joshua's history, as recorded in the book bearing his name, that at least there is no record of children who might be his heirs. Joshua a type of Christ,' etc.—*Sermons on Subjects of the Day*, p. 155.

Note 12.

P. 140, Section 2. 'Our own sin and penance,' etc.—'At Christmas we joy with the natural unmixed joy of children, but at Easter our joy is highly wrought and artificial in its character . . . the feeling at Easter is not unlike the revulsion of mind on a recovery from sickness. . . . In sickness the mind wanders from things that are seen into the unknown world ; it turns back into itself, and is in company with mysteries ; it is brought into contact with objects which it cannot describe, which it cannot ascertain. It sees the skirts of powers and providences beyond this world, and is at least more alive, if not more exposed, to the invisible influences, bad and good, which are its portion in this state of trial. And afterwards it has recollections which are painful, recollections of distress, of which it cannot recall the reasons, of pursuits without an object, and gleams of relief without continuance. And what is all this but a parallel feeling to that, with which the Christian has gone through the contemplations put before his faith in the week just passed, which are to him as a fearful harrowing dream, of which the spell is now broken ? The subjects, indeed, which have been brought before him are no dream, but a reality,—his Saviour's sufferings, his own misery and sin. But, alas ! to him at best they are but a dream, because, from lack of faith and of spiritual discernment, he understands them so imperfectly. They have been to him a dream, because only at moments his heart has caught a vivid glimpse of what was continually before his reason,—because the impression it made upon him was irregular, shifting, and transitory,—because even when he contemplated steadily his Saviour's sufferings, he did not, could not, understand the deep reasons of them, or the meaning of his Saviour's words,—because what most forcibly affected him came through his irrational nature, was not of the mind but of the flesh . . . of his own discomfort of body, which he has been bound, so far as health allows, to make sympathise with the history of those sufferings which are his salvation. And thus I say his disquiet during the week has been like that of a bad dream, restless and dreary ; he has felt he ought to be very sorry, and could not say why—could not master his grief, could not realise his fears, but was as children are, who wonder, weep, and are silent, when they see their parents in sorrow, from a feeling that there is something wrong, though they cannot say what.'—*Parochial and Plain Sermons*, 'Keeping Fast and Festival,' vol. iv. pp. 334 ff.

The illustration taken from mental experiences during sickness and convalescence seems derived from the preacher's own experience during his illness in Sicily. 'I . . . fell ill of a fever . . . my servant thought I was dying, and begged for my last directions. I gave them . . . but I said, "I shall not die." I repeated "I shall not die, for I have not sinned against the light, I have not sinned against the light." I have never been able quite to make out what I meant.'—*Apol.*, pp. 34-35. Compare the long memorandum, 'My Illness in Sicily,' published in Miss Moseley's *Life and Correspondence of Cardinal Newman*, vol. i. pp. 363-78.

NOTE 13.

P. 158. 'For each truth,' etc.—A favourite idea with Newman. It will be found most fully developed in the *Grammar of Assent*, chap. v. sec. 2. The sum of what he there says is given in *Select Treatises of St. Athanasius*, etc., vol. ii. pp. 316-17. 'Let it be observed that the mystery lies, not in any one of the statements which constitute the doctrine, but in their combination. The meaning of each proposition is on a level with our understanding. . . . God is a Father ; God is a Son ; God is a Holy Spirit : the Father is not the Son. . . . God is numerically one ; there are not three gods. In which of these propositions do we not understand what is meant to be told us ? For devotion, then . . . the mystery is no difficulty. . . . The difficulty . . . is not in understanding each sentence of which the doctrine consists, but in its incompatibility (taken as a whole, and in the only words possible for conveying it to our minds) with certain of our axioms of thought, indisputable in themselves, but foreign and inapplicable to a sphere of existences of which we have no experience whatever.' Again, 'Much as is idly and profanely said against the Creed of St. Athanasius as being unintelligible, yet the real objection which misbelievers feel, if they spoke correctly, is, that it is too plain. No sentences can be more simple, nor statements more precise, than those of which it consists. The difficulty is not in any one singly ; but in their combination. And herein lies a remarkable difference between the doctrine of the Holy Trinity, and some modern dogmatic statements on other points, some true, and some not true, which have at times been put forward as necessary to salvation. Much controversy, for instance, has taken place in late centuries about the doctrine of justification, and about faith ; but here endless perplexities and hopeless disputes arise, as we all know, as to what is meant by " faith," and what by "justification" ; whereas most of the *words* used in the Creed to which I have referred are only common words, used in their common sense,' etc.—*Parochial and Plain*

Sermons, 'The Mystery of the Holy Trinity,' vol. vi. p. 347. Cp. *ib.* vol. iv. p. 289, 'The Mysteriousness of our Present Being.'

NOTE 14.

P. 164. 'Nine orders in three hierarchies.'—A pencil note shows that the preacher consulted Petavius, and Bail, the author of *La Théologie Affective,* etc. Both these authors followed the pseudo-Dionysius *De Coelesti Hierarchia.*

> 1st Hierarchy—Seraphim, cherubim, thrones.
> 2nd Hierarchy—Dominations, virtues, powers.
> 3rd Hierarchy—Principalities, archangels, angels.

'Each appellation of the Beings above us manifests their God-imitating characteristics of the Divine Likeness' [Dionysius]. Thus, to give one example, 'The appellation . . . of the Thrones denotes their manifest exaltation above every grovelling inferiority, and their supermundane tendency towards higher things' [*ib.*]. In the case of the lowest order or choir, the Angels, contentment is their characteristic virtue. Perhaps this suggested to Dante the reply made by a soul in the first or lowest Heaven, that of the Moon, to the question, 'Do ye feel the want of a higher place?'

> Frate, la nostra volontà quieta
> Virtù di carità, che fa volerne
> Sol quel ch'avemo, e d'altro non ci asseta.
> Se disiassimo esser più superne,
> Foran discordi gli nostri disiri
> Dal voler di colui, che qui ne cerne.[1]

NOTE 15.

P. 177, Section 15. 'Progress.'—'In the province of physiology and moral philosophy, our race's progress and perfectibility is a

[1] 'Brother, a virtue of charity sets at rest our will, which makes us wish that only which we have, and lets us not thirst for aught else. If we desired to be more on high, our desires would be out of harmony with the will of Him who distributes us here.'—*Paradiso,* iii. 70-76; Butler's translation.

dream, because Revelation contradicts it, whatever may be plausibly argued on its behalf by scientific inquirers.'—*Idea of a University*, p. 273. In other words, the history of man on this planet is to end in Antichrist and the triumph of wickedness.

NOTE 16.

P. 184, Section 2. 'Keble's poem.'—Presumably the following stanza :—

> 'Reason and Faith at once set out
>   To search the Saviour's tomb ;
> Faith faster runs, but waits without,
>   As fearing to presume,
> Till Reason enter in, and trace
> Christ's relics round the holy place—
> "Here lay His limbs, and here His sacred head,
> And who was by to make His new-forsaken bed?"'
>   *The Christian Year*, St. Thomas' Day.

NOTE 17.

P. 197, Section 2. 'Yet familiar to children.'—See *Grammar of Assent*, pp. 112-16, from which the following passage may be quoted :—' Supposing he [*i.e.* a child] has offended his parents, he will all alone and without effort, as if it were the most natural of acts, place himself in the presence of God, and beg of Him to set him right with them. Let us consider how much is contained in this simple act. First, it involves the impression on his mind of an unseen Being with whom he is in immediate relation, and that relation so familiar that he can address Him whenever he himself chooses ; next, of One whose good-will towards him he is assured of . . . further, of One who can hear him . . . and who can read his thoughts . . . lastly, of One who can effect a critical change in the state of feeling of others towards him. That is . . . this child has in his mind the image of an Invisible Being, who exercises a particular providence among us, who is present everywhere, who is heart-reading, heart-changing, ever accessible, open to impetration.'

NOTE 18.

P. 205, Section 5. ' Could.'—Probably an unconscious reminiscence of Isaias v. 4 in the Authorised Version ; ' What could have been done more to my vineyard.' The Vulgate reads 'Quid est quod debui ultra facere vineae meae.'

NOTE 19.

P. 222, Section 2. 'What is Faith ? Why,' etc.—The ejaculatory *why* and the word *heart* a little later on show that the preacher is using not scientific but popular or colloquial language. It is in colloquial language, therefore, that we shall find illustrations of his meaning. With his ' secret inward sense,' etc., compare such expressions as ' In his secret heart he knows well enough,' or,—supposing a man to be arguing for arguing's sake, making out a case—such appeals to his true self as ' Do you in your heart of hearts believe what you are saying ?' or ' What is after all your conscientious belief ? The ' secret inward sense ' in ' heart ' and ' conscience ' applied to a belief which comes in the first place from an external source, *i.e.* the fact that there is a Revelation, need only mean an *intense* belief, though the choice of the words may well have been influenced by the thought of the yet more secret and inward workings of divine grace on the heart. For faith viewed as something learned from without see other sermons, especially those on pp. 313-19.

NOTE 20.

P. 291, Section 2. 'This day.'—'They *all* discard (what they call) gloomy views of religion ; they all trust themselves more than God's word . . . and are ready to embrace the pleasant consoling religion natural to a polished age. They lay much stress on works on *Natural Theology*, and think that all religion is contained in these ; whereas, in truth, there is no greater fallacy than to suppose such works to be in themselves in any true sense religious at all. Religion, it has been well observed, is something *relative to us*; a system of commands and promises from God *towards* us. But how are we concerned with the sun, moon, and stars? or with the laws of the universe? how will they teach us our *duty*? how will they speak to *sinners*? They do not speak to sinners at all. They were created *before* Adam fell. They "declare the *glory* of God," but not His *will*. They are all perfect; all harmonious; but that brightness and excellence which they exhibit in their own creation, and the Divine benevolence therein seen, are of little moment to fallen man. We see nothing there of God's *wrath*, of which the conscience of a sinner loudly speaks. So that there cannot be a more dangerous (though a common) device of Satan than to carry us off from our own secret thoughts, to make us forget our own hearts, which tell of a God of justice and holiness, and to fix our attention merely on the God who made the heavens; who is *our* God indeed, but not God as manifested to us sinners, but as He shines forth to His angels, and to His elect hereafter.

'When a man has so far deceived himself . . . at once he misinterprets and perverts the whole tenor of Scripture. . . . We are expressly told that "strait is the gate" . . . that they who do not obtain eternal life "shall go into everlasting punishment." This the dark side of religion; and the men I have been describing cannot bear to think of it. They easily get themselves to believe that those strong declarations of Scripture do not belong to the present day, or are figurative. They have no language in their heart responding to them. Conscience has been silenced. The only information that they have received concerning God has been from Natural Theology, and that speaks only of benevolence and harmony; so they will not credit the plain word of Scripture.'—*Parochial and Plain Sermons*, 'The Religion of the Day,' vol. i. pp. 317-19.

EDITOR'S NOTES

p. 2. These *titles* (seat of wisdom, gate of heaven) are from the *Litany of Loreto*. *Vita, dulcedo* (life, sweetness) are from the *Hail, Holy Queen*.

p. 3. *Confiteor*: the *I Confess* (Prayer said during the penitential rite at Mass).

p. 4. cf. *Certain Difficulties felt by Anglicans in Catholic Teaching* Vol 1 pp. 354–5; *Certain Difficulties felt by Anglicans in Catholic Teaching* Vol 2 pp. 335–6; *Sermon Notes* pp. 327–9.

p. 4. *the Church having a hold upon them*: in the sense that one submits to the authority of the Church and its future infallible guidance.

p. 5. *Maldonatus*: Juan Maldonado, SJ (1534–1583), a Spanish theologian who produced Gospel Commentaries. The theme of Mary Magdalen is developed in *Discourses to Mixed Congregations* p. 71.

p. 7. *The boy hid the fox* under his tunic where it gnawed into his stomach, but he could not admit the pain (being Spartan) and so died. It occurs in *Helena* by Evelyn Waugh (1963 ed.) pp. 54–5.

p. 7. *'pudebat me esse pudentem'* ('I was ashamed of being ashamed'): (Augustine, *Confessions* 2, 9, 9).

p. 9. *'hidden from thine eyes'*: Luke 19:42.

p. 12. *hand and foot*: cf. I Cor. 12:15.

p. 22. *Turris Davidica* (tower of David): a title in the *Litany of Loreto*. *'Ecce ancilla Domini'* ('Behold the handmaid of the Lord'): Mary's reply to the angel (Luke 1:38).

p. 23. *coelum animatum*: (heaven is full of life) a possible reference to Augustine, *De Civitate Dei* 22, 30, 1.

p. 24. The quotation is from Acts 14:22.

p. 24. '*de porta inferi*': ... *from the gate of hell, the lion's mouth and the deep lake may it not swallow them up*: The Offertory Antiphon of the Requiem Mass before Vatican II's reform.

p. 25. *St Felicity* (3rd century martyr): saw Dinocrates in a place of pain, and having prayed then saw him in heaven. *St Malachy* (1094–1198) saw his dead sister first in black and after his prayers, finally clothed in glory.

p. 25. *pain of sense*: positive sufferings which afflict the soul, i.e. fire. '*with me in paradise*': Luke 23:43.

p. 28. Both poems by Lord Byron published in 1816 and 1814 respectively. *The Giaour* is a derogatory term for a non-Muslim used by Turks. In the poem, he ends his days in a monastery.

p. 30. see Gen 6:2.

p. 31. '*It already worketh*': namely, the mystery of lawlessness (see 2 Thess. 2:7).

p. 33. see infra pp. 230–1.

p. 36. '*dust thou art*': Gen. 3:19.

p. 37. *the natural soul*: in the sense of Aristotle's principle of material life.

p. 38. The devil answered her 'I am that wicked one who is deprived of the love of God.'

p. 39. Newman translates from the *Vulgate* of Isa. 57:20 see the introduction to this edition, p. xxviii.

p. 39. *poena damni* means exclusion from the beatific vision; *poena sensus* is the material suffering inflicted.

p. 41. *animula blandula* (a somewhat agreeable little soul): quotation from an elegy written on the life of the Emperor Hadrian.

p. 41. Philip II rebuked his courtiers for telling him a lie. Mary Magdalene of Pazzi trembled because of her fear of divine judgement.

p. 41. *ictus oculi* (in the twinkling of an eye): I Cor. 15:52.

p. 42. see Matt. 10:29–31.

p. 47. *Nunc et in hora mortis nostrae*: Now and at the hour of our death (from the *Hail, Mary*).

p. 47. St Peter's, Broad Street, Birmingham (now demolished, and part of the site of the International Convention Centre).

p. 52. *Great difference between religious truth and scientific*: refer to *The Idea of A University* pp. 51–53 where Newman talks of the various types of knowledge.

p. 59. *Dagon*: the god of the Philistines (1 Sam. 5:3).

p. 60. *Catholic Hours*: before the recent reform these were: Matins and Lauds, Prime, Terce, Sext, None, Vespers and Compline. See Tract 75, p. 4. *silva*: the material.

p. 60. *St Aloysius Gonzaga, SJ* (1568–1591): an early Jesuit saint who died as a result of nursing plague victims.

p. 61. *Oratorium Parvum*: the Lay Association attached to the Congregation of the Oratory. See *Lectures on the Present Position of Catholics*, p. xci (Millennium Edition) for a description.

p. 65. *otium cum dignitate*: a peaceful life with honour (Cicero, *Pro Sestio* 45.98).

p. 67. *Johann J. Döllinger* (1799–1890): a German theologian who was appointed to the chair of ecclesiastical history at Munich in 1826. He wrote a history of the Church in 1840, of which see Vol. 1 p. 42f.

p. 68. *Quare fremuerunt gentes*: why do the nations tremble (Ps. 2:1).

p. 70. *buying and selling*: the reference is to Luke 17:28.

p. 75. *had He not willed to feel it*: see *Mental Sufferings of Our Lord in His Passion Discourses to Mixed Congregations* pp. 324–343.

p. 75. *mole ruit sua*: fell by its own weight (Horace, *Carmen Seculare*, 4, p. 65.

p. 76. *Quis custodiet*: who is to guard the guards? (Juvenal, *Satires*, 6, p. 347).

p. 77. *Vox populi*: the whole quotation is *The voice of the people is the voice of God*. Attributed to Alcuin (735–804) in a letter to Charlemagne.

p. 81. '*Shall a mother forget her sucking child?*': Isa. 49:15.

p. 82. '*narrow is the way*': Matt. 7:14.

p. 83. *Oratorium Parvum*: see note ref. p. 61.

p. 83. *Paley's Evidences*: Newman treats of William Paley (1743–1805) the author of the *Evidences of Christianity* (1794) in *Lectures on Justification* pp. 127–8.

p. 85. *The whole creation groaning*: Rom. 8:22.

p. 85. *the sweet nard filled the house*: John 12:3.

p. 85. *multitudo fidelium*: the faithful multitude.

p. 87. *St Leo 1400 years ago*:

> Through the bishops the care of the universal Church would converge on the see of Peter and nothing should ever be at odds with this head.
> Leo to Anastasius, ML 54.675 *c.* AD446

p. 88. '*Hedge them in*': Luke 19:43.

p. 88. *St Alphonsus* says:

> The dying sinner shall be tortured by remorse of conscience, by the assaults of the devils, by the fears of eternal death.

p. 89. *St Andrew Avellino*: a contemporary of St Philip Neri (1521–1608) who died of apoplexy and is often invoked against sudden death for this reason.

p. 91. *sin was imputed to Him*: Isa. 63:1f; John 9:24.

p. 93. According to St Gregory of Nyssa, St Gregory the Wonderworker (d.268) was favoured with an apparition of the Blessed Virgin Mary and received a revelation about the Trinity in the form of a Creed.
St Justina: a third-century martyr who suffered for her virginity.

p. 95. *Mane nobiscum Domine*: stay with us, Lord (Luke 24:29).

p. 96. *put off all His glory*: Phil. 2:7.

p. 97. *the gloominess of Catholicity*: Newman wrote in his Private Journal for 21 January 1863 'As a Catholic, my life is dreary, not my religion'. *Autobiographical Writings* p. 254.

p. 97. *'Peace, peace when there is no peace'*: Ezek. 13:10.

p. 97. *'The end is the trial'*: cf. 1 Pet. 3:12; Matt. 10:32.

p. 99. *'My Lord and my God'*: John 20:28.

p. 100. *Curis acuens mortalia corda*: The spear moving the hearts of men.

p. 103. *Alcester Street*: the Oratory's first residence in Birmingham 1849–1852.

p. 103. *A NET*: Ps. 10:9.

p. 104. *inviolata, intemerata*: inviolate, chaste. Titles of the Virgin Mary in the *Litany of Loreto*.

p. 105. *'I have waited for thy salvation'*: Gen. 49:18.
Limbo Patrum: the abode of pre-Christian holy persons; see Luke 16:22.

p. 108. *poena damni*: see note ref. p. 39.

p. 111. *All men in God's wrath*: Eph. 2:3.

p. 113. *Congratulamini mihi, quia cum essem parvula* (Rejoice with me since I am a child): the Responsory to the eighth reading of the third Nocturn on the feast of the Maternity of the Blessed Virgin Mary in the former breviary.

p. 113. *Gaudere cum guadentibus*: Rom. 12:15.
ἐπιχαιροκακια: malignant joy in another's misfortune or *schadenfreude*.

p. 115. *Father Claver, St Peter Claver* (1580–1654): proclaimed patron of the missions to black people in 1888.

p. 116. *Lady Olivia Acheson*: daughter of the Earl of Gosford and benefactor to many Catholic causes. She fell ill in Birmingham on 26 December 1851 and died on 28 March 1852.

p. 117. *advocata nostra*: our advocate (from the *Hail, Holy Queen*).

p. 117. *St Irenaeus*: 'He who from the Virgin is Emmanuel.'
Adversus Haereses 3, 19, 1. MG 7, p. 938.
St Agnese in Piazza Navona at that time possessed a picture of the Blessed Virgin Mary and the Saints over the high altar.

p. 118. *Thomas Scott* of Aston Sandford (1747–1821): spoke on the power of prayer in *Essays on the Most Important Subjects in Religion* (London, 1814) p. 390.

p. 119. *de congruo*: out of fairness, see p. 296.

p. 119. memorials: for Newman's views on the subject see *Meditations and Devotions* p. 611 where he leaves exact instructions.

p. 122. *Septem Dolorum*: Seven Sorrows (of BVM).

p. 122. *the war*: the Crimean War had just begun.

p. 124. *propter Deum*: for God himself (as opposed to ourselves).

p. 125. *Melliflui facti sunt coeli*: the reference is to Isa. 45:8. It is the Introit of the Fourth Sunday of Advent in the pre-Vatican II liturgy.

p. 127. The readings are taken from the Second Sunday after Pentecost, but Newman preaches on the Eucharist.

p. 128. The illegible words are *to alter it*.

p. 128. '*The world is in wickedness*': I John 5:19.

p. 134. *a circle of holy beings*: see Rev. 4:4.

p. 136. *memory make them continuous*: see *Discourses to Mixed Congregations* pp. 328–9.

p. 137. *Monstra te esse Matrem*: 'Show yourself a Mother' from the hymn *Ave Maris Stella*.

p. 139. *St Gregory insists*: 'If the Spirit lifted us up above, while the flesh did not tempt us, it would by that very uplifting prostrate us the worse in the fall of pride'. *Morals on the Book of Job* 19, 6, 12 ML 76 p. 102.

p. 139. *St Jerome in Breviary*: in his Commentary on Matthew 19. ML 29.135.

p. 140. *... though man had not sinned*: the view put forward by Bl. Duns Scotus (d.1308).

p. 142. *St Rose*: St Rose of Lima (1586–1617).

p. 143. *Balaam and the angel*: Gen. 28:20.

p. 143. *Desideria efficacia et sterilia*: moral theologians divide desires into those which attain their object (*efficacia* = effective) and those who are ineffective.

p. 144. '*I came not to call*': Matt. 9:13.
'*Two shall be in the field*': Matt. 24:40.
'*Ten virgins*': Matt. 25:1f.
'*He that persevereth*': Matt. 24:13.
'*Many that are first*': Matt. 19:30.

p. 147. The Indian Mutiny began in April 1857.

p. 149. '*Ephpheta*': Mark 7:34.
in solidum: taken together, en bloc.

p. 151. *Zingis*: alternative spelling for Genghis (Khan) (1167–1227).
Timour: alternative spelling for Timur Beg (Tamerlane) (1335–1405).

p. 152. *Zohrab The Hostage* (1832): a novel by James Morier (1780–1849) who was secretary to the British legation in Persia 1809–1815.

p. 152. *Francesco Guicciardini* (1483–1540): author of *La Istoria d'Italia* and other historical works.
Ludovico Muratori (1672–1750): great savant and historian, author of the *Annali d'Italia*.

p. 153. *... wounded Highlanders*: at Culloden (16 April 1746).

p. 154. '. . . *they will be downright demons*': official news correspondents did not arrive until 1858. Lurid second-hand accounts which were later found to be exaggerated were widely published. See *The Times* editorial 6 August 1858.

p. 158. '*Thou hast hid these things . . .*': Luke 10:21.

p. 159. *Blessed Sebastian Valfrè* (d.1710) of the Turin Oratory.

p. 160. *the Achilli fund*: the Newman Defence Fund established to defray the expenses of the trial.
Their present troubles: Austrian forces were defeated in June, 1859 at Magenta, near Turin.

p. 161. *The scribe . . . asks for 'eternal life'*: Luke 10:25.

p. 161. *God . . . is the only stay . . .* See *God the Stay of the Soul, Parochial and Plain Sermons* V, p. 22.

p. 162. *Mere appearances . . .*: the Body and Blood of Christ are really present. The bread and wine are appearances according to the teaching of Trent.

p. 166. the *sermon* is No. 29 in *Parochial and Plain Sermons* V. The quotation is from John 5:4.

p. 167. *St Frances of Rome* (1384–1440): said to have been guided for the last twenty-three years of her life by an archangel.

p. 167. *linked to a soldier*: Acts 28:16.

p. 167. *St Anthony (in Cassian)*: in his second Conference *On Discernment* he calls it 'very rightly good sense' *Conferences of Cassian*, tr. Com Luibheid (Classics of Western Spirituality, New Jersey, 1985), pp. 62–4.

p. 169. '*Honour to whom honour*': Rom. 13:7.

p. 170. δια τηνφαινομενην ὕβριν: on account of the manifest injury.

p. 171. *St Ignatius of Antioch* (1st century) and *St Barlaam* who died under torture at Antioch in the fourth century.
O cacodaemons . . . and halters?: from Tertullian, *Ad Scapulam*, 5; quoted by Newman in *The Via Media* I, p. 14.

p. 176. *excitation* is spiritual arousal.
Now is the acceptable time: 2 Cor. 6:2.

p. 181 τόποι: passages: *cardo*: hinge.

p. 182. *Onesimus*: see Letter to Philemon.

p. 183. *'that every mouth should be stopped'*: Ps. 63:11.
the penitent thief: John 20:28.
'My Lord and my God': John 21:21.

p. 185. *'Who is he that overcometh ...'*: I John 5:5.

p. 186. ...*'He will give thee the desires of thy heart'*: 2 Chron. 6:16.

p. 189. *complacentia*: according to St Francis de Sales 'By which we may truly assert that we belong to God who is also our possession' *Treatise on the Love of God* 5.5.

p. 189. *Taurobolium*: the killing of bulls, as in the Mithras cult.

p. 192. *dignus vindice nodus*: unless the problem merits God's intervention.

p. 193. *'Pray without ceasing'*: 1 Thess. 5:17; Jas. 5:16f.

p. 194. ... *labour till the evening*: Ps 104:23. This was the Scripture verse for Newman's first and last sermon preached as an Anglican.

p. 195. *'Come let us reason together'*: Isa. 1:18.

p. 196. *'against thee only have I sinned'*: Ps. 51:6.

p. 200. *We veil our crosses*: the custom of veiling crosses and statues from Passion Sunday (5th Lent).

p. 200. *Abraham had first 'seen' Him*: Gen. 22.
the 'expectation of the nations': Matt. 12:21.

p. 203. *'Yet a little time ...'*: John 16:17.

p. 206. *our 'enemies may come about us'*: Luke 19:43.

p. 206. *'What shall I do?'*: Luke 10:25.

p. 207. *necessitate medii*: the necessary means to achieve the end.

p. 212. *It is dedicated to St Peter*: St Peter's, Broad Street was rebuilt in 1871 see note to p. 103.
the Holy See in its troubles: Pius IX rejected the Law of Guarantees and considered himself a prisoner of the Vatican after 1871.

p. 213. *Tower of Siloam*: Luke 13:4.

p. 214. *no one can say 'Jesus is the Lord ...'*: I Cor. 12:3.

p. 215. *as France*: it was the time of the Paris Commune after the defeat of France by Prussia.

p. 216. '*Ye shall not be as the nations*': Lev. 20:23.

p. 217. '*I fast twice a week*': Luke 18:12.

p. 217. '*I will have mercy and not sacrifice*': Matt 9:13.

p. 217. '*His blood be upon us ...*': Matt 27:28.

p. 218. *Julian the Apostate*, Flavius Claudius Julianus (331–363): see Gibbon, *Decline and Fall*, vol. 19.

p. 219. *The mustard seed*: Matt 13:31–2.

p. 219. '*Stones – children of Abraham*': Matt. 3:9.
'*Many shall come*': Luke 13:29.

p. 220. *he might simply leave Rome*: theologians are divided as to whether the papacy is linked to Rome in such a way that it can never be separated.

p. 221. *Satan the god of this world*: John 12:31; Matt. 4:8.
'*Michael and his angels*': Rev. 12:7.

p. 222. *a sense of the duty to obey Him*: see infra pp. 313–19.

p. 223. *their faith failed*: Matt. 26:56.

p. 223. '*Not to all the people*': Acts 10:41.
five hundred brethren at once: I Cor. 15:6.
'*some doubted*': Matt. 28:17.

p. 225. *not even the angels*: Mark 13:32.

p. 225. *the Truth called Antichrist*: I John 2:18.

p. 227. *'many Antichrists'*: I John 4:3.

p. 228. *Orval*: Brother Aubertin (d.1837), a religious of Orval, admitted that the 'prophecy' which he had published was in fact his own work and did not come from the fifteenth century. *The Rambler* (1849, p. 73) has the circular sent by the Bishop of Verdun.

p. 230. *Ignorance of the Scriptures is indeed ignorance of Christ*: Jerome, *Commentary on Isaiah*, Prologue ML 24, 27.

p. 231. *Horsley's letter*: Bishop Samuel Horsley (1733–1806) warned of a design to undermine Christianity by multiplying and encouraging sectaries ... Governments will pretend an indifference to all. *Discussions and Arguments* p. 107.

p. 231. *Malvenda*: Tomás Malvenda (1566–1622) in his book *De Antichristo* (Lyons, 1647) attacks Luther and the Reformers but also deals with the spread of the Gospel throughout the world and speculates about the existence of Christianity in America before Columbus and in China before Marco Polo.

p. 234. *'Ye shall be as gods'*: Gen. 3:5.

p. 234. *'My spirit shall not always'*: Gen. 6:3.
'The Spirit intercedes': Rom. 8:26.

p. 235. *'If ten persons'*: Gen. 18:32.

p. 236. *St Gregory Thaumaturgus* (d.268); Bishop of Neocaesarea in Pontus. There were reportedly seventeen Christians when he arrived as bishop in 238 and only seventeen pagans when he died.

p. 237. *St Philip Neri* (1515–1595); the founder of the Oratory and a worker of miracles during and after his life.

p. 237. *'Unless we see signs'*: John 4:48.

p. 240. *He has created and bought us*: I. Cor. 6:20; 7:23.

p. 242. *'Eye hath not seen'*: I Cor. 2:9

p. 242. *The world has its 'depth'*: Eph. 3:18.

p. 242. *'all the kingdoms of the earth'*: Matt. 4:8.

p. 251. *ninety-nine angels*: Matt. 18:12.

p. 252. *a great multitude*: Rev. 7:9.

p. 253. *four wounds*: ignorance, wickedness, weakness and disordered desire. *Summa Theologica* of St Thomas Aquinas, I–II Q 85 a 3c.

p. 253. *'salvation of the Jews'*: I John 5:19.

p. 253. *'Moses' seat'*: Matt. 23:2.

p. 254. *'Flee from the wrath to come'*: Matt. 3:7.

p. 254. *'salvation from the Jews'*: John 4:22.

p. 255. *Protestant translation*: burnt because it was regarded as tainted with heretical teaching and commentary.

p. 256. *'tradition'* hands on in its entirety the word of God committed to the apostles by Christ and the Holy Spirit to their successors (*De Divina Revelatione* n. 9-Vatican II).

p. 257 *The Seen and Unseen Worlds*: see *Parochial and Plain Sermons* IV:13 'The Invisible World'.

p. 258. *'marrying and giving in marriage'*: Matt: 24:38.

p. 258. *This is one which has spread* ...: the feast of the Sacred Heart was extended to the whole Church in 1856.

p. 263. *The Te Deum calls them an army*: 'The white-robed army of martyrs praise you.'

p. 263. *The most horrible deaths*: they died by crucifixion, flaying alive, stoning, by the sword, beheaded, boiled in oil (St John survived miraculously).

p. 266.. *Enoch 'walked with God'*: Gen. 5:24.
our Lord joined them ...: Luke 24:13ff.

p. 267. *Jesus Christ the same yesterday . . .*: Heb. 13:8.

p. 270. '*I will repent by and bye*': *Henry IV Part I* Act 3 Sc. 3.

p. 270. *The willing plunge*: see 'When I looked forward to my purgatory, It ever was my solace to believe, That ere I plunged amid the avenging flames, I had one sight of Him to strengthen me' (*Dream of Gerontius, Verses on Various Occasions*, p. 347).

p. 271. *St Vincent Ferrer*: Fr Louis Bail in *La Théologie Affective* (Paris, 1847) relates that because of the contrition of one of his penitents, St Vincent saw him removed from purgatory to heaven.

p. 272. '*partakers of the divine nature*': 2 Pet. 1:4.

p. 273. *the sceptre shall have departed from Judah*: Gen. 49:10.

p. 274. *they wonder at their own great works*: Eccles. 2:4.

p. 274. *homuncio*: alternative spelling for homuncule.

p. 275. *Lex orandi lex credendi*: the standard of worship is the standard of faith.

p. 276. ἡ ἀνομια: iniquity or lawlessness.

p. 277. *Isaac was the child of promise*: Gen. 22; Heb. 11:17–18.

p. 278. *a remnant*: I Kings 19:18; Rom. 11:4.

p. 281. *Sursum corda*: Lift up (your) hearts.

p. 282. *Credo quia impossibile*: I believe because it is (humanly) impossible.

p. 286. '*Lord, wilt thou at this time*': Acts 1:6.

p. 287. '*Abraham the friend*': 2 Chron. 20:7.

p. 293. *naturalia remanserunt integra*: they remained with their natural gifts intact (a theological expression).

p. 293. *infideles et reprobati*: unfaithful and reprobate.

p. 296. *de congruo*: out of fairness, rather than justice (which is de condigno).

p. 297. *even if man had not fallen*: see infra p. 140.

p. 299. *The Two Standards* of the Spiritual Exercises of St Ignatius – of Christ and Lucifer (Week 2 Day 4).

p. 299. *State of the Pope*: he was in Gaeta in exile after the revolution of 1849.

p. 301. *four empires*: Dan. 7:17 and Rev. 13:5.

p. 301. *Docetae*: they doubted that the Son of God had come in the flesh. *Dupuis*: Charles Dupuis (1742–1809) propounded a cosmogony based on the signs of the zodiac.

p. 304. *Catechismus Romanus*: 'Not only by virtue of his divinity but also of his humanity' Chapter 7 Q. 2.

p. 304. '*Sitteth on the right hand*': sharing the very glory of the Father.

p. 305. *Wisdom iv*: 'The righteous man who has died will condemn the ungodly who are living' (Wisd. 4:16).

p. 307. *Sacramenta mortuorum*: Sacraments of the dead in the sense of dead in sin, therefore Penance and the Anointing of the Sick.

p. 308. *Four properties*: incapable of suffering, filled with beauty and radiance, with the capacity to obey the soul promptly, possessing a spiritualised nature.

p. 310. *Catechismus ad Parochos*: the Catechism designed for Parish clergy.

p. 310. κατηχειν: to resound in one's ears, to din into one, or to catechise.

p. 311. *all the counsel of God*: Acts 20:27.

p. 315. *Still a veil*: a reference to the veil over the tabernacle in the Church.

p. 316. '... *no one can be saved*': Acts 4:12.

p. 318. Illegible word is *Christ*.

p. 318. '*Catholic my surname*': Pacian of Barcelona (4th century) ML 13. 1055.

p. 318. *'infants in grace know'*: I Cor. 3:1.

'Jesus is the Lord': I Cor. 12:3.

Disciplina arcani: the reserve shown by Christians concerning the truths of the faith.

p. 319. *Consubstantial*: of one being with the Father – against the Monophysite heresy.

p. 319. *Theotokos*: Mother of God. The title was declared at the Council of Ephesus in 431 but not incorporated into any Creed.

p. 320. *tremunt potestates*: the powers are in awe before you (from the *Common Preface*).

p. 322. *His Fathers only converse*: 'The daily use of the word of God in a simple familiary and efficacious manner, very different from the usual style of preachers.' *St Philip Neri* (Ponnelle & Bordet, London, Sheed & Ward, 1937), p. 322.

p.322. *the 'narrow way'*: Matt. 7:13.

p. 325. *Distinguo*: I clarify my point further.

p. 328. εὐσεβεις: devout pious people (Acts 2:3ff).

p. 328. *'. . . rather than a soul fail'*: perhaps a reference to the providential mercy of God in sending his angels to humanity *Summa Theologica* Q 113a 1 and 2.

p. 328. *Dr A*: Dr Thomas Arnold who died in 1842. Rumours of this incident were common although Stanley makes no reference in his standard biography.

p. 329. *'My sheep hear Me'*: John 10:27.

p. 330. *St Francis de Sales*: 'Jacob was so penetrated with joy on beholding Rachel as to shed tears, so no sooner has our heart found its God and received the first effects of his mercy in the gift of faith, than it is animated with the sweetest sentiments of love.' *Treatise on the Love of God* 2.15.

p. 331. *O felix culpa* (O Happy fault): from the *Exultet*, the Holy Saturday Sequence.

p. 332 *Doyle's Catechism*: 'Knowledge is a gift of God by which we know and understand the will of God ... Counsel is a gift of God by which we discover the frauds and deceits of the Devil, and are not deceived by him.' James Doyle, *An Abridgement of The Catechism of Christian Doctrine* (Dublin, 1828).

p. 333 *appetitus in alterum*: desire or longing for the other.

Scriptural texts for Masses on Sundays and feastdays (prior to 1969)

	Epistle	*Gospel*
Advent 1	Rom. 13:11–14	Luke 21:25–33
Advent 2	Rom. 15:4–13	Matt. 11:2–10
Advent 3	Phil. 4:4–7	John 1:19–28
Advent 4	1 Cor. 4:1–5	Luke 3:1–6
Christmas Night	Tit. 2:11–15	Luke 2:1–14
Christmas Day	Heb. 1:1–12	John 1:1–14
within the Octave	Gal. 4:1–7	Luke 2:33–40
Circumcision	Acts 4:8–12	Luke 2:21
Epiphany	Isa. 60:1–6	Matt. 2:1–12
Holy Family	Col. 3:12–17	Luke 2:42–52
1 Epiphany	Rom. 12:1–5	Luke 2:42–52
2 Epiphany	Rom. 12:6–16	John 2:1–11
3 Epiphany	Rom. 12:16–21	Matt. 8:1–13
4 Epiphany	Rom. 13:8–10	Matt. 8:23–27
5 Epiphany	Col. 3:12–17	Matt. 13:24–30
6 Epiphany	I Thess. 1:2–10	Matt. 13:31–35
Septuagesima	1 Cor. 9:24–27; 10:1–5	Matt. 20:1–16
Sexagesima	2 Cor. 11:19–33; 12:1–9	Luke 8:4–15
Quinquagesima	1 Cor. 13:1–13	Luke 18:31–43
1 Lent	2 Cor. 6:1–10	Matt. 4:1–11
2 Lent	1 Thess. 4:1–7	Matt. 17:1–9
3 Lent	Eph. 5:1–9	Luke 11:14–28
4 Lent	Gal. 4:22–31	John 6:1–15
Passion Sunday	Heb. 9:11–15	John 8:46–59
Palm Sunday		Matt. 21:1–9
	Phil. 2:5–11	Matt. 26:1–75
Easter Day	1 Cor. 5:7–8	Mark 16:1–7
Low Sunday	I John 5:4–10	John 20:19–31
2 Easter	I Pet. 2:21–25	John 10:11–16
3 Easter	I Pet. 2:11–19	John 16:16–22
4 Easter	Jas. 1:17–21	John 16:5–14
5 Easter	Jas. 1:22–27	John 16:23–30
Ascension	Acts 1:1–11	Mark 16:14–20
Sunday after Ascension	1 Pet. 4:7–11	John 15:26–27; 16:1–4
Pentecost	Acts 2:1–11	John 14:23–31
Trinity	Rom. 11:33–36	Matt. 28:18–20
Corpus Christi	1 Cor. 11:23–29	John 6:56–59
Sacred Heart	Eph. 3:8–12, 14–19	John 19:31–37

1 Pentecost	1 John 4:8–21	Luke 6:36–42
2 Pentecost★	1 John 3:13–18	Luke 14:16–24
3 Pentecost	1 Pet. 5:6–11	Luke 15:1–10
4 Pentecost	Rom. 8:18–23	Luke 5:1–11
5 Pentecost	1 Pet. 3:8–15	Matt. 5:20–24
6 Pentecost	Rom. 6:3–11	Mark 8:1–9
7 Pentecost	Rom. 6:19–23	Matt. 7:15–21
8 Pentecost	Rom. 8:12–17	Luke 16:1–9
9 Pentecost	1 Cor. 10:6–13	Luke 19:41–47
10 Pentecost	1 Cor. 12:2–11	Luke 18:9–14
11 Pentecost	1 Cor. 15:1–10	Mark 7:31–37
12 Pentecost	2 Cor. 3:4–9	Luke 10:23–37
13 Pentecost	Gal. 3:16–22	Luke 17:11–19
14 Pentecost	Gal. 5:16–24	Matt. 6:24–35
15 Pentecost	Gal. 5:25–26; 6:1–10	Luke 7:11–16
16 Pentecost	Eph. 3:13–21	Luke 14:1–11
17 Pentecost	Eph. 4:1–6	Matt. 22:34–46
18 Pentecost	1 Cor. 1:4–8	Matt. 9:1–8
19 Pentecost	Eph. 4:23–28	Matt. 22:1–14
20 Pentecost	Eph. 5:15–21	John 4:46–53
21 Pentecost	Eph. 6:10–17	Matt. 18:23–35
22 Pentecost	Phil. 1:6–11	Matt. 22:15–21
23 Pentecost	Phil. 3:17–21; 4:1–3	Matt. 9:18–26
24 Pentecost	Col. 1:9–14	Matt. 24:15–35
Peter and Paul	Acts 12:1–11	Matt. 16:13–19
Assumption	Jud. 13:22–25; 15:10	Luke 1:41–50
All Saints	Rev. 7:2–12	Matt. 5:1–12
Immaculate Conception	Prov. 8:22–35	Luke 1:26–28

★ or Sunday within the Octave of Corpus Christi